US NATIONAL SECURITY REFORM

This collection of essays considers the evolution of American institutions and processes for forming and implementing US national security policy, and offers diverse policy prescriptions for reform to confront an evolving and uncertain security environment.

Twelve renowned scholars and practitioners of US national security policy take up the question of whether the national security institutions we have are the ones we need to confront an uncertain future. Topics include a characterization of future threats to national security, organizational structure and leadership of national security bureaucracies, the role of the US Congress in national security policy making and oversight, and the importance of strategic planning within the national security enterprise. The book concludes with concrete recommendations for policy makers, most of which can be accomplished under the existing and enduring National Security Act.

This book will be of much interest to students of US national security, US foreign policy, Cold War studies, public policy and International Relations in general.

Heidi B. Demarest is an Officer in the US Army and Director of the American Politics program in the Department of Social Sciences at the US Military Academy.

Erica D. Borghard is an International Affairs Fellow at the Council on Foreign Relations, placed at JPMorgan Chase and US Cyber Command.

ROUTLEDGE GLOBAL SECURITY STUDIES

Series Editors: Aaron Karp and Regina Karp

Global Security Studies emphasizes broad forces reshaping global security and the dilemmas facing decision-makers the world over. The series stresses issues relevant in many countries and regions, accessible to broad professional and academic audiences as well as to students, and enduring through explicit theoretical foundations.

Nonproliferation Policy and Nuclear Posture
Causes and Consequences for the Spread of Nuclear Weapons
Edited by Neil Narang, Erik Gartzke and Matthew Kroenig

North Korea, Iran and the Challenge to International Order
A Comparative Perspective
Patrick McEachern and Jaclyn O'Brien McEachern

Stable Nuclear Zero
The Vision and Its Implications for Disarmament Policy
Edited by Sverre Lodgaard

US Grand Strategy in the 21st Century
The Case for Restraint
Edited by A. Trevor Thrall and Benjamin H. Friedman

US National Security Reform
Reassessing the National Security Act of 1947
Edited by Heidi B. Demarest and Erica D. Borghard

For more information about this series, please visit: https://www.routledge.com/Routledge-Global-Security-Studies/book-series/RGSS

'Seventy years after America's national security institutions were formed in the wake of the Second World War, this book assesses their evolution and how they are holding up under today's challenges. The contributors' views will inform scholars and policy-makers alike and provoke debate on how best to retain our strategic advantage.'

—*Ambassador Douglas Lute,*
Former US Permanent Representative to NATO, USA

'The disruptions of the early 21st Century are proving at least as challenging as those that led to the creation of the National Security Act over seventy years ago. This impressive volume is a must-read for any practitioner or scholar seeking to assess the durability of our current national security system, the conditions that might give rise to further change, and the prospects for successful reform.'

—*Dr Kathleen Hicks, Senior Vice President,*
Henry A. Kissinger Chair, and Director, International Security Program,
Center for Strategic and International Studies, USA

'West Point's Senior Conference pulled together some of the most deeply thoughtful scholars and practitioners of American national security to kick the tires on the 1947 National Security Act and determine whether it's still road-worthy for the nation's needs. As a participant in the conversations, what struck me most was how the gravity of West Point's culture depoliticized debates, a rarity on these important issues in our polarized time. This terrific book conveys the most important intellectual contributions from those debates about the structure and processes of American national security – it deserves a wide audience in classrooms, among policy practitioners, and our concerned citizens.'

—*Dr Kori Schake, Deputy Director-General,*
International Institute for Strategic Studies, UK

US NATIONAL SECURITY REFORM

Reassessing the National Security Act of 1947

Edited by Heidi B. Demarest and Erica D. Borghard

Routledge
Taylor & Francis Group

LONDON AND NEW YORK

First published 2019
by Routledge
2 Park Square, Milton Park, Abingdon, Oxon OX14 4RN

and by Routledge
711 Third Avenue, New York, NY 10017

Routledge is an imprint of the Taylor & Francis Group, an informa business

British Library Cataloguing-in-Publication Data
A catalogue record for this book is available from the British Library

Library of Congress Cataloging-in-Publication Data
Names: Demarest, Heidi Brockmann, 1979- editor. | Borghard, Erica D., editor.
Title: US national security reform: reassessing the National Security Act of 1947 /
edited by Heidi B. Demarest and Erica D. Borghard.
Description: 1st edition. | Abingdon, Oxon; New York, NY: Routledge, 2018. |
Series: Routledge global security studies | Includes bibliographical references
and index.
Identifiers: LCCN 2018008055| ISBN 9780815398462 (hardback) |
ISBN 9780815399582 (pbk.) | ISBN 9781351171564 (e-book)
Subjects: LCSH: National security–United States. | National security–Law and
legislation–United States. | United States. National Security Act of 1947. |
National security–United States–Decision making.
Classification: LCC UA23 .U777 2018 | DDC 355/.033573–dc23
LC record available at https://lccn.loc.gov/2018008055

ISBN: 978-0-8153-9846-2 (hbk)
ISBN: 978-0-8153-9958-2 (pbk)
ISBN: 978-1-351-17156-4 (ebk)

Typeset in Bembo
by Deanta Global Publishing Services, Chennai, India

CONTENTS

CONTRIBUTORS

Deborah Avant is a Professor and Director of the Sié Chéou-Kang Center for International Security and Diplomacy at Josef Korbel School of International Studies, University of Denver, USA.

Richard K. Betts is the Arnold A. Saltzman Professor and Director of the Saltzman Institute of War and Peace Studies at Columbia University, USA.

Meena Bose is the Executive Dean at Peter S. Kalikow School of Government, Public Policy and International Affairs, Hofstra University, USA.

Risa A. Brooks is the Allis Chalmers Associate Professor of Political Science at Marquette University, USA.

David S. C. Chu is the President of the Institute for Defense Analyses.

I. M. (Mac) Destler is the Saul Stern Professor of Civic Engagement at the University of Maryland School of Public Policy, USA.

Andrew F. Krepinevich, Jr. is the President and Chief Operating Officer of Solarium LLC.

Douglas L. Kriner is a Professor of Political Science at Boston University, USA.

Thomas G. Mahnken is the President and Chief Executive Officer of the Center for Strategic and Budgetary Assessments.

Walter Russell Mead is the James Clark Chase Professor of Foreign Affairs and Humanities at Bard College, USA.

Barry R. Posen is the Ford International Professor of Political Science at Massachusetts Institute of Technology, USA.

ACKNOWLEDGMENTS

The editors would like to thank each of the contributors to this volume, whose creativity and expertise continue to inspire us beyond the completion of this project. We owe a debt of gratitude to Andrew Humphrys and the editorial team at Taylor & Francis, without whose boundless patience and professionalism this volume would not exist. We are also deeply appreciative of the leadership, ideas, and support of Brigadier General Cindy Jebb, Colonel Suzanne Nielsen, and our colleagues in the Department of Social Sciences at the United States Military Academy.

The ideas expressed in this volume are those of the authors and editors alone, and do not reflect the official position of the Department of Defense, the Department of the Army, or the United States Military Academy.

INTRODUCTION

How should we think about national security reform?

Heidi B. Demarest

On July 26, 1947, Congress passed legislation that purported to "provide a comprehensive program for the future security of the United States."[1] Unquestionably, the National Security Act of 1947 forever changed the way America organizes for and conducts national security policy. The Act established a Secretary of Defense and the Joint Chiefs of Staff to "provide for the effective strategic direction of the armed forces and for their operation under unified control," created the National Security Council as an advisory body to the president to improve integration and cooperation between national security agencies, and outlined the duties of a new Central Intelligence Agency, which was intended to coordinate intelligence activities across the government.[2] Even for people who live and work in places far removed from the national security establishment, it would be difficult to imagine America without the Secretary of Defense or the CIA. Yet, that nation existed as recently as 75 years ago.

This volume is the product of many conversations about what people in another 75 years might think about how our nation approaches national security policy. Is the National Security Act of 1947 durable enough to persist unscathed? Or has the world changed so significantly over the better part of the past century that our existing institutions and frameworks require reimagining? Will future national security challenges seem unrecognizable and render our current institutions and practices defunct?

Eleven experts who study the national security establishment, many of whom have practical experience in government, took up this topic in 2016 at West Point, New York in the midst of a contentious presidential election. Their perspectives are predictably diverse. All of them, however, would agree that the future is likely to present challenges to American national security incomparable to the past, and that *some* degree of evolution will be required to confront these challenges successfully—though, remarkably, the majority of these scholars agree that the power to enact these changes lies within the executive branch today. The extent and character of a national security enterprise metamorphosis and the mechanism by which it occurs provide rich fodder for debate among our contributors and our readers.

Consider the backdrop to the National Security Act of 1947. National security policy centered on the Cold War after recent combat experience in World War II. A bipolar distribution of power in the international security environment provided relative stability. The Marshall Plan and the establishment of the North Atlantic Treaty Organization reassured European allies and promoted economic growth. President Truman eschewed isolationism and eagerly supported the fledgling United Nations, amid a domestic policy agenda focused on economic prosperity. Congress managed to work with the president to achieve meaningful legislation on domestic policy issues.

But organizational problems within the national military establishment and foreign policy community abounded. The nation's experience in World War II had exposed gaps in how coherently America executed national security policy in support of strategic aims. The military services acted in parallel but with fierce independence; the president's intelligence support structure lacked prioritization and oversight; and executive agencies responsible for implementing the president's strategic guidance did so largely without regard to one another. The National Security Act of 1947 did not solve these problems all at once. In fact, President Truman opposed the creation of the National Security Council, fearing it would usurp his executive authority, and flat-out refused to attend its meetings. It took the better part of a decade for the institutions created by the National Security Act to find their footing, assisted by intentional ambiguity within the law.[3]

The contributors to this volume consider the evolution of each of three threads over the past 70 years—global threats and the international security environment; the domestic political landscape; and institutional obstacles within the national security enterprise—and ground their recommendations for national security reform in their characterizations of the present and the future, in contrast with the past.

Global threats and the international security environment

Most experts in this volume agree that the post-Cold War world is more dangerous, more complex, and altogether more worrisome than the stable bipolar world order to which America had become accustomed in the 20th century. Future national security policymakers will have to address not only the contemporary dangerous consequences of religious fundamentalism, terrorism, fractured regional alliances, or regional state powers that possess nuclear weapons, but also revisionist powers like China, Russia, and Iran that invite the once-negligible possibility of great power conflict. As Andrew F. Krepinevich, Jr. notes, rival states are closing the gap with the U.S. in their ability to project military power, and both Krepinevich and Walter Russell Mead warn of the erosion of deterrence as a viable or effective approach to American foreign policy in a world where the best defense is a good offense. Barry R. Posen characterizes the same geopolitical trend away from bipolarity as a "diffusion of power," eventually dispersing to multipolarity, where not only states but individuals and groups retain the ability to pose credible threats and use weapons and tactics once employed exclusively by states. And then, there is cyberspace. This entirely new domain has expanded the scope of potential threats, adversaries, and capabilities far beyond what the architects of the National Security Act could have imagined.

Scholars oriented on the distribution of power in the international arena also agree on one principle when it comes to national security reform: all efforts are futile in the absence of a clearly defined strategy. Thomas G. Mahnken's call to clarify, prioritize, and resource our strategic goals is accompanied by the observation that change will not occur or persist without executive support, and Mahnken is joined by Krepinevich and Posen in the opinion that an overhaul of existing institutions is unwarranted and unlikely without a clear strategic vision. It remains to be seen whether President Trump's America First national security strategy provides the guidance, direction, and executive backing required to tinker with the organizational structure of the national security enterprise. Authors offer their own proposals aimed at preparing for the future in the absence of a grand strategic vision: Walter Russell Mead recommends full-throated support of the technology revolution, likening American foreign policy to a video game in which the player advances to more complex and demanding levels, and calls for investment in reimagining the Pentagon's bureaucratic routines. Barry R. Posen challenges would-be national security officials to become more educated and attuned to how other nations work, and to invest time in the kind of strategic forecasting befitting of a nation interpreting political intelligence and employing diplomacy in support of national priorities and interests. But the majority of these recommendations, the authors concede, are not statutory. Many could be implemented today with existing authorities.

Domestic politics

The absence of American grand strategy lamented by some of our contributors is explained by others who study American political behavior and institutions. These experts acknowledge a variety of circumstances within American government that hobble our efforts to create grand strategy and execute effective national security policy. The range is broad. Rising personnel costs within the Department of Defense and increases in mandatory spending threaten economic stability and act as political third rails. Overreliance on contractors to perform services for the American military abroad and a corresponding refusal to acknowledge it obscures all options but a one-size-fits-all-conflicts military response to international crises. Increased polarization in the electorate and the legislature, along with greater secrecy and control of sensitive information by the executive, has resulted in an increase in executive power and a relative decline of congressional oversight of foreign policy. The proposed solutions to these problems are as diverse as their scope.

First, the temptation is to throw up our hands at the domestic political environment. In this post-2016 era, we are all spectators observing the actions of a divided government within a starkly divided society. No amount of reform to the National Security Act of 1947 will induce the electorate toward moderation, so to the extent that our problems are caused by or are a function of political polarization, we may just have to wait it out.

But there *are* some steps we might consider taking within the political arena. Risa A. Brooks encourages us to begin with first principles of national strategy: how might we structure the strategic decision-making process in a way where more people would agree that it makes sense? Strategy, Brooks continues, should reveal clear relationships between means and ends and employ some degree of causal logic. Strategy should be integrated across multiple dimensions and instruments of national power. All of this is possible to achieve through well-designed national security institutions, a thorough understanding of the decision-making process of key policy actors and advisors, or with high-quality content and analysis of information used in national security decision-making. In particular, Brooks contends that presidents ought to seek greater self-awareness in their decision-making, a caution that Douglas L. Kriner would likely agree with. Each time the executive retains exclusive access to information about a highly classified mission in the name of national security, the system of checks and balances as imagined by the Founders erodes. To shore up the system of legislative oversight as originally designed and attempt to check the growing assertion of executive power, Kriner argues, Congress needs to build up their capacity from the inside. Stronger national security committees can do much to alleviate the information asymmetry with the executive branch and help Congress perform the role they were meant to fulfill in our democracy.

All of these proposed solutions lead to increased attention, acknowledgment, and discussion of the myriad problems in national security decision-making. Our collective inability to admit that we have problems within the national security enterprise hinders our ability to fix them, as Deborah Avant notes. Not only have we seemed to have decided as a nation that military might is the correct instrument to use when responding to national security crises, despite our experiences in the global war on terror and our subsequent attempts to counter and prevent violent extremism, but we have neglected to collect, analyze, and catalogue the lessons we learned through hard-won practice. Avant is adamant that we must first eschew debates over *solutions* in favor of gathering diverse voices to discuss *problems* in order to move forward in the current domestic political environment.

Again, only a few of these proposals—primarily the reorganization and redistribution of responsibilities within existing congressional committees—lend themselves to the kind of reform reminiscent of the National Security Act of 1947. All else can be accomplished in the present political environment through force of personality or will, using the apparatus in place today.

National security institutions

But surely some concrete improvements can be made to the brick-and-mortar institutions charged with formulating and implementing national security policy. After all, the National Security Act of 1947 created agencies and institutional arrangements that have remained generally static—isn't it time these agencies adapted to confront the more strenuous challenges in the contemporary national security environment? Our experts, for the most part, agree that some changes are in order. But those changes are already within the power of the executive branch to make.

Executive personalities and management styles have always influenced each administration's approach to national security policy in the spaces between formal institutions and defined responsibilities, and the Trump administration is no exception. Meena Bose takes a retrospective look at six presidents and their preferences for engaging with and managing the National Security Council apparatus and its members. Again, the National Security Act of 1947 established the Council as an advisory body to the president, and intended the National Security Council staff to improve coordination and integration of national security policy among executive agencies. In practice over time, this has happened with varying degrees of success. A president who maintains personal involvement in national security policy-making is judged, unsurprisingly, to have presided over a more efficient and successful national security policy process, though the formal apparatus is virtually identical across administrations. Bose also discusses the role of the National Security Advisor, and deduces that that most important responsibilities of the person holding that position are to run the National Security Council staff and ensure the quality of analytic products provided to decision-makers. Not all National Security Advisors have embraced these responsibilities.

Mac Destler would respond to Bose's conclusions by arguing that the National Security Advisor faces an uphill battle wrangling the contemporary National Security Council staff. This is not because the quality of the president's special assistants for national security has declined, but rather that the number of staff has risen exponentially and become too unwieldy to realize its intended value. As both Bose and Destler acknowledge, centralizing national security decision-making within the White House does little to bolster the flexibility and agility of the policy process; a growing staff only places greater demands for time on the relatively few close personal advisors to the president, and creates unnecessary bottlenecks at the top. Both authors are optimistic about a more streamlined, effective national security policy process given an executive with the personality to devote personal time and attention to the NSC and the desire to cut the staff back to more manageable levels; again, these suggested improvements require no action on the part of Congress.

Neither do David S. C. Chu's recommended adjustments to the resource allocation process within the Department of Defense rely on congressional intervention. Chu's institutional focus is on the office of the Secretary of Defense, whose role was created by the National Security Act and subsequently strengthened by follow-on amendments. The Pentagon's budgeting process has been in place since 1961 and the dawn of Secretary of Defense Robert McNamara's era of cost-effective analysis. Opponents and criticism of the budgeting process for national defense abound. The budget process is insensitive to developments in the world that impact American grand strategy; its ability to reflect American grand strategy is questionable; and we are largely unable to assess how well past budgets were implemented and use those lessons in the future (a criticism Deborah Avant echoes and applies to the military's application of resources to the current fight against violent extremism). To address these problems, Chu recommends starting with people. What is the right mix of personnel to accomplish the military's missions? What level of flexibility ought to be incorporated into manning, based on the nation's strategic interests and likely engagements throughout the world? What is the mission driving the planning process within the Department of Defense? These questions, of course, begin with firm executive preferences expressed early enough to affect the unrelenting budgeting machine devised by Secretary McNamara—and creativity on the part of military decision-makers. Even within the unwieldy Department of Defense, it appears enough latitude exists to make substantive improvements to legacy institutions without the help of the legislative branch.

Another perspective on change

The first chapter of this book appears to undercut the entire premise of the volume. Richard K. Betts argues that if the National Security Act of 1947 isn't broken, we shouldn't be so quick to fix it. And, as the chapters unfold across a variety of perspectives—by assessing global threats and the national security environment, evaluating contemporary domestic political behavior and institutions, and the structure of national security institutions themselves—the authors generally fall in line with Betts. Institutions must function (and are indeed designed to do so) despite wide variation over time of the people who inhabit them. Betts points to several problems and mistakes borne out through the current institutional structure, and concludes that failures are a result of individual personalities, rather than systemic errors in process. The Congress, despite its ability to enact revolutionary reforms to affect the way the United States government organizes for national security, cannot enforce the process as intended or imagined. And, in a nod to a deep tradition of scholars who examine how changes occur and decisions are made in bureaucracies dealing with complex problems, Betts ultimately recommends an evolutionary approach to reform. Even small changes may create unforeseen problems and exacerbate the admittedly inefficient practice of national security policy.

What, then, is the point of this book, if not to call for a new National Security Act? Is the National Security Act of 1947 and its subsequent amendments adequate for the challenges of the next 75 years? Fortunately, each chapter contains a rich critique of how national security policy is formulated or implemented, and proposes steps that can be taken today to improve our processes and institutions. The essays in this volume formed the foundation of a second discussion about national security reform in 2017 at West Point, where practitioners informed by the scholars' work devised a series of concrete steps for policymakers responsible for devising, executing, or providing oversight of American national security. The summary of the discussion is included as an afterword, along with the list of practitioners who helped create it. Whether or not you agree with the recommendations for reform, it serves as but one example of the type of thinking provoked by this collection of diverse essays. And, as we believe everyone whose work is included in this book would agree, creative and critical thinking about our national security apparatus has only grown in importance during an unorthodox era of the American experience.

Notes

1 80th Cong., 1st Sess., Public Law 253, Sec. 2.
2 Ibid.
3 Douglas T. Stuart, *Creating the National Security State: A History of the Law That Transformed America*, Princeton: Princeton University Press, 2012, 8–9.

1

THE DURABLE NATIONAL SECURITY ACT

Richard K. Betts

The National Security Act of 1947 is now well past normal retirement age but like many other baby boomers is still working full-time. As the Trump revolution unfolds, should we expect to see it junked?

Even before Trump there were calls to update the fundamental statutory basis for national security decision and implementation, as young up-and-comers looked impatiently at the seemingly outmoded attitudes and waning capacities of elders they wished would step aside. The urge to replace is natural for those who focus on blunders in the substance of national security policy and assume results would have been better if the process of policymaking had been different. Or it seems natural to frustrated toilers inside the Beltway as they focus on barriers to accomplishing the specific priorities of interest to them among the complex mix of purposes in national security.

If we look beyond the intuition stoked by immediate dissatisfactions the case for major change is unclear. Dissatisfaction is largely about the speed and results of the existing structure and process. Speed is blunted in large part by the conflict of complex competing interests and the checks and balances that protect them. This is the price of democratic government in general. Results, in turn, depend on the wisdom of incumbents who act through the existing process. At some level, judgment about the success or failure of institutions is not independent of the policy that comes out of them, but designers can only aim for structures and processes that will *enable* a proper process or decision; they cannot select the individuals who accede to power over time and inhabit the structures. Office holders come and go, true institutions must endure for generations. Successful institutions set and bound the conditions in which government operates and provide incentives and opportunities for fallible incumbents to do their best. Institutions must work despite wide variation over time in officials' ideologies, experience, and sensibility, and through tidal changes in the political, economic, and social conditions that surround them.

A bad structure may hamper good designs of wise incumbents, but a good structure cannot prevent bad initiatives or foolish ones. In short, it is important to focus on the difference between institutions and outcomes or the difference between a design that optimizes one purpose and a design that "satisfices" across the board when many purposes conflict. Fixing particular problems opens the door to other problems.

There are two main managerial issues to be handled over time: horizontal and vertical. The horizontal one is when to add new organs, as technology changes and new functions or policy problem areas emerge. In principle, this should also mean when to retire obsolete organs, although this hardly ever happens, so the complexity of the system tends to grow. The vertical issue is where the balance should be struck between the benefits of centralization and decentralization of authority.

Among the tests of how well an institutional system manages these adaptations are whether it works to reveal issues requiring consideration and decision, provides relevant information and options to policymakers, and produces clear and deliberate actions rather than accidental or unrecognized ones. A system must enable these processes even if it cannot force a president and his lieutenants to take proper advantage of them – a big issue in the evolving Trump era. Enabling requires some balance between organizational pluralism and decentralization to represent relevant concerns, and integration and centralization to impose direction and coherence on choices. The National Security Act and the several amendments and additions to it have accomplished these aims imperfectly, but better than the less developed system before 1947, and probably as well on balance as a system that might be designed differently. In the United States since 1947 failures in national security policy have been due far more to high politics and misjudgments than to the managerial apparatus established by the Act.

When attention focuses on the difference between institutions and results, and one considers whatever else is on offer, the National Security Act still looks like a solid foundation. This does not mean that no changes in the system are needed. New problems can sometimes prove revolutionary – today, for example, the rapid emergence of cybersecurity as a fundamental priority for all elements of government and the civilian economy. The question is whether necessary adaptations cannot be thoroughly accomplished within the limits of existing legislation. No structure remains perfectly suited for a mission over long spans of evolving conditions and challenges, and any that is successful must evolve along with its context, but the institutions designed in 1947 and the 1949 amendments to the Act, tweaked occasionally since, have proved remarkably able to perform their functions through changing times.

Strategic revolution, institutional evolution

What was the impetus for the Act? Consensus on peacetime American activism in the world, and maintenance of a large standing military establishment, is now deeply rooted in American politics, but in 1947 it was new. Within government the National Security Act gave support to the direction in which the United States had been firmly headed since Pearl Harbor. The idea of isolationism had always been exaggerated anyway. The United States had been deeply involved in Asia since 1898 and in Latin America earlier; isolationism applied in effect to abstention from the European balance of power. Events of the 1930s and subsequent global catastrophe discredited that abstention and World War II left Washington with dramatically expanded political, economic, and military roles, both outside and inside the country.

Outside, the war had left revolutionary changes in world order: economic unipolarity and politico-military bipolarity. With the rest of the West in ruins, both revolutions in world order seemed to demand American leadership. Inside, all of the American government had grown rapidly, first in the New Deal, then in the mobilization for war. Both outside and inside the country these expansions naturally generated efforts to organize and integrate the proliferation of participants and mechanisms of policymaking and implementation. Outside, the point was to unite allies in reliable and effective collaboration well before war, to avoid the mistakes of the 1930s. Inside, the point was to bring coherence to a complex array of organizations that had emerged haphazardly and grown quickly.

On the inside, there was an anti-statist tradition that remained an undercurrent and constrained some aspects of Cold War mobilization.[1] The domestic consensus for sustaining muscular government across the board, however, lasted nearly half a century, from Roosevelt until Reagan. Although that consensus has faltered since then it is useful to remember that none of the three Republican presidents between 1945 and 1981 challenged the main institutions of the New Deal. In any case, the consensus (or to be accurate, the elite consensus) on international activism, and thus for maintaining robust national security institutions, has lasted longer than the public's favorable view of government in general. Civilian political leaders are rated low in public opinion surveys but the military remains more respected and popular than almost all other domestic institutions. Commitment to forward-leaning foreign policy has been stronger among the American elite than in mass opinion, but it endures and controls, brushing off political challenge from losers such as Robert Taft, George McGovern, Pat Buchanan, Ralph Nader, or Ron and Rand Paul. (Donald Trump has tilted erratically in the direction of retrenchment when he rails about free-riding allies, but has more often indulged his contradictory instinct toward belligerence.) The domestic reflection of the global mission at its dawn was the reshaping of the policymaking system in the 1947 Act.

The principal early efforts to organize and integrate in the outside world were the United Nations (UN) and North Atlantic Treaty Organization (NATO), multinational organizations led by the United States. Many had high hopes for the UN at its birth and assumed it would play an important material role in peace enforcement. In an exclamation in 1950 that now seems quaintly naïve after more than six decades of international violence, Secretary General Trygve

Lie responded to Assistant Secretary of State John Hickerson's news that North Korea had invaded the South in June 1950 by blurting, "My God, Jack, that's a violation of the United Nations Charter!"[2] The UN's utility, however, has remained primarily diplomatic, while NATO in Europe and bilateral alliances elsewhere have been the effective instruments for the prevention and prosecution of America's wars.

In the late 1940s American economic hegemony, represented in the Marshall Plan and its bureaucratic embodiment, the Economic Cooperation Administration (ECA), underwrote NATO's political and military counterweight to the threat from Moscow. The USSR was ravaged by the war, but left with military forces controlling half of Europe and ideological influence, via Communist parties, within the countries of the other half. As time went on, the overwhelming American economic dominance was eroded as Europe, Japan, and the Soviet Union recovered, but bipolarity endured and intensified – politically, as electoral challenges from western Communist parties were blunted and the two blocs solidified, and militarily, as Moscow developed nuclear weapons – and the peacetime fielding of large conventional forces on both sides continued.

NATO was the main event in external integration. As Robert Osgood emphasized more than a half-century ago, it was an unprecedented alliance in two respects. First, it was a peacetime commitment by the United States to immediate involvement in a European war – the "entangling alliance" against which Washington's Farewell Address had warned, but which the lessons of the 1930s were seen to require. Along with the Marshall Plan which preceded it, the North Atlantic Treaty marked the Republican Party's enlistment in the Cold War consensus, as Senator Arthur Vandenberg's support trumped Robert Taft's opposition.

Osgood's second emphasis remains NATO's most significant aspect today: "NATO is unique among peacetime alliances. In fact, it has assumed tasks of multinational planning, decision, and action that few wartime alliances have performed."[3] It evolved quickly from a simple guaranty pact into a highly integrated transnational *institution*. As with any alliance, members pledged to come to each other's defense in event of war (although the limits of this Article 5 promise have traditionally been overlooked).[4] NATO went further. It established joint command structures, mechanisms, and peacetime deployments as well as a formal North Atlantic Council (NAC) for regular consultation and deliberation. Institutionalization underwrote the presumption of automaticity in the mutual commitment. In the early days some, especially Dwight Eisenhower, thought the peacetime forward presence of U.S. forces in the integrated defense plan would be temporary as Western Europe recovered and created, in effect, tripolarity.[5] Instead, permanent peacetime deployment was assumed after the 1950s as Washington pushed the strategic concept of flexible response on the allies.

Fatefully, NATO's unique institutionalization was not replicated in Asia. There was no NEATO for Northeast Asia. In principle, there was multinational military action in Korea, via the UN Command, but in practice, especially after the 1953 truce, deterrence in Korea was a bilateral affair between Washington and Seoul. Starting in 1955, with the French withdrawal from Indochina, there was a Southeast Asia Treaty Organization (SEATO) but it never developed beyond a hollow shell. Indeed it was almost immediately moribund, although it did take twenty years to die officially after proving irrelevant to the main conflict of its time, the second Indochina war.

In one sense there was less need in Asia for the unprecedented military integration of NATO because the main asset to be defended, Japan, was protected by a water barrier, unlike Germany and France, and the geography of the peninsula limited the conventional force that Communist powers could bring to bear on the short front. The other military challenges in Asia were primarily revolutionary movements, as in Vietnam, against which maximizing a conventional force was not the main problem. The absence of a clearly mobilized and articulated multinational deterrent, however, did enable North Korean miscalculation in 1950. Today the absence of a multinational security organization also reflects the continuing hesitancy of countries in the region to commit to united deterrence of Chinese expansion.

Postwar demobilization proceeded even as the 1947 Act was passed – conscription lapsed in that year, although it was soon renewed when the Berlin Blockade began in 1948 – but much of the organization of U.S. military forces to backstop bipolarity was in place or nascent by the time of the 1947 Act. Forerunners of the system of unified and specified commands that came to implement the global sweep of U.S. military operations in the Cold War grew out of the preceding war and subsequent occupations: the army's European Command and Far East Command, and the Strategic Air Command formed in the Army Air Force the year before the Act made the service independent. The Joint Chiefs of Staff (JCS), which had grown out of the Joint Board in early 1942, became permanent. Similarly, modest centralization of foreign intelligence functions already occurred with the Central Intelligence Group (CIG) before the Act made it into the Central Intelligence Agency (CIA). Many postwar planners hoped for fundamental changes that would truly unify the armed services and consolidate organizations, but resistance (especially from the navy) kept the final legislation from going that far.[6] For the institutions to carry out U.S. policy, the National Security Act clarified, codified, and extended the institutional evolution that originated in World War II.

The bumper sticker for the main effects of the 1947 Act would be "coordinating pluralism." Some officials, frustrated by the complexity of overlapping and independent units involved in planning and operations during World War II, hoped for dramatic consolidation of functions. After the pulling and hauling that produced the Act this did not happen; duplication and overlaps largely survived, although they became subject to higher-level oversight, and over time, some greater discipline. Three new organizations, however, were crucial management innovations. Establishment of the Department of Defense (DoD) did not merge the separate services, but it did create a civilian hierarchy that could arbitrate, choose, or direct among the services more effectively than before.[7] Establishment of the Director of Central Intelligence (DCI) did not merge the intelligence functions of the military services' and State Department's intelligence units, but it did create more coherent mechanisms for getting information and analysis to the top. Establishment of the National Security Council (NSC) did not streamline the bureaucracies, but did formalize and regularize the process of representing them in ultimate decisions.

Organizing for decision and direction

For developing policy the 1947 Act created novel organs to accomplish coordination, the inadequacy of which had been proven during the war. The Department of Defense, the biggest and most important of the organizational innovations, has persisted as a giant conglomerate combining large and diverse military forces, technological research and development, complex and expensive procurement programs, and a dense corps of civilian managers. Over time the crucial evolutions have been the growth and clout of staff in agencies of the Office of the Secretary of Defense (OSD), the elaboration and thickening of the system of peacetime combatant commands worldwide (known as "the CINCs," or Combatant Commanders in Chief, until Donald Rumsfeld changed the designation), and a major ratchet in unification of the armed services through a strengthened JCS since the Goldwater-Nichols reform.

The CIA did not take control of separate intelligence services but limited centralization did occur under the CIA director's other hat, the more senior position of Director of Central Intelligence (DCI). This second, more important, hat was consistently misunderstood outside the intelligence community (IC). One institutional change that was more radical than evolutionary was the warrant for covert political operations abroad that was given to the CIA. Even this grew out of wartime – the Office of Strategic Services (OSS) – but it heralded the routinization of a function never before common for the United States in peacetime. Covert action was at best only vaguely authorized in the 1947 legislation, which directed the agency "to perform such other functions and duties related to intelligence affecting the national security as the National Security Council may from time to time direct."[8] (More specific authorization for covert action came from the council later in the year via directive NSC 4A and, in 1948, NSC 10/2.) At the time, DCI Roscoe Hillenkoetter resisted taking responsibility for the function, which is really a matter of policy execution rather than intelligence collection, but the CIA was stuck with it when Secretary of State George Marshall refused to let the State Department take it.[9]

As the small group of the most senior policymakers, the NSC was to preside over consideration of issues that cut across departmental concerns. The closest thing to the NSC under the old system was the State-War-Navy Coordinating Committee (SWNCC), but that did not operate at the highest level as the NSC would – as, in effect, a subset of the cabinet.[10] The National Security Act itself also mandated the council "to advise the President with respect to the integration of *domestic*, foreign, and military policies" and "to assess and appraise the objectives, commitments, and risks of the United States in relation to our actual and potential military power."[11] Truman and Eisenhower added the secretary of the treasury to the normal attendees at NSC meetings, to integrate consideration of domestic and military policies, but for most of the past half-century the NSC has not been known as a forum for considering fiscal or other elements of domestic policy, despite their relevance to security policy. (Instead, even as NSC activity in foreign affairs expanded, a separate entity was created to deal with the most essential domain of national security: the Homeland Security Council.)

Hardly anyone now remembers, but the original idea for the NSC differed from what most see as its role today. In the mind of James Forrestal, the first secretary of defense, who had chafed under what he saw as Franklin Roosevelt's freewheeling initiatives during the war, the NSC would regularize consultation and constrain and discipline the president. As time passed, it would evolve into more of the reverse: an enforcement arm of the president over the departments.

In the policy process the council proper (meaning the statutory members),[12] the group meant to confer with and influence the president, is not what many think of anymore when they hear "National Security Council." Instead most think of the NSC *staff*, which began as primarily a paper-shuffling conduit from the departments but evolved into the president's own staff. For a while the Obama administration even took the word "Council" out of the name for the unit, calling it simply the National Security Staff (NSS), implicitly a purely White House organ. The term "National Security Advisor" did not come into usage until the 1970s and was not in the authorizing legislation, which specified only an executive secretary to direct the staff. This position evolved into Special Assistant (and, under Nixon, simply Assistant to the President) for National Security Affairs. (In the rank inflation of recent times the bulked-up staff came to include numerous "Special Assistants" to the President.) All this reflects the extent to which the NSC staff and its head originated as managers of departmental participation in policy formulation but developed into policy players in their own right – a development that became controversial with Henry Kissinger, as it has been periodically ever since.[13] It can be no surprise that activist presidents become inclined to hold as many of the reins as possible in the White House rather than leave policy to the vagaries of bureaucracy. The assertive role of the National Security Advisor recedes at some points, especially as it did twice under Brent Scowcroft, but tends to return.

The controversy over whether the NSC staff should shape policy or simply coordinate it went with the widening of the staff's purview. As the NSC evolved it became a forum for discussing all of foreign policy rather than focusing on aspects related to war and peace, as originally envisioned. The staff became a collection of mini-departments paralleling the bigger bureaucracies in Defense, State, Treasury, and the intelligence community. From a number around twenty in the early 1960s the NSC's professional staff grew to about a hundred in the second George W. Bush administration.[14] Under Obama that size reportedly more than doubled and provoked wide resentment within the departments for its tendency to micromanage.

How well has the system worked?

The system operates for whoever runs it, and cannot always compensate for other determinants of results: the balance of power in the outside world that enables the United States to work its will or prevents it from doing so; the limitations of information available to the system, whoever may be in charge; and especially the vagaries of personality and the incidence of bad judgment by the individual office holders due to ignorance, ideology, recklessness, vanity, wishful thinking, reticence, or other subjective factors and human frailties.

For example, reticence, encouraged by the awesomeness of presence at Olympus, is an often underestimated subverter of formal process. Chester Cooper, who had doubts about the war in Vietnam, recounts:

> The President, in due course would announce his decision and then poll everyone in the room – [National Security] Council members, their assistants, and members of the White House and NSC staffs … . "Mr. X, do you agree?" "I agree, Mr. President." During the process I would frequently fall into a Walter Mitty-like fantasy: When my turn came I would rise to my feet slowly, look around the room and then directly at the President, and say very quietly, "Mr. President, gentlemen, I most definitely do *not* agree." But I was removed from my trance when I heard the President's voice saying, "Mr. Cooper, do you agree?" And out would come a "Yes, Mr. President, I agree."[15]

This subjective problem is not susceptible to fixing through legislation. At the same time that Cooper admitted that human failure, however, he also demonstrated that the official formal products mandated by the NSC system – National Intelligence Estimates (NIEs) on Vietnam – were for the most part remarkably accurate.[16]

It is reasonable to assume that national security policy in the Cold War would have been worse in the absence of the integrating reforms of the 1947 Act, because the underdeveloped system of the pre-1940 era couldn't handle the load – it simply afforded less availability of information, fewer specialized organs, and inadequate top-level coordination of the departments. No one suggests returning to the less articulated and less centralized system of a century ago. In the course of the past seventy years, moreover, needed additions and expansions could be accomplished through simple executive order or specific legislative authorizations that did not reshape the overall structure – for example, the creation of the National Security Agency (NSA) in 1952, the Defense Intelligence Agency (DIA), and the Arms Control and Disarmament Agency (ACDA) in 1961, or the replacement of the Atomic Energy Commission (AEC) by the Nuclear Regulatory Commission (NRC) and Energy Research and Development Administration (ERDA) in 1974.[17] It is hard to see how a system of enhanced coordination that is markedly different in form from what has evolved since 1947 would necessarily have made policy better. Among the failures in Cold War policy, which would have been reversed if organizations different from the DoD, CIA, and NSC had been created?

It would be hard to ascribe much of the responsibility for the two biggest disasters in the time since the 1947 Act – the Vietnam War and the second war against Iraq – to the institutions that were in place as a result of the Act and its additions. There were many fateful mistakes in deciding for both wars and prosecuting them, but few that could be attributed to faulty strictures of policymaking organs. Contrary to common assumptions, American leaders did not stumble into Vietnam with no idea of what they were getting into; the commitment was due to the conviction at the highest level that there was no acceptable alternative to preventing Communist victory.[18]

As for Iraq, organizational dynamics of the legislatively formalized system did not push Bush and company to decide for war, because they did not take full advantage of the system. Indeed, there apparently was never any formal examination of the question of whether to go to war or any formal NSC meeting to debate the decision. Legislation can establish structure but it cannot enforce process.

President Trump would do well to contemplate the lesson from this case: policymakers ignored or overrode the checks and balances on their judgment that the system afforded. Secretary of Defense Donald Rumsfeld was well aware that most professionals in the U.S. Army thought the lean invasion force he wanted would be too small to stabilize the country, and he was well aware that the State Department was pushing for more planning for the aftermath of combat. He suppressed the first because he wanted to show that the technical "Revolution in Military Affairs" enabled military success with lean forces, and suppressed the second in order to avert postwar entanglement in the country. These were decisions made not because of the organization of the policymaking process but because of Rumsfeld's personal judgment and confidence. In the same vein Secretary of State Colin Powell's reservations about the plan for war were not suppressed by the apparatus of decision-making but were soft-pedaled by Powell himself and, such as they were, simply rejected by President Bush, who favored Rumsfeld.

A partial exception to the exoneration of process was the October 2002 National Intelligence Estimate (NIE) on Iraq's weapons of mass destruction. Although it did not cause the war, since Bush's decision preceded the estimate, it did provide the excuse for it, when a more accurate estimate would have made it difficult to sell the decision for war to Congress and the public. But even here the main problem was the individual judgment of intelligence managers about how to package the presentation of the analysis rather than the information or analysis itself that came out of the system. The actual evidence behind the estimate turned out to be meager, which might be an indictment of the quality of the institutions responsible for collecting intelligence, but on balance it is fair to say that the estimate's conclusion was wrong for the right reason.[19] It is very difficult psychologically and politically to differentiate judgment of process and results. Reviewing the criticism of the 2002 policy process by the Senate Select Committee on Intelligence Robert Jervis points out:

> We like to think that bad outcomes are to be explained by bad processes, but this needs to be demonstrated rather than assumed ... . If I am right that although some serious (and correctable) errors were made, the processes were not as flawed as the [Senate] reports claim, this is good news in that the system was not horribly broken, but bad news in that there are few fixes that will produce more than marginal (but still significant) improvements ... . We need to avoid equating being wrong with having made avoidable and blameworthy errors. SSCI [the Senate Select Committee on Intelligence] in particular falls into this trap, as is shown by the fact that it almost always equates reasonable, well-grounded inferences with those that proved to be correct. *We can see the problem by asking the obvious counterfactual: would the same report have been written if the estimates had turned out to be correct? This is implausible, yet it is what SSCI implies.*[20]

It is not clear that, before the decision to assault Iraq, intelligence collection would have been improved by any difference in the structure of the intelligence community that could have been established by legislation, which must design the community for all seasons.

Should we change the system?

If the structure of the national security policy system is out of date, how is it out of date? The main points of the redesign of the system in 1947 were consolidation, centralization, and coordination. The first of these has not been a persistent priority. Efforts to streamline functions that outside generalists see as redundant often lead to piling a new coordinating mechanism on top of the old units rather than eliminating them. (For example, Secretary of Defense McNamara had hoped the creation of DIA could absorb most of the three service intelligence agencies, but the latter regenerated and remained about as large as ever.) Continued interest in centralization and coordination has been more prominent.

The NSC staff was barely foreseen in the National Security Act, emerged gradually as a coordinating unit, and has drifted fitfully toward the centralizing mission. This trend has probably gone too far in recent times with the radical expansion of the NSC staff. Nixon and Kissinger's extreme centralization of foreign policy in the White House was controversial long ago, but it was accomplished more by ignoring or circumventing the professional bureaucracies in State and Defense than by duplicating them. It is hard to see how an NSC staff now numbering in the hundreds is not a parallel bureaucracy. If reducing the staff is desirable, however, this should ideally be done by executive direction within existing legislation; a hard and fast numerical cap in law could prove problematic under unforeseen future circumstances.

The original impetus for the 1947 Act was unification of the armed services and greater integration remained a continuing concern long after its passage. It is hard to make the case, however, for significant further moves in that direction. The Goldwater-Nichols reforms late in the Cold War accomplished nearly all the additional integration that should be desired. There are changes at the margin that might still make sense – for example, merging the several separate service war colleges into the National War College, an option considered at the time of the original Act but rejected because of service resistance. A similar case was made for the merger of the three nuclear weapons laboratories after the Cold War, and rejected then too. These two particular consolidations, however, would be incidental for defense policy in general, and it is uncertain that reducing the variety of educational institutions would be desirable anyway. When recommended economization is a minuscule portion of defense spending, vested interests and their rationales, which may even be correct, trump the recommendation.

Consolidation of military services was a principal goal of the 1947 Act and its amendments. What about the possible need for new *additional* services? Important changes in the milieu of military action have arisen since 1947. One is the use of outer space for intelligence and combat functions. Going back to the 1990s some in the Air Force and elsewhere thought that the nature of new space operations was radically different from traditional operations on land, sea, and in air and that a separate Space Force was the logical adaptation to the military results of scientific progress. Support for such radical change did not grow, however, and Space Command appears to be performing adequately.

There is one issue area which intuition suggests should logically require major reorganization: cybersecurity. First, in a short time cyber concerns have gone from incidental matters to fundamental challenges for the economic prosperity and politico-military security – indeed, potentially, the survival – of contemporary civilization. Both domestic and foreign policies are inevitably putting a far higher premium on dealing with emerging problems in cyberspace. Second, this whole realm of technology and society's utter dependence on it was completely unforeseen in the National Security Act or any of the legislative adjustments of it. As with intelligence, all departments and government functions have a stake in cybersecurity, so centralization in a single new agency would not remove the other departments from involvement. Nevertheless, the position of the National Security Agency and its twin, Cyber Command, as the dominant institutions in the business may not be the optimal organizational solution to the question. As yet there is no vigorous movement or coherent rationale being promoted for radical reorganization of units and functions concerned with cyber conflict, but change of some sort – whether it be a central agency for cybersecurity or something else – is one of the few obvious candidates for consideration.

Otherwise, sensible proposals for change in the national security system should be evolutionary rather than revolutionary. All sensible observers realize that in practice any system will fall down sometimes, if only because officials who design and operate it are fallible. Some, however, believe that *in principle* all good things could go together and policy could be more or less perfected if the ideal system for organizing interests, priorities, and consideration of options could be discovered and engineered. This is an illusion, because in real life all good things in any general category of human endeavor hardly ever go together. All too often, optimizing one function must detract from another. Consolidation reduces inefficiency but penalizes concerns whose representative units are merged or streamlined. Centralization improves consistency of purpose but reduces checks and balances. Checks and balances reduce the odds of precipitous action and mistakes from zealotry or ignorance, but also erect obstacles to innovation, initiative, speed, and reform. In these tradeoffs, reorganizations that tilt in favor of one interest against another eventually are questioned as mistakes due to shortchanging the first interest emerge.

Does change always help?

Most mechanisms or norms have two edges. For example, should military leaders simply salute and keep their mouths shut when civilian leaders direct them to undertake actions they believe will fail, or should they be expected to let Congress, or even the press and public, know their professional judgment and disagreement? Those concerned with keeping the military in their proper place to protect democracy from men on horseback tend to believe the first, others concerned with maximizing awareness of representatives and citizens in a democracy may want the second. Civilian officials in the Obama administration reportedly felt undermined by leaks from military leaders when making decisions about the level of effort in Afghanistan.[21] But was the behavior of the Joint Chiefs of Staff in 1965 preferable, when their doubts that the Johnson administration plans for war in Vietnam would succeed were not made known to the public?[22]

Basic reforms of the system are – and should be – rare. There are significant short-term costs in disruption of work and confusion of results when reorganization changes missions and lines of authority, so the longer the term between necessary reorganizations, and the more limited the necessary changes, the better. Depending on what is counted there have been numerous reorganizations but only a few major structural changes in the national security policy system. For seven decades since the National Security Act one might cite only the 1949 amendments (which for practical purposes might be lumped with the 1947 Act), the 1958 defense reorganization, the 1986 Goldwater-Nichols legislation, the creation of the Department of Homeland Security in 2002, and the Intelligence

Reform and Terrorism Protection Act (IRTPA) of 2004. Establishment of permanent intelligence oversight committees in Congress in the mid-1970s was comparable in importance, but that reform did not affect the executive institutions established by the National Security Act.

None of this means that there have not been other major changes of practice. For example, the size and power of agencies in the Office of the Secretary of Defense are radically greater than in the 1950s. The burgeoning of OSD provoked resistance in the military and criticism in Congress, especially as Secretary of Defense Robert McNamara used the Office of Systems Analysis to challenge the positions of the services and JCS. The evolution of OSD, however, was immanent in the establishment of the DoD by the 1949 amendments.

The few major reorganizations since 1947 have smoothed out lines of authority and increased integration. On balance the benefits probably dominate, but there are costs to such progress. Centralization increases the capacity for quick and decisive action. Pluralism or redundancy retards that capacity, but it also reduces errors due to submerging particular perspectives or risks. The complexities and controversies of national security issues preclude clear verdicts on how much major reorganizations improve policy outcomes, or which if any should be judged ineffective or counterproductive. To reflect on the balance of risks in reform, consider one that might be a case where benefits do not outweigh costs: the 2004 IRTPA. Its main provisions were the legal requirement to break down "stovepipes" and maximize sharing of intelligence among the various agencies of the IC, and the establishment of a new Director of National Intelligence (DNI), both to avert failures of coordination seen as contributing to the September 11th surprise.

The first, improved sharing of intelligence, has a second edge, which seemed less apparent in the aftermath of September 11th but which comes back periodically: heightened risk of breaches in secrecy. The 9/11 Commission and legislators in 2004 focused on the breakdown in collaboration between the CIA and the Federal Bureau of Investigation (FBI) before September 11th. They did not focus on the danger represented by the Aldrich Ames espionage scandal of a few years earlier – the hemorrhage of sensitive secrets to Russia, which had prompted complaints in Congress about having allowed one individual such wide access to sensitive information. A decade after the IRTPA the second edge came back again with Bradley/Chelsea Manning's wikileaks and yet again with Edward Snowden's revelation of the sensitive intelligence collection activities of the National Security Agency (NSA). These incidents create natural pressures for reversion to more compartmentation in order to limit damage when custodians of secrecy go bad.

The second edge of the DNI reform has been the introduction of a new layer of bureaucracy – the unit known as the Office of the Director of National Intelligence (ODNI) – in an intelligence system that was already beset by bloat, and in which the function of the DNI already existed, albeit widely unrecognized.[23] The DNI issue must be understood in the context of the prevalent misunderstanding mentioned earlier: almost no one among journalists, public commentators, and even anyone in government outside the intelligence community ever understood that the old DCI, the office established by the 1947 Act, could have accomplished what the DNI was designed to do. That is because few understood that the DCI was a two-hatted job. Except among professionals in the IC, he was invariably referred to as "director of the CIA," never by his proper title of Director of Central Intelligence, which covered the *additional* responsibility of coordinating the rest of the intelligence community. The higher coordination function was not accomplished as thoroughly as it might have been because the DCI's responsibility was never matched by sufficient authority, due to resistance from the Defense Department. The seldom recognized fact remains that the old DCI did not accomplish everything the new DNI was designed to do because the president did not overrule the other departments and invest the DCI with more direct control of their intelligence functions. As it turned out, the new DNI also wound up circumscribed and limited in authority, for some of the same reasons that the old DCI had been. More decisive centralization would require making the DNI into the cabinet Secretary of Intelligence.

So an alleged benefit of the 2004 IRTPA was the separation of the old DCI's two jobs. Many believed that combining the CIA director and community coordinating functions in one person (the old DCI) was too big a job, or that it represented a conflict of interest, privileging the CIA over other agencies in the community. These arguments were incorrect. First, the secretary of defense has a far larger and more diverse set of responsibilities, yet there is no lobby to break that position up. Indeed, the point of creating the DoD in the first place was to establish unitary control over disparate organizational leviathans. Second, if the Central Intelligence Agency established in 1947 was not supposed to be truly central, first above equals rather than among them, what was the point of the agency's name? The cost to separating the jobs is that the top coordinator's ability to implement centralizing missions is limited by the loss of his or her own troops in the CIA – troops that are the practical assets for shepherding his or her initiatives when the other departments succeed in resisting the allocation of enough personnel, or their best, to the DNI. The separation of the two hats has probably encouraged some of the expansion in ODNI, which comes at the cost of further bureaucratic complexity. Of course there are benefits from the specifics of the DNI legislation, but there is no consensus in the intelligence community that they outweigh the costs of more bureaucratization and layering.

Whether or how the system that has evolved under the National Security Act should be changed substantially depends on many considerations, but more than any other one thing, on opinions about the relative costs and benefits of centralization and decentralization. Such opinions vary with economic ideology and policymaking experience. In contrast to much else in national policy in our prolonged season of polarization, opinions on these managerial questions do not vary as obviously or consistently with party or left-right ideological divisions. On other matters Republicans have tended to favor less centralization than

Democrats, but national security is the one area of policy where Republicans favor strong government. In a Republican administration Donald Rumsfeld turned out to be the most dictatorial secretary of defense since Robert McNamara under the Democrats. Opinion on the proper balance is more likely to vary with the level of perspective: bureaucrats in particular agencies that have interests which conflict with other agencies may be more likely to see the virtues of decentralization, while highest-level policymakers overseeing the whole national security landscape may be more likely to value tighter control from the top.

Policy, strategy, and organization

The National Security Act was spurred by the rapid and radical change in U.S. foreign policy, military activity, and commitments. Just over four decades later almost as radical a change occurred in the strategic milieu: the end of the Cold War and, at least for quite a while, of great power competition altogether. If policy objectives and military requirements change drastically, doesn't that naturally imply that the policy system for decision and implementation warrant drastic change too?

American military activity did not change drastically, however, when both the Soviet threat and worldwide Marxist-Leninist movements collapsed. In fact, in the fifteen years after the Berlin Wall opened the United States undertook more than twice as many wars as it did in the forty-odd years of the Cold War (Iraq I, Kosovo, Afghanistan, Iraq II vs. Korea and Vietnam), and its military has been engaged in combat continually since 2001. While the frequency of combat is greater than in the Cold War, the scale so far is not, but great power conflict has also reemerged with conflict over Ukraine and islands in the South China Sea. Military challenges are not yet as big as they were from World War II to 1989, but they have not reverted to what they were before 1941.

One might ask whether radical change in the policymaking system should be undertaken if the United States ever comes to radical change in basic national security policy, such as shedding the role of globocop and sugar-daddy for cheap-riding allies, ratcheting down the amount of America's global military activism. After all, the National Security Act was prompted by the change in the other direction, expansion of commitments. Some changes in managerial particulars would of course go naturally with any big change in activity and responsibilities, but no general reversion to the scale of military activity before 1941 is in the cards. Trump's "America First" instincts point in different directions, toward restraint on humanitarian intervention but activism on counterterrorism. In any event, the rationales for organization of the system depend primarily on its size and complexity, not the particulars of who the foreign adversaries of the moment are.

The case for moving toward a mobilization strategy was persuasive for a long time after the Cold War ended. This would involve reorienting the roles of active and reserve forces, military personnel policy in general, research and development and military procurement, organization of the defense industrial and production base, and other functions.[24] If that were ever undertaken seriously it would indeed involve major changes in military personnel, procurement, research and development, and other functions. The idea never had any serious constituency, however, and it is harder to contemplate a mobilization strategy in the past several years, when Chinese and Russian activities have raised the prospect of great power conflict again. It is improbable that national leaders will adopt the logic of Barry R. Posen's case for reducing U.S. burdens to a budget of 2.5 percent of GDP.[25] Trump aims to spend more on the military, not less. If leaders were to spend significantly less, however, the American profile in international security would still remain far greater than it was before the mid-20th century, and the case for dismantling many of the organizations legislated in 1947 would be weak.

The world has changed a lot since 1947 but has not become far simpler. Nor have technological and economic functions become simpler; rather they have grown ever more complex. Only radical simplification in the context and substance of national security policy would make a case for reducing the complexity of the system for policymaking and implementation. At some point technical changes might mandate wholesale reorganization but so far the centralizing and coordinating reforms of the 1947 Act and subsequent piecemeal reorganizations have worked at least as well as any radically new system plausibly would. It's not broke, so let's not fix it.

An earlier version of this essay entitled "Don't Retire the National Security Act" appeared in *The American Interest,* vol. 12, no. 4, February 9, 2017. www.the-american-interest.com/2017/02/09/dont-retire-the-national-security-act/.

Notes

1 See Aaron L. Friedberg, *In the Shadow of the Garrison State: America's Anti-Statism and Its Cold War Grand Strategy* (Princeton: Princeton University Press, 2000). Some developments cushioned the tension between these attitudes. For example, demography enabled conscription to be maintained without actually forcing most young men into service. Ibid., chap. 5, and Samuel P. Huntington, *The Common Defense: Strategic Programs in National Politics* (New York: Columbia University Press, 1961), pp. 59, 240, 371, and 435 on legislative consideration of Universal Military Training as an alternative to Selective Service.

2 Quoted in Glenn D. Paige, *The Korean Decision: June 24–30, 1950* (New York: Free Press, 1968), p. 95. The UN did then go on to fight its only war in history, albeit relying on the United States as its executive agent. The Korean War is the only one fought under a UN Command (which persists in South Korea to this day, pending formal termination of the war). The UN gave a mandate for the 1991 war against Iraq, but without a UN Command for it.

3 Robert E. Osgood, *NATO: The Entangling Alliance* (Chicago: University of Chicago Press, 1962), p. 1.

4 Article 11, stating that members would carry out the treaty "in accordance with their respective constitutional processes," provided the escape hatch. On how the issue was finessed, see Dean Acheson, *Present at the Creation: My Years in the State Department* (New York: W. W. Norton, 1969), pp. 280–281. NATO participation in the war in Afghanistan has proved to be a coalition of the willing, and Article 5 has been shaken

since post-Cold War NATO expansion as unexpected tension with Russia led some to question whether it should apply to vulnerable new members like the Baltic states.

5 Marc Trachtenberg, *A Constructed Peace: The Making of the European Settlement, 1945–1963* (Princeton: Princeton University Press, 1999), p. 148.

6 Demetrios Caraley, *The Politics of Military Unification: A Study of Conflict and the Policy Process* (New York: Columbia University Press, 1966); John C. Ries, *The Management of Defense: Organization and Control of the U.S. Armed Services* (Baltimore: Johns Hopkins Press, 1964), chaps. 4, 6, 7, 8; Huntington, *Common Defense*, chap. 2.

7 The original 1947 legislation created the "National Military Establishment" with military service secretaries holding prominent positions. The Department of Defense was established in the 1949 amendments to the Act.

8 National Security Act of 1947 (Public Law 253, 80th Congress, July 26, 1947), 61 Stat. 495, Sec. 102 (d) (5).

9 Arthur B. Darling, *The Central Intelligence Agency: An Instrument of Government to 1950* (University Park, PA: Pennsylvania State University Press, 1990), pp. 256–265 (reprint of official study by CIA History Staff, originally completed in 1953); Anne Karalekas, "History of the Central Intelligence Agency," in U.S. Senate Select Committee to Study Governmental Operations with Respect to Intelligence Activities, Final Report: *Supplementary Detailed Staff Reports on Foreign and Military Intelligence*, Book IV, 94th Cong., 2d sess., April 1976 (Report no. 94–755), pp. 25–31.

10 Ernest R. May, "The Development of Political-Military Consultation in the United States," in Aaron Wildavsky, ed., *The Presidency* (Boston: Little, Brown, 1969).

11 National Security Act, Sec. 101 (a) (emphasis added).

12 President, vice president, secretaries of state and defense, a few other high-level agency heads that changed over time such as the director of the Office of Civil and Defense Mobilization, and non-member statutory advisers such as the JCS chairman and director of National Intelligence.

13 The counterargument to the assertive model for the NSC staff was etched in detail in I. M. Destler, *Presidents, Bureaucrats, and Foreign Policy: The Politics of Organizational Reform* (Princeton: Princeton University Press, 1972), pp. 121–142, 254ff, and passim, and Destler, "National Security Management: What Presidents Have Wrought," *Political Science Quarterly* 95, no. 4 (Winter 1980–1981).

14 http://orchestratingpower.org/Chapter09/NSC%20Staff%20Size.pdf.

15 Chester Cooper, *The Lost Crusade: America in Vietnam* (New York: Dodd, Mead, 1970), p. 223.

16 Chester Cooper, "The CIA and Decision-Making," *Foreign Affairs* 50, no. 2 (January 1972); this article surveyed the record of NIEs revealed in the leaked Pentagon Papers.

17 Creation of the Department of Homeland Security in 2002 went further than most such adaptations, absorbing numerous units from throughout the government, but still fit within the 1947 system.

18 For the full argument see Leslie H. Gelb with Richard K. Betts, *The Irony of Vietnam: The System Worked* (Washington, DC: Brookings Institution, 1979). The policymaking pathologies assessed in James C. Thomson, Jr.'s classic post-mortem were not driven by the bureaucratic structure and process of the 1947 Act. Thomson, "How Could Vietnam Happen? An Autopsy," *The Atlantic* (April 1968).

19 Richard K. Betts, *Enemies of Intelligence: Knowledge and Power in American National Security* (New York: Columbia University Press, 2007), pp. 114–123.

20 Robert Jervis, "Reports, Politics, and Intelligence Failures: The Case of Iraq," *Journal of Strategic Studies* 29, no. 1 (February 2006), pp. 13–14 (emphasis added).

21 Bob Woodward, *Obama's Wars* (New York: Simon & Schuster, 2010), chaps. 11–14, 18, 21–23, 25, 28.

22 H. R. McMaster, *Dereliction of Duty: Lyndon Johnson, Robert McNamara, the Joint Chiefs of Staff, and the Lies That Led to Vietnam* (New York: HarperCollins, 1997); Richard K. Betts, *American Force: Dangers, Delusions, and Dilemmas in National Security* (New York: Columbia University Press, 2012), chap. 9.

23 Paul R. Pillar, *Intelligence and U.S. Foreign Policy: Iraq, 9/11, and Misguided Reform* (New York: Columbia University Press, 2011), pp. 295–307; Betts, *Enemies of Intelligence,* pp. 150–156.

24 Richard K. Betts, *Military Readiness: Concepts, Choices, Consequences* (Washington, DC: Brookings Institution, 1995), chap. 8; Betts, "American Strategy: Grand vs. Grandiose," in Richard Fontaine and Kristin M. Lord, eds., *America's Path: Grand Strategy for the Next Administration* (Washington, DC: Center for a New American Security, May 2012), pp. 35–40.

25 Barry R. Posen, *Restraint: A New Foundation for U.S. Grand Strategy* (Ithaca, NY: Cornell University Press, 2014), p. 163.

2

IMPROVING STRATEGIC ASSESSMENT IN THE EXECUTIVE BRANCH

Lessons from the scholarly literature

Risa A. Brooks

In an era in which the United States faces a dizzying array of security challenges in the international arena, political leaders' abilities to engage in effective strategic assessment is vital. Less clear is how well prepared are the institutions and individuals central to national security affairs for this formidable task. In Washington, complaints abound about the size and roles of the NSC, dysfunction in the "interagency," and the overall agility and responsiveness of the national security establishment. The particulars vary across administrations, but it often seems that regardless of who is in office, no one is fully satisfied with how major strategic and foreign policy decisions are made.[1]

Beyond calls for change in these institutions and practices, however, there is surprisingly little positive analysis and understanding of *what should be* the overarching method for analyzing and choosing strategies in the executive branch. We lack limited understanding of what are the essential elements of sound strategic assessment and what might be done to promote it.

In this essay, I look to academic scholarship related to national security decision-making to see what lessons might be gleaned about the factors that affect strategic assessment and, in turn, how to improve it at the highest levels of government. Rather than focusing on specific recommendations, I seek to identify general principles and approaches for conceptualizing the ingredients of good strategic assessment. Although this essay is framed as an academic review of the scholarly literature, it also has a practical goal: to encourage circumspection and critical appraisal of the implicit "theories" that inform how analysts and practitioners approach national security reform.

Specifically, in the first half of this essay, I identify three different approaches to conceptualizing the core elements of strategic assessment: an approach that focuses on organizations and bureaucracies; one that focuses on the practices and qualitative features of deliberative processes; and one that emphasizes the content and substance of the information and analysis that informs those deliberative processes. These approaches emerge from scholarly literatures related to international crisis decision-making, bureaucratic politics, presidential politics, political psychology and studies of intelligence and civil-military relations.[2] In the second half of the essay, I identify several insights or lessons that follow from this analysis. I begin, however, by clarifying what I mean by strategic assessment.

What is "good" strategic assessment?

In this essay I employ a broad definition of strategic assessment: it is the means through which top officials arrive at a set of actions in response to particular security challenges, and more broadly choose how to employ resources and instruments of statecraft to secure the country.[3] Strategic assessment, generally speaking, involves identifying, evaluating, comparing and choosing among different alternatives. These strategies may focus on a specific issue, such as how to manage a regional conflict (e.g., disputes over the territorial waters in the South China Sea); broad, long-term security challenges (e.g., the "rise" of China); or, in some instances, on overarching principles for how to organize and employ military and diplomatic resources in order to safeguard the country's core security interests (e.g., "grand strategy").

While foreign policy-making involves myriad defense or security issues at different levels of the government, strategic assessment describes a subset of activities by top officials and political leaders in the national security arena. It heavily involves the executive branch, including the Executive Office of the President, including the NSC and White House Staff, the Cabinet, the Director of National Intelligence and members of the Intelligence Community (IC), and senior advisors close to the president. Also important, although not always considered as part of strategic assessment, is the (indirect) role of executive departments and staffs that supply analyses that inform their superiors' evaluations and decisions.

Evaluating what constitutes "good" strategic assessment can be challenging.[4] Intuitively, it makes sense that good strategic assessment is that which produces good strategy: strategy that advances the security goals of the state. Yet measuring strategic assessment with reference to the outcomes it produces is problematic for several reasons. Analysts may disagree with the strategic choices of a president and then infer that the process by which they are chosen is flawed. George W. Bush for example is commonly criticized for the nature of strategic assessment prior to the decision to go to war against Iraq in 2003. But some have found that the administration's decision-making process exhibited some favorable qualities and was not as pathological as critics of the war contend.[5] One person's efficacious strategy—and by extension the process of strategic assessment that produces it—may be another's misguided and flawed endeavor.

Measuring strategic assessment by looking at international outcomes is also problematic because even good strategy (and good strategic assessment) can produce bad outcomes. The result of a state's interaction with another state depends not just on its strategy, but on the strategy of the opposing state, as well as exogenous factors.[6] In addition, strategies are evaluated and chosen under conditions of uncertainty. Hence, a well informed and conceived strategy may nonetheless fail to achieve its aims if the state of the world ultimately diverges from what is reasonably anticipated. Finally, good strategy may also not always be necessary to attain desired outcomes. A state may at times achieve its goals through uncoordinated and improvised actions if the strategic faults of an adversary, or other conditions, allow it. For these reasons, a strategy may yield an adverse or positive international outcome for reasons unrelated to its merits.

Still, what leaders and their publics ultimately care about *is* the quality of the strategy produced by the state. Rather than focus on the outcome or content of strategy, an alternative is to focus on its properties. There are several attributes an ideal-typically "good" strategy is likely to exhibit, at least in the abstract.[7]

First, conceptually, it will be informed by a reinforcing set of assumptions and causal logics connecting actions and policies. That is, there will be "theory" implicit in the strategy about how it is supposed to achieve its goals and that theory will inform what actions the state takes. A strategy that provides for actions that reflect broadly different assumptions and causal logics about how to produce victory, concessions, or some other preferred outcome is likely to produce waste and contradictions. Although it may often remain implicit, strategy should reflect a clear and consistent conceptualization of means–end relationships and causal logic.

Second, and related, the strategy or grand strategy will be integrated across a number of dimensions.[8] It will promote and reflect political goals and rely, as much as is feasible, on a reinforcing set of diplomatic, military and economic measures (the variety of which will depend on the issue at stake). In the ideal this involves a synthesis of actions in the diplomatic, military and economic realms, such that they are coordinated and work together in support of objectives. Sound strategies will also reflect the resources and capabilities available to a state, both in hard material terms, and with respect to the political constraints that affect the use of resources. Since perfect integration across all dimensions is impossible to achieve, an effective strategy also will be based on an explicit evaluation of the contradictions and tradeoffs that must be made, especially when those involve compromising other national interests and goals.

Third, an effective strategy will be truly "strategic" in the sense of premising a state's actions on an understanding that outcomes in international relations are the product of the interdependent choices of different actors.[9] The actions by one state shape the choices of its allies and competitors, and so on. Without anticipating the responses of opponents to one's course of action, and incorporating that assessment into the initial choice of strategy, a strategy may produce unforeseen and unintended consequences.

Fourth, an effective strategy should be formulated and modified in context of robust estimates of the uncertainties inherent in any international situation. In the ideal, an effective strategy is premised on more than a static incorporation of probabilities; it is adapted to shifting levels of certainty and regular reevaluations about what is known, not known, and with what confidence either can be judged. Also vital is an understanding of the stakes or implications of different uncertainties for the management of the issue at hand, and therefore what unknowns matter, and with what consequences.

This abstract description of an "ideal" strategy may rarely, if ever, be observed in practice. These properties, however, provide a general sense of the goal of strategic assessment and what attributes an intrinsically effective strategy is apt to exhibit. They provide a benchmark or standard against which we might evaluate and judge strategies—and the processes of strategic assessment that produce them.

Three ways of conceptualizing strategic assessment

What causes good strategic assessment? Under what conditions are leaders likely to devise strategies with the requisite properties? There is surprisingly little consensus about the answers to these questions. In fact, there are at least three different ways of thinking about what factors shape assessment and what is likely to matter most for the quality of these processes. Below I discuss these three different approaches.

The bureaucracy and organizational structure approach

A first way of approaching strategic assessment focuses on the structure and configuration of the entities that are involved in national security affairs. The focus is on the composition, roles, responsibilities and authority of different bureaucratic or organizational units and relations among them.

From this perspective, the quality of strategic assessment will vary with the strength of the government's organizational structures and bureaucracy.[10] Improving strategic assessment will often depend on effective organizational change and institutional reform. The key to producing a good process of strategic assessment is to configure the right institutions. The assumption is that improvements in underlying deliberative and analytical capacities and conventions will follow from organizational reform. Process and norms matter, but they derive fundamentally from structure.

Central to this approach are (albeit sometimes implicit) assumptions about the nature of organizations and the impact of bureaucratic biases on policy-making. These are perhaps best captured in Graham Allison and Morton Halperin's seminal research on the importance of "government politics" on national security processes, which involves different approaches to understanding the impact of organizations and bureaucracy on policy-making.[11] An "organizational process" model conceptualizes policy decisions as the output of competition among a variety of organizational units within the government, which each had its own ways of doing business, as well as priorities to protect and advance. Organizations churn along, fueled by their standard operating procedures and cultural codes, and decisions emerge as outputs of those processes. The "bureaucratic politics" model focuses on the personalities and ambitions of major actors in the bureaucracy who fight to promote their institution's power and resources. Bureaucracies expand their authority by monopolizing information and claiming unique expertise. They cling to their domains of responsibility, lest another entity trespass on their "turf."[12]

Organizational reform, from this approach, aims to mitigate the pathological effects of parochialism, bureaucratic competition and to create more buy-in and cooperation across units. The goal is to change incentives, perspectives and priorities of actors within the relevant entities so that they align each other and with the functional demands of their mission and tasks. As one analyst captures the motivating assumptions: "Most basically, people respond to incentives, and incentives arise from organizational structure."[13]

The emphasis on institutional change and reorganization is common in efforts to advance national security reform. As Eikenberry observes, the U.S. has a long tradition of reform through organizational reconfigurations, either on a large or small scale. As he characterizes the impulse driving such efforts:

> A comprehensive and effective United States national security strategy must take stock of the capacity of the relevant government machinery to plan and implement. To move beyond mere aspirations requires a deep understanding of the organizational structures and administrative capabilities of the agencies charged with formulating and executing the policies, programs and processes associated with that strategy.[14]

Indeed, many of the country's most significant reforms related to national security matters have aimed to promote better coordination and efficiencies through organizational change.[15] The seminal change was the National Security Act of 1947. Subsequent changes include the Goldwater-Nichols Acts of 1986, which enhanced the advisory role of the Chairman of the Joint Chiefs, and the Intelligence Reform and Terrorism Prevention Act of 2004,[16] which created the Office of the Director of National Intelligence (ODNI) and designated the director the principal advisor to the president on intelligence matters; it also created the National Counterterrorism Center, whose director reports both to the president and the DNI about overarching counterterrorism initiatives. Within the National Security Council there also have been several modifications and adjustments, including, for example, the decision by the Obama administration in 2009 to combine the Homeland Security Council and National Security Council staffs with the intent of enhancing efficiencies and coordination.[17]

More recently consider, for example, the proposals of the congressionally mandated Project on National Security Reform (PNSR). Its working groups identified a range of problems and issues in the allocation of responsibilities and mandates of national security institutions.[18] Its 2008 report diagnoses the deficiencies of national security architecture in terms that resonate strongly with a "government politics" approach. It highlights imbalances in the allocation of responsibilities and problems with the mandates of executive departments, alongside a system that overcentralizes management in the White House. As the report concludes, "Taken together, the basic deficiency of the current national security system is that parochial departmental and agency interests, reinforced by Congress, paralyze interagency cooperation even as the variety, speed, and complexity of emerging security issues prevent the White House from effectively controlling the system."[19] The core recommendations amount to a significant redesign to emphasize "integrated effort, collaboration and agility."[20]

The decision-making "process" approach

The second approach focuses less on problems of bureaucracy and organizations and more on the qualitative features of advisory processes and the norms and practices observed within them. This is prevalent in the sizable literature on foreign policy-making and crisis decision-making within the United States' executive branch. The unit of analysis is the "advisory system," or the way in which individuals engage with information and each other in small-group forums. These advising systems are shaped by multiple factors, which are only partly, and often weakly, related to organizational structures and institutional features.

The key elements are often defined differently, but there are several common themes within the literature on national security decision-making about the major features of these processes. In particular, analysts often focus on: (1) what individuals and views are represented in advisory forums; (2) what are the informal rules or conventions for discussion and how well are dissenting and marginal perspectives incorporated; (3) with what decision-rules are outcomes determined; and (4) how is information managed to avoid the pathological effects of cognitive biases on small-group decision-making. In particular, one commonly cited precondition for sound assessment is that, "advocates should exhibit an 'adequate degree of diversity of views'."[21] Multiple advocacy is an essential component of a sound process.[22]

As Jervis summarizes the implicit ideal typical process:

> Researchers call for leaders and their foreign policy apparatuses to seek diverse information and views, to develop a "level playing field" where no department or individual has an unfair advantage in convincing the president, and to try to avoid making decisions prematurely, before the information has been surveyed and many options developed. Relatedly, although policies should not be changed lightly, decision makers should be ready to examine new information, monitor the success of their policies, and be prepared to reconsider and change.[23]

Advisory systems are judged, sometimes implicitly, against a standard of "procedural rationality."[24]

A principal aim of this scholarship, in turn, is to explain why departures from the standard of procedural rationality occur, and therefore why an evaluative (or strategic assessment) process might prove deficient. In general, scholars tend to emphasize two sources of weaknesses: those caused by motivated and unmotivated biases.

Unmotivated biases originate in the cognitive shortcuts on which individuals rely in managing and processing information and are predicable, pervasive and generally common errors.[25] They include confirmation bias, which involves selective interpreting of information to support pre-existing views; premature cognitive closure, in which minds are made up rapidly and closed to new information; attribution bias, in which behaviors are attributed to an actor's personality and character, rather than his or her situation or context; and overconfidence in regard to probability of success of a chosen course of action.[26]

Motivated biases originate in the emotional or psychological needs and impulses of a leader or decision-maker. They reflect that person's character or personality[27] and therefore are often idiosyncratic and particular to the specific individuals involved in the deliberative process. They include phenomena such as an individual's impulse to limit search and analysis in order to moderate stress and reduce cognitive dissonance; the desire to discount information that presents a challenge to one's self-image; the tendency to discount or neglect the survey of options that result in negative consequences, or are contrary to the individual's preferences or world view. Also included are demands on a president to eliminate actions that would result in negative political consequences for him or her domestically[28] and a tendency to resist recognizing and incorporating explicit value tradeoffs when choosing a course of action.[29]

The unit of analysis within this scholarship is often the president's advisory system.[30] To explain variation, scholars often emphasize the impact of the president's character, psychology, political imperatives, and "managerial style" on the quality of deliberation.[31] For example, as Schafer and Crichlow observe, leaders who place a high value on "control" within a process might exclude individuals whose viewpoints or personalities challenge their authority and the orderliness of the situation.[32] A leader that is averse to conceptual complexity might preempt an exhaustive analysis of probabilities or uncertainties out of discomfort with the so-called empirical "gray zone." These processes can then yield defects, or departures from procedural rationality, such as inferior search and evaluation of information, and unsystematic survey of goals and options.

A subset of this scholarly literature focuses less on individuals, and more on the particular psychological pressures that originate in small groups and how those create distortions and departures from procedural rationality. These include the classic concept of groupthink and its more recent conceptual counterpart, "polythink." Groupthink describes a process in which maintaining group conformity and cohesion is paramount.[33] So powerful is the need to maintain group harmony, and avoid a possibly disruptive and rancorous search process, that it contributes to pathologies in the deliberation about alternative courses of action.[34]

The demand to achieve and maintain consensus about a course of action results in the suppression of dissenting views and disconfirming information.

In contrast, "polythink" describes:

> A group dynamic whereby different members in a decision-making unit espouse a plurality of opinions and offer divergent policy prescriptions, and even dissent, which can result in intragroup conflict and a fragmented, disjointed decision-making process. Members of a polythink decision-making unit, by virtue of their disparate worldviews, institutional and political affiliations, and decision-making styles, typically have deep disagreements over the same decision problem. Consequently, members of polythink-type groups will often be unable to appreciate or accept the perspectives of other group members, and thus will fail to benefit from the consideration of various viewpoints.[35]

Polythink therefore describes the inverse of groupthink, in which differences among the participants in deliberation result in a truncated and dysfunctional deliberative process.

In short, what these studies have in common is a motivating hypothesis that good decisions require a good process—and that the process does not depend on organizational structure primarily or even fundamentally, but on participants' psychology, worldviews, group and interpersonal dynamics.[36]

The "analytical" approach: focusing on the substance and quality of analysis

The final approach focuses on the specific analytical tools and methods that shape the information and insights upon which decision-makers rely in strategic assessment. This might be seen as a third level of analysis in conceptualizing assessment. An organizations and bureaucracies approach focuses on structures, rules and procedures. A process approach focuses on the qualitative manner in which deliberation and decision-making occurs. An approach that emphasizes analytics, then, refers to the specific tools and methods that inform the *content* and *quality* of the substance and information evaluated within such processes.

This approach is perhaps developed within the scholarly literature on intelligence, but it has implications for strategic assessment more broadly. That literature highlights the ways in which causal beliefs, an analyst's theory and methodology can shape the way in which information is evaluated and decisions are made.

An excellent example of this approach is Robert Jervis's diagnosis of the causes of the "intelligence failure" associated with the United States' failure to find WMDs in Iraq in 2003.[37] A detailed review of his argument helps illuminate the key aspects of the analytical approach. Jervis argues that while problems of organizational structure and process contributed to weaknesses in intelligence on the WMD issue,[38] a variety of deficiencies in the *quality* of analysis also contributed to the flaws in intelligence. Among these was a failure by analysts to make comparisons and adequately to develop alternative explanations for behaviors of the Iraqi regime that were observed. For example, the fact that Saddam Hussein was concealing the foreign procurement of items that might be used for a weapons program with deceptive practices like front companies, was taken as evidence that he was pursuing a covert WMD program; neglected was comparison with other non-military items, which would have shown that he used front companies widely and would have cast doubt on the idea that he was trying to hide something in particular.[39]

Jervis also argues that CIA officers might have paid closer attention to "negative evidence."[40] This would have involved inferring observations about what should have been observed if Saddam Hussein was pursuing WMD. Looking for and not seeing those actions would have raised doubts about whether the conjecture (the regime has WMD, but is hiding it) was accurate. As it was, the lack of evidence was not problematized and was instead attributed to the regime's efforts at denial and deception; the alternative explanation (that it simply did not have a WMD program) does not appear to have been given much attention. The IC "treated deception and denial as a given rather than as a hypothesis to be tested, and they never asked what information might indicate that activities were absent rather than being hidden."[41]

Similarly, the IC failed to distinguish between the conclusions it made that were based on fact and those that originated in inferences drawn about the meaning of those facts. As I describe in detail below, beliefs about how the world works provide the scaffolding for interpreting facts and making judgments about their significance. Hence, the limited facts known about the state of the WMD program were married with inferences about the incentives facing Saddam Hussein's autocratic regime to acquire the weapons; these inferences were not always clearly separated from the known facts. As Jervis puts it, "deductions and indirect inference are central to the enterprise of understanding. The real problem was that the ICs and policymakers were unaware of the extent to which the conclusions rested on these kinds of judgments."[42]

In short, what Jervis highlights in his analysis of the WMD failure is an important aspect of strategic assessment more broadly: the analytical skills and approaches of those involved in the evaluative process. It is not just *what* people believe that matters, but *how well they think* and the analytical skills they have acquired and put to use in preparing for and engaging in the deliberative process.

Lessons for improving strategic assessment

Below I discuss several lessons that can be drawn from this scholarly literature for strategic assessment, and efforts to enhance its quality. I highlight several broad themes.

Moving beyond an emphasis on organizations

A first lesson relates to the pervasiveness of the "organizational structure" approach in how improvements in strategic assessment and national security policy-making are often conceptualized. As noted above, these approaches emphasize altering things such as the size, roles, chains of command, responsibilities, and coordinating functions of organizational units. The implicit argument is that changes in structure are the key to promoting better analytical and decision-making processes.

It might be better, however, to treat this view as a hypothesis rather than a fact. How important is organizational structure to sound processes of assessment within and across institutions? How important is the structure—of the NSC or of the way the president consults advisors and staff, for example—for strategic assessment?

Indeed, organizational structure may only somewhat or indirectly affect deliberative or assessment processes. Studies, for example, have shown only a limited impact of the structure of a president's advisory processes on their quality. Haney found little relationship between a leader's managerial style (e.g., whether it is formalistic, competitive, or collegial) and the quality of decision-making in different presidential administrations.[43] As Haney describes it, "Another readily noticeable feature of the findings is that there is no obvious, direct relationship between a particular advisory structure and the decision process that results."[44] "While the specific pathology may differ, all types of advisory systems are prone to weaknesses (and strengths) of one kind or another.[45]

Perhaps other factors, such as the psychological and immaterial dynamics that shape the decision-making process, or the analytical capacity of participants, are also important, or even more impactful than structural factors. At the least, it is important to understand that changing institutions or tweaking organizational structure represents just one approach for how to promote better national security policy. Practitioners might seek to conceptualize "national security reform" to incorporate more of the insights from the decision-making process or analytical approaches.

Multiple advocacy and the ingredients of good process

Another set of lessons relates to what actually makes for a "good" deliberative process. As noted above, a consistent theme in the literature is the importance of "multiple advocacy" as a key ingredient for sound assessment. Incorporating individuals with different perspectives is one way to hedge against the distortions introduced by small-group decision-making biases and cognitive shortcuts in information processing.

Less considered is what should be the basis of "multiple advocacy." What *kind* of diversity of views is important and are there parameters or limits to the intensity of constructive divergence? One way to operationalize diversity is to focus on the executive departments (Defense, State, Treasury, etc.) and whether they have equal access and influence in the president's advisory system; here a diversity of views is operationalized as a representation of different bureaucratic perspectives.

Incorporating individuals based on their bureaucratic positions, jobs and responsibilities, however, is just one way of conceptualizing "multiple advocacy." The attributes that individuals bring may vary beyond their expertise or bureaucratic position. Axes of disagreement may not coincide with organizational boundaries and issues may be multidimensional.[46] For this reason, it might be useful to focus on the overall configuration of preferences about a particular set of issues among those represented in advisory processes, which may be influenced by bureaucratic position, but may also reflect the personal values and perspectives of an individual.

This raises the question of how much "preference divergence" is constructive in strategic assessment. Relevant here is a theme in the civil-military relations scholarship on the importance of "structured conflict" in providing for comprehensive search and analysis. What Eliot Cohen calls the "unequal dialogue" hinges on intense debate between political and military leaders, which is managed by a capable and authoritative political leader. Too much conflict in priorities among civilian and military leaders can be dysfunctional to strategic assessment, as can too little preference divergence, such that there is insufficient search and debate.[47] This relates to Mintz and Wayne's finding that advisory processes benefit when they reflect a middle ground between cohesion and dissent, in what they call a balance between "convergence and divergence in group members' views."[48]

It might also be important to consider the impact of the overarching world view of the participants. Consider how Alexander George characterizes the fundamentals of the foreign policy decision-making process. He argues that it involves:

> (1) information about the situation [and global context]; (2) substantive knowledge of cause-and-effect relationships that is relevant for assessing the expected consequences of alternative courses of action; and (3) a way of applying the values and interests engaged by the problem at hand in order to judge which course of action is "best" and/or least costly and which, therefore, should be chosen.[49]

George's framing is instructive in two respects. First, it highlights that strategic assessment is an inherently conceptually based exercise. Those engaged bring their individual intellectual dispositions, beliefs and first premises to the process. Whether consciously or not, participants' assumptions and knowledge about how inter-state behavior operates shapes the content and direction of debate.[50] They bring different beliefs about the utility of military force, multilateral action and diplomacy. Also important are beliefs about causality and therefore expectations about the responses different actions will elicit from an opponent, or what factors and features of the strategic context are considered salient and elevated in discussion. How individuals weigh the significance of events is "tied to their beliefs about world politics, the images of those they are dealing with, and their general ideas if not ideologies."[51] When world views diverge two individuals can observe the same fact and interpret its significance differently. "Facts do not speak for themselves" and however objective they may appear, they must be interpreted through existing theories and beliefs.[52]

Second, George's comments highlight that strategic assessment is a values-based exercise. That is, participants bring to the table different valuations of the importance of costs and risks of different actions and outcomes. They bring different conceptions of the "national interest" and how aggressively the country should invest in things such as humanitarian interventions, regime change, or the centrality of safeguarding human rights and civil liberties to the United States' security. In short, the grand-strategic world views of those engaged are likely to shape the process and analysis considerably.[53]

"In turn, achieving "structured conflict" may require that participants in advisory processes share first-order preferences and beliefs and assumptions about the state of the world. This might seem to conflict with the principles of multiple advocacy, which require that diverse perspectives be represented. Although provocative in this regard, the point is worth considering. A divergence of views about a particular issue is different from a divergence in causal beliefs about how international politics operates and value judgments about the national interest. Presidents may be best able to deliver on the goals for which they were elected when they can rely on advisory processes and individuals who share their general worldview. President Obama, for example, was criticized for having too many people who shared first premises and world views within his administration.[54] Yet he did not start out that way; rather early in his first administration he sought to establish a "team of rivals" among his advisors.[55] The abandonment of that approach may reflect the difficulties of deliberation and evaluation when individuals are so far apart as to impede effective deliberation. The dynamics of polythink suggest that trying to assess options among individuals who have fundamentally divergent views of how the world works may prove intractable.[56] In short, in making for a sound assessment process, the configuration of individuals' preferences and world views may be as important as incorporating a diversity of expertise and bureaucratic perspectives."

Finally, there is one other potentially useful way of thinking about who might be represented to ensure a sound process. One might look for individuals with specific analytical abilities or intellectual dispositions to help promote comprehensive and creative search and analysis. This follows in part from the analytical approach discussed above. In addition, some individuals may exhibit particular traits and capacities that render them especially good analysts. They might also be included in deliberative processes to the extent that one is able to select for individuals in such a manner.[57] Psychological research shows that some individuals are not as beholden to particular preexisting beliefs and theories as others when evaluating novel situations.[58] This is the finding of the "Good Judgment

Project,"[59] which was started by three psychologists to explore aptitudes in forecasting; their research identified a class of individuals who are "actively open-minded" and can readily accommodate to uncertainty, demonstrate agility in synthesizing information and at arriving at judgments about its implications. In short, ensuring good strategic assessment may involve thinking creatively about who is represented, and what intellectual strengths they bring to the process.

The limits of "good" process

That a good process is necessary or important to sound strategic assessment, however, should also not be taken as given. Once again, underlying this approach is a hypothesis: that good process promotes good decisions. Demonstrating a systematic empirical link between process and outcomes has often proven problematic, however, in part for the reasons discussed at the start of the essay: analysts disagree about what counts as a good outcome. As Renshon and Renshon put it, "the quest for criteria by which to judge the quality of decisions has proved to be complex, necessary, and thus far elusive."[60] Without a benchmark for measuring "good" outcomes, it is difficult to establish that good processes generate them.

In fact, there is good reason to expect that a good process may sometimes produce bad outcomes.[61] In part this is the result of the endemic uncertainty and significant challenges inherent in formulating strategy, noted above.[62] An advisory process may yield an informed and astute decision, but that does not alleviate the underlying fact it may prove inadequate to achieving its stated goals.

Alternatively, at least at times, good processes may be simply irrelevant for devising effective strategies. After all, there is a wealth of study of "leadership" that belies the idea that structures or process are determinative or even central to shaping outcomes and yielding effective strategy.[63] As Alexander George describes it, "Sound decisions by executives do not always require vigilance or consensus within the group."[64] Rather, more important may be the quality of a leader's judgment, which "resides in the experience and intuition of a decision-maker."[65] As Renshon and Renshon observe, quoting George:

> There are a number of reasons this might prove to be true in practice, but among the most important is that "the conscious exercise of leadership in a crisis situation in order to direct the focus of group deliberations away from options already discarded for good reasons and towards issues where the executive feels the a particular need for group input is a legitimate response to the constraints on decision making."[66]

Good leadership may at times substitute for sound process.

Finally, the conventional framing of "good" and "bad" processes may be too narrowly conceived. Processes also vary in other dimensions, privileging different values and political imperatives. A system that maximizes flexibility and responsiveness may come at the expense of one that favors comprehensiveness and inclusivity. A process that lacks checks and balances and therefore is efficient may also be vulnerable to capture, while one that has many built-in safeguards may be biased toward the status quo. These tradeoffs, moreover, may have serious implications for the choices facing those proposing reform initiatives. For example, while the need for greater sharing of information with the IC is well established, as Jervis notes, reducing compartmentalization is not without risks. Compartmentalization limits damage due to security breaches and the free flow of information could facilitate destructive acts should someone infiltrate IC systems.[67] In other words, it may be just as important to think about what values and attributes should be prioritized in strategic assessment, as to think about what qualifies as a good or bad process.

Challenges and opportunities for improving strategic assessment

A final lesson that emerges from the scholarly literature analyzed above is that there are inherent challenges to any effort to promote improvements in strategic assessment. Successful efforts to improve the capacity of political leaders to engage in strategic assessment will have to acknowledge and work with or around these obstacles.

Some of these obstacles are well known, such as the challenges facing effective bureaucratic reform. Hence, evaluation of the circumstances in which reform is possible, and when it has proven more or less efficacious is important. One study, for example, found that organizational changes were more likely to be effective when spearheaded by the executive branch.[68]

Also among these challenges are the incentives inherent in political leadership and presidential politics.

> A number of the biases that policy makers bring to bear are motivated— i.e., involve political and psychological reasons why they need to structure their worlds in a certain way. This means that they will resist reforms that, while sound in the abstract, would make their lives more difficult.[69]

For example, "Surveying many options may seem good in practice, but when a decision must be made, it may seem to be subverting the unity of purposes."[70] Reevaluating and reviewing policy is apt to be interpreted as vacillation, indecision, and lack of strategic focus.[71] Politically, admitting that your strategy requires compromises and tradeoffs in other valued goals can be untenable.[72] In other words, there are going to be areas in which politics or personalities inhibit the prospects for change and little can be done to overcome them.

The scholarly literature suggests, however, that there are in other respects some positive, if unconventional, things that can be done to improve deliberation and decision-making. One central insight of the analytical approach is that the training of those involved in the act of evaluating information and deriving insights is critical—whether that be the principals engaged in strategic assessment at the apex, or their supporting staffs. By rendering individuals more aware of common inferential biases and of the benefits and features of deductive argumentation and hypothesis-testing, the quality of analysis within different entities and levels of the government may improve. As the analytical skills of decision-makers or the subordinates who support them are enhanced, strategic assessment is apt to improve.

In addition, presidents may also learn to think more self-consciously about their own advisory systems. There is evidence that exposing decision-makers to the pitfalls and biases that beset deliberative processes may be valuable.[73] It may be a starting point for improving assessment, especially in areas where political and psychological imperatives do not inhibit improvement.[74] There are, for example, several known instances in which self-aware leaders consciously adjusted their strategic assessment processes to mitigate pathologies.[75]

Scholars also can play an important, indirect role in improving strategic assessment, especially in improving the analytical basis of assessment discussed above. To this end, scholars should continue to make the case that abstract general theory is useful and essential in applied settings, while converting the insights of their research into tractable policy advice.

Scholars might also do more to demonstrate the value of training in analytical approaches and methodological issues.[76] Those knowledgeable in social science methods do not always make clear the practical implications of the analytical tools and approaches on which they rely.[77] Doing so is essential to demonstrate to political leaders and practitioners that investment in such training will have practical value in an applied setting. This is essential given the time pressures, stresses and demands on policymakers' time and attention.

Notes

1 Derek Chollet, "What's Wrong with Obama's National Security Council," *Defense One*, 26 April 2016. www.defenseone.com/ideas/2016/04/whats-wrong-obamas-national-security-council/127802; Karen De Young, "How the Obama Administration runs Foreign Policy," *Washington Post*, 4 August 2015; Daniel DePetris, "Trump's Dysfunctional NSC a Threat to National Security" *Reuters*, 9 August 2017. www.reuters.com/article/us-depetris-nsc-commentary/commentary-trumps-dysfunctional-nsc-a-threat-to-national-security-idUSKBN1AP1T2.

2 Note that these perspectives are not commonly compared by scholars, or necessarily understood as alternative approaches to strategic assessment (most do not even use that terminology).

3 When analyzing strategic assessment many scholars focus specifically on the development of a country's military strategy in armed conflict, in which the civilian and military leadership are often central actors Here I use "strategy" to refer not just to the specific military approach employed in a war, but the overall political-military approach adopted toward an armed conflict, or security issue. Scott Gartner, *Strategic Assessment in War* (Yale University Press, 1997); Richard K. Betts, "Is Strategy an Illusion?" *International Security* 25, no. 2 (Fall 2000), pp. 5–50; Barry R. Posen,

The Sources of Military Doctrine: France, Britain, and Germany Between the World Wars (Ithaca, NY: Cornell University Press, 1984).

4 Jonathan Renshon and Stanley A. Renshon, "The Theory and Practice of Foreign Policy Decision Making," *Political Psychology* 29, no. 4 (2008), p. 518; Deborah Welch Larson, [book review] *Perspectives on Politics* 10, no. 1, (March 2012), p. 227.

5 The Iraq 2003 war has been alternatively deemed a case of groupthink and polythink (see discussion of these concepts later in the chapter). Renshon contends, however, that the deliberative process associated with the war contained elements often associated with a good process. Alex Mintz and Carly Wayne, *The Polythink Syndrome: U.S. Foreign Policy Decisions on 9/11, Afghanistan, Iraq, Iran and ISIS* (Stanford University Press, 2016), chapter 5; Stanley A. Renshon, *National Security in the Obama Administration* (Routledge, 2010), p. 67.

6 Renshon and Renshon, "Theory and Practice of Foreign Policy Decision Making," p. 525; Risa A. Brooks, *Shaping Strategy: The Civil-Military Politics of Strategic Assessment* (Princeton University Press, 2008), p. 10; Mark Schafer and Scott Crichlow, *Groupthink versus High-Quality Decision Making in International Relations*, (New York: Columbia University Press, 2010).

7 This framing is my own, but builds on a typology that appears in Risa A. Brooks, "Introduction," in Risa A. Brooks and Elizabeth Stanley, eds., *Creating Military Power: the Sources of Military Effectiveness* (Stanford University Press, 2007).

8 On the importance of integration, see Posen, *The Sources of Military Doctrine*.

9 Betts, "Is Strategy an Illusion?"

10 The scholarship on civil-military relations emphasizes the importance of overcoming bureaucratic biases such as these. In his classic book, *The Sources of Military Doctrine*, Barry Posen, for example, argues that political intervention is essential to innovation and to ensuring means-end integration in politico-military strategy. Without such intervention, the organizational biases that afflict military organizations can prevent innovation and integration. Feaver also argues that political oversight of the military is essential, given that the military's preferences commonly diverge from political priorities; the political principal must intervene to prevent destructive forms of agency slack that could result in inferior outcomes and failure for military to execute political decisions. In both cases, political control over military activity is necessary to neutralize organizational biases Peter Feaver, *Armed Servants: Agency, Oversight and Civil-Military Relations*, (Cambridge: Harvard University Press, 2005).

11 Graham Allison and Morton Halperin, "Bureaucratic Politics: A Paradigm and Some Policy Implications," *World Politics* 24 (1972), pp. 40–79. Also see Allison's classic, *Essence of Decision* (Boston: Little Brown, 1971). Also see William W. Newmann, *Managing National Security Policy* (Pittsburg: University of Pittsburg Press, 2003), pp. 19–37; Alex Mintz and Karl DeRouen Jr., *Understanding Foreign Policy Decision-Making* (Cambridge University Press, 2010), pp. 70–75.

12 Mintz and DeRouen, *Understanding Foreign Policy Decision-Making*, p. 71; Newmann, *Managing National Security Policy*, p. 20.

13 Gordon Nathan Lederman, "Restructuring the Intelligence Community," in Peter Berkowitz, ed., *The Future of American Intelligence* (Hoover Press, 2005), chapter 3, p. 93.

14 Karl W. Eikenberry, "Toward a National Security Strategy," *Defining Ideas*, 4 June 2015, p. 3.www.hoover.org/research/toward-national-security-strategy.

15 Since the passage of the National Security Act of 1947, a vast number of briefs and analyses about shortcomings and proposed reforms have been written. See, for example, those related to the Intelligence Community and to the NSC. Kenneth Warner and J. Kenneth McDonald, "US Intelligence Community Reform Studies Since 1947," *Center for the Study of Intelligence*, April 2005. See also, for example, the list of reports by the CRS. www.fas.org/sgp/crs/intel/index.html. On the NSC, there are many examples and proposals for reform. For a sample of commentaries on these see I. M. Destler and Ivo Daadler, "A New NSC for a New Administration," Brookings,

15 November 2000. www.brookings.edu/research/a-new-nsc-for-a-new-adminis-tration; Russell Berman, "Republicans Try to Rein in National Security Council," *The Atlantic*, 20 May 2016. www.theatlantic.com/politics/archive/2016/05/republi-cans-try-to-shrink-the-national-security-council/483596; Shawn Brimley, Julianne Smith and Jacob Stokes, "Reforming the National Security Council: What the Next President Needs to Know," War on the Rocks, 1 July 2015. http://warontherocks.com/2015/07/reforming-the-national-security-council-what-the-next-president-needs-to-know and "Enabling Decision: What the Next President Needs to Know," Center for a New American Security, 24 June 2015. www.cnas.org/sites/default/files/publications-pdf/CNAS%20Report_NSC%20Reform_Final.pdf; Karen De Young, "White House Tries for a Leaner NSC," *Washington Post*, 15 June 2015. www.washingtonpost.com/world/national-security/white-house-tries-for-a-leaner-national-security-council/2015/06/22/22ef7e52-1909-11e5-93b7-5eddc056ad8a_story.html.

16 Richard A. Best Jr., "Intelligence Reform After Five Years: The Role of the Director of National Intelligence (DNI)," Congressional Research Service, 22 June 2010. www.fas.org/sgp/crs/intel/R41295.pdf.

17 Spencer Hsu, "Obama Combines Security Councils, Adds Offices for Computer and Pandemic Threats," *Washington Post*, 27 May 2009. www.washingtonpost.com/wp-dyn/content/article/2009/05/26/AR2009052603148.html.

18 The PNSR was established by Congress as a nonpartisan effort to study the national security infrastructure and develop recommendations for reform. "Forging a New Shield," Project on National Security Reform, Executive Summary, November 2008. http://0183896.netsolhost.com/site/wp-content/uploads/2011/12/pnsr-forg-ing_exec-summary_12-2-08.pdf.

19 See "Forging a New Shield," Executive Summary, p. viii.

20 "Forging a New Shield," p. xi.

21 Alexander George and Eric Stern, "Harnessing Conflict in Foreign Policy Making: From Devil's to Multiple Advocacy," *Presidential Studies Quarterly* 32, no. 3, pp. 484–508. Cited in Renshon and Renshon, "The Theory and Practice of Foreign Policy Decision Making," p. 526.

22 Alexander George, "The Case for Multiple Advocacy in Making Foreign Policy," *American Political Science Review* 66 (September 1972), pp. 751–795.

23 Jervis references Alexander George, *Presidential Decisionmaking* (see Note 36). See Robert Jervis, "Bridges, Barriers and Gaps: Research and Policy," *Political Psychology* 29, no. 4 (2008), p. 378. Also, on core components of an advisory process, see Patrick J. Haney, *Organizing for Foreign Policy Crises* (University of Michigan Press, 2002), p. 48; Renshon and Renshon, "The Theory and Practice of Foreign Policy Decision Making," p. 518. Schafer and Crichlow, pp. 63–66.

24 Deborah Welch Larson, [book review] *Perspectives on Politics* 10, no. 1 (March 2012), pp. 227–228; Gartner, *Strategic Assessment in War*, p. 41; Christopher Tuck, *Confrontation, Strategy and War Termination* (London: Routledge, 2013), p. 12; Herbert Simon, "From Substantive to Procedural Rationality" in Spiro Latsis, ed., *Method and Appraisal in Economics* (Cambridge University Press, 1976), pp. 129–149.

25 Daniel Kahneman and Stanley Renshon, "Hawkish Biases," in Trevor Thrall and Jane Cramer, eds., *American Foreign Policy and the Politics of Fear: Threat Inflation Since 9/11* (New York: Routledge, 2009).

26 Mintz and Carly, *Polythink*, pp. 19–20.

27 As Renshon and Renshon describe it, "A motivated bias is a systematic distortion of information acquisition or appraisal caused by the decision makers' psychological investment in a certain view or understanding regardless of the facts. The somewhat misleading conventional terms 'cognitive error' or 'bias,' in contrast, are not moti-vated by any desire to reduce cognitive dissonance or maintain well-being." See "The Theory and Practice of Foreign Policy Decision Making," p. 512.

28 Alex Mintz, "How Do Leaders Make Decisions: A Poliheuristic Approach," *Journal of Conflict Resolution* 48, no. 1 (2004), pp. 3–13.

29 As Jervis observes about the importance of these tradeoffs, "In fact, people often manage to underestimate such trade-offs, or even not to perceive them at all. It is as though they believe in a benign deity who has arranged things so that the policy that is best on one dimension is superior to the alternatives on several other independent dimensions as well." Jervis, "Bridges, Barriers and Gaps: Research and Policy," p. 581.

30 As one set of analysts describes it, "While the basic organizational units or structures, as described above, in national security domain may endure across administrations, how a deliberative process actually works varies. Who and in what manner the president, his staff and top advisors relies on the NSC or engages informal or ad hoc working groups and advisory settings varies across and within administrations over time and in relation to substantive issue." Alan G. Whittaker, Shannon A. Brown, Frederick C. Smith, and Elizabeth McKune, "The National Security Policy Process: The National Security Council and Interagency System," August 2011, p. 24. https://issat.dcaf.ch/Learn/Resource-Library/Policy-and-Research-Papers/The-National-Security-Policy-Process-The-National-Security-Council-and-Interagency-System.

31 See the many works by Margaret Hermann on "Leadership Trait Analysis." Margaret Hermann, "Explaining Foreign Policy Behavior Using the Personal Characteristics of Leaders," *International Studies Quarterly* 24, no. 1, pp. 7–46; Schafer and Crichlow, *Groupthink Versus High-Quality Decision Making*, p. 43. Fred Greenstein, "Can Personality and Politics Be Studied Systematically," *Political Psychology* 13, no. 1 (1992), pp. 105–128.

32 Schafer and Crichlow, *Groupthink Versus High-Quality Decision Making*, p. 14.

33 Ibid., p. 6.

34 Some of the defects include the illusion of invulnerability, stereotyping the outgroup, collective rationalizations, self-censorship, pressuring dissenters, seeking unanimity and the like. These problems then generate failures to consider available information, truncated search, failing to compare the utility of different options, etc. Schafer and Crichlow, *Groupthink Versus High-Quality Decision Making*, p. 24.

35 Ibid., p. 3.

36 Ibid., p. 247; Mintz and Wayne, *Polythink*; Alexander George, *Presidential Decision-making in Foreign Policy: The Effective Use of Information and Advice* (Boulder, CO: Westview Press, 1980).

37 Jervis concludes that the conclusion that the regime was developing the weapons was made with unwarranted confidence, and should have been more contingent, reflective of underlying uncertainties. Robert Jervis, *Why Intelligence Fails: Lessons from the Iranian Revolution and Iraq War* (Cornell University Press, 2010), p. 149. For the issues discussed here, see pp. 136–153.

38 For example, the fact that the DCI was the head of the IC as well as the CIA meant dissenting views were not always heard from INR or DOE. Jervis, *Why Intelligence Fails*, p. 144.

39 Jervis, "Bridges, Barriers and Gaps: Research and Policy, pp. 584–585.

40 Jervis, *Why Intelligence Fails*, p. 151.

41 Ibid., p. 139.

42 Ibid., p. 149.

43 Haney, *Organizing for Foreign Policy Crises*.

44 Haney, *Organizing for Foreign Policy Crises*, p. 135. Also see Renshon and Renshon, "The Theory and Practice of Foreign Policy Decision Making," p. 518.

45 Mintz and Wayne, *Polythink*, p. 21; John Burke and Fred Greenstein, *How Presidents Test Reality* (New York: Russell Sage, 1989).

46 As one analysts puts it, "we must be careful to distinguish decision process from effective policy substance." Stanley Renshon, *National Security in the Obama Administration: Reassessing the Bush Doctrine* (London: Routledge, 2010), p. 69.

47 Eliot Cohen, *Supreme Command: Soldiers, Statesmen, and Leadership in Wartime* (New York: Free Press, 2002); Brooks, *Shaping Strategy*.

48 Mintz and Wayne, *Polythink*, p. 6.

49 George, *Presidential Decisionmaking in Foreign Policy*, p. 25.

50 This is separate and distinct from the cognitive biases that may shape how information is managed, which are discussed later in the chapter.

51 Jervis, *Why Intelligence Fails*, p. 170.

52 Ibid., p. 170.

53 Posen, *The Sources of Military Doctrine*, p. 13.

54 Stanley A. Renshon, *National Security in the Obama Administration: Reassessing the Bush Doctrine*, (New York: Routledge, 2009). p. 64; Bret Stephens, "Obama's Team of Conformists" *Wall Street Journal*, 9 December 2008.

55 Joe Klein, "National Security Team of Rivals," *Time*, 21 November 2009; Stephens, "Obama's Team of Conformists"; Renshon, *The Bush Doctrine Reconsidered*.

56 Mintz and Wayne, *Polythink*, p. 3.

57 Stanley Renshon and Deborah Larson, eds., *Good Judgment in Foreign Policy: Theory and Application* (Lanham, MD: Rowman and Littlefield, 2002).

58 Philip Tetlock, *Expert Political Judgment: How Good Is It? How Can We Know?* (Princeton, NJ: Princeton University Press, 2005).

59 See Alix Speigel, "So You Think You're Smarter than A CIA Agent," NPR.org 2 April 2014. Michael Horowitz, "Good judgement in forecasting international affairs," Washington Post Monkey Cage 26 November 2013. www.npr.org/sections/parallels/2014/04/02/297839429/-so-you-think-youre-smarter-than-a-cia-agent; www.washingtonpost.com/news/monkey-cage/wp/2013/11/26/good-judgment-in-forecasting-international-affairs-and-an-invitation-for-season-3; http://ericfarr.net/tag/kahneman.

60 Renshon and Renshon, "The Theory and Practice of Foreign Policy Decision Making," p. 522.

61 The Iraq 2003 war is a case in point. It has been called a case of groupthink and polythink. Alternatively, in a less common view, Renshon contends that the deliberative process associated with the war contained elements often associated with a good process. Mintz and Wayne, *Polythink*, chapter five; Renshon, *National Security in the Obama Administration*, p. 67.

62 Betts, "Is Strategy an Illusion?".

63 Schafer and Crichlow, *Groupthink Versus High-Quality Decision Making*.

64 See Alexander George, "From Groupthink to Contextual Analysis of Policymaking Groups," in Paul Hart, Eric Stern, and Bengt Sundelius, eds., *Beyond Groupthink: Political Group Dynamics and Foreign Policymaking* (Ann Arbor: University of Michigan Press, 1997) pp. 44, 48–49. Quote appears in Renshon and Renshon, "The Theory and Practice of Foreign Policy Decision Making," p. 520.

65 Deborah Welch Larson, "Good Judgment in Foreign Policy: Social Psychological Perspectives," in Renshon and Larson, *Good Judgment in Foreign Policy*, p. 7.

66 Quote appears in George, "From Groupthink to Contextual Analysis," p. 45 and is cited in Renshon and Renshon, "The Theory and Practice of Foreign Policy Decision Making," p. 520.

67 Jervis, *Why Intelligence Fails*, p. 187.

68 Drew Cramer and Grant Mullins, "Lessons Learned from Prior Attempts at National Security Reform," Project on National Security Reform, Overarching Issues Working Group. Undated manuscript.

69 Jervis, "Bridges Barriers and Gaps: Research and Policy," p. 577. For example, engaging in a procedurally rational deliberative process may jeopardize perceptions of a president's leadership if the public concludes it is compromising decisive action in favor of a careful survey of alternatives. Similarly, acknowledging that achieving one goal internationally may come at the expense of a key principle or other valued objective may be interpreted as inadequacy or inefficacy.

70 Jervis, "Bridges, Barriers and Gaps: Research and Policy," p. 580.

71 Ibid., p. 580.

72 Ibid., p. 580; Joshua Rovner, *Fixing the Facts: National Security and the Politics of Intelligence*, (Ithaca: Cornell University Press, 2011). On other obstacles see Renshon and Renshon, "The Theory and Practice of Foreign Policy Decision Making," p. 517.

73 Renshon and Renshon, "The Theory and Practice of Foreign Policy Decision Making," p. 531; Jervis, *Why Intelligence Fails*, chapter four.

74 Larson, "Good Judgment in Foreign Policy: Social Psychological Perspectives," p. 4; Alexander George, *Presidential Decisionmaking in Foreign Policy*.

75 Haney, *Organizing for Foreign Policy Crises*; Schafer and Crichlow, *Groupthink Versus High-Quality Decision Making*. Renshon and Renshon, for example, propose leadership training that would render leaders more self-aware of their particular approach in decision-making. They also suggest focusing on aspects of the deliberative processes that might be more easily "de-biased" than others and suggest building off the track record of such changes in advocating fixes. Renshon and Renshon, "The Theory and Practice of Foreign Policy Decision Making," pp. 528–530.

76 See, for example, the insights in Jervis, *Why Intelligence Fails*, pp. 179–196.

77 For example, a problem such as "selecting on the dependent variable" may sound like an absurd abstraction to those unacquainted with the concept. But if explained properly in an applied setting, it can be an illuminating insight: discerning the causes of war, deterrence failure, regime change, and other important phenomena by studying only instances in which these events occurred may obscure the fact that the very same apparent causes were present in cases where the events did not occur. Hence, examining both positive and negative cases of an event can help an analyst avoid misunderstanding the true causes of some real-world problem. For a discussion of the problem in context of the Iraq war WMD failure see Jervis, *Why Intelligence Fails*, p. 191.

3

BENT BUT NOT BROKEN?

Inter-branch politics, checks and balances, and the contemporary national security state

Douglas L. Kriner

Perhaps no individual at the Constitutional Convention did more to promote the unity, energy, and dispatch of the presidential office than James Wilson.[1] However, while Wilson favored a robust presidency, he also strongly supported the decision to entrust the bulk of war powers in the fledgling Republic to the legislative branch. At the Pennsylvania Ratifying Convention, Wilson lauded this allocation as a chief virtue of the new Constitution: "The system will not hurry us into war; it is calculated to guard against it. It will not be in the power of a single man, or a single body of men, to involve us in such distress."[2] While presidential war power ebbed and flowed over the first century and a half of the national experience, Congress always remained of paramount importance. As late as December 6, 1941, President Franklin Roosevelt found himself severely hamstrung by a Congress that retained a firm grip on power in military affairs. While Roosevelt could materially aid the Allied effort, direct intervention against Nazi Germany or Imperial Japan was unthinkable until the surprise attack on Pearl Harbor.[3] Within a decade of World War II's conclusion, however, the pendulum of power over foreign affairs had swung dramatically from one end of Pennsylvania Avenue to the other.

The National Security Act of 1947 began to create an institutional framework that enabled the president to become the preeminent actor directing American foreign policy in the post-World War II era. Congress was pushed into a decidedly secondary role. Despite several attempts over the intervening decades to claw back some of the power that gradually accreted to the executive branch, Congress faces a series of well-known institutional barriers that have largely hamstrung its efforts to use its formal powers to check the post-1945 president in the international arena. This ascendance gave birth to the paradigm of a seemingly "imperial presidency."[4]

Such claims of presidential imperialism are at best overstated and at worst seriously misleading in that they distort the extent to which inter-branch politics have remained at the forefront of foreign policymaking since 1945. Congress is not irrelevant in the international arena. Rather, Congress has consistently exerted influence – in some circumstances, considerable influence – on concrete policy outcomes through more informal means. The institutional clashes are often not as direct and dramatic as a straightforward reading of *The Federalist Papers* might lead us to expect. Congress does not routinely block military action by refusing to declare war or terminate ongoing military ventures by exercising its power of the purse. However, by employing a wide variety of tools Congress does succeed in raising the political costs for the president of pursuing foreign policies of which the legislature disapproves. Mindful of these political costs, presidents often adjust their conduct of foreign policy accordingly.[5]

However, the last 25 years have witnessed two significant exogenous shocks that have threatened to uproot the tenuous system of informal, primarily political checks and balances that underlay the post-1947 national security state: first, the end of the Cold War, and second the terrorist attacks of September 11, 2001, and the emergence of the limitless and endless global war on terror. Have these shocks fundamentally upset the balance of power and *modus vivendi* between the branches?

A growing body of scholarship across disciplines has begun to address these questions. For example, within political science, scholars focused on military action in particular have concluded that even in a post-Cold War and post-9/11 world, many of the informal constraints on the commander-in-chief remain in place.[6] Congress remains relevant, even in an era of clearly augmented executive power. Within legal scholarship, a growing number of voices has similarly argued that while the Madisonian ideal of formal checks and balances may have all but disappeared, it has been replaced by a broader system of accountability in which inter-branch conflict and politicking remain of paramount importance.[7]

This chapter aims to contribute to scholarship in this vein by examining three features of contemporary politics that threaten to weaken the informal checks upon which Congress has relied to impose some measure of constraint on an ascendant executive for most of the post-1945 era. First, as has been well documented by congressional scholars, partisan polarization has increased dramatically since the passage of the National Security Act of 1947, with the contemporary polity reaching levels of polarization not seen since the turn of the 20th century.[8] Divided government and the presence of strong majorities of opposition partisans on Capitol Hill have always served as catalysts for Congress to exercise the tools at its disposal to raise the political costs of pursuing foreign policy with which the legislature disagrees. The alignment of partisan and institutional incentives has always bolstered congressional efforts to constrain presidential overreach in foreign affairs. However, in an increasingly polarized world, open inter-institutional conflict over the conduct of foreign relations has become almost exclusively a feature of divided government. By contrast, in unified government during periods of intense partisan polarization, partisan incentives to defend a co-partisan president all but drown out the institutional drive to maintain a check on an assertive executive.

Second, the chapter examines the threat to the inter-branch balance of power posed by increased secrecy and heightened executive branch control of information relating to multiple aspects of the global war on terror, both foreign and domestic. Presidents have always enjoyed and exploited informational asymmetries to gain institutional advantage vis-à-vis other institutional actors in the foreign policy realm. However, the imperatives of a post-9/11 world have tilted the balance even further toward the president with potentially serious consequences for other actors' capacity to exercise a political constraint on presidential power.

Finally, recent years have given rise to extraordinarily broad claims of presidential power, foremost among them brazen assertions that the president enjoys broad latitude to act as commander in chief, immune from any constraint imposed by other political actors. Also particularly important is the interaction of such claims with an intense demand for secrecy. For example, some of the boldest claims have asserted the power to limit other branches' access to information. Paradoxically, this may be less of a problem in areas like military action itself, which (when not covert) are highly public. In such cases, extraordinary assertions of presidential power can be contested by Congress and other actors in the public sphere. In these conditions, the political constraint may still be operative. However, in many other areas this political constraint may never be triggered if the president's actions are kept from public purview.

Of course, some may question whether a diminishing of Congress' influence over foreign policymaking is troubling at all. Even many longtime Congress scholars lament that the intensely polarized contemporary Congress is institutionally broken.[9] More fundamentally, Congress' very constitutional design may undermine its capacity to engage in effective and efficient foreign policymaking.[10] Finally, electoral incentives encourage most members of Congress to approach foreign policy questions parochially rather than holistically.[11] Given these institutional weaknesses, an increasingly executive-dominated process may often produce more normatively positive policy outcomes.

While Congress' foreign policy failings are legion, we would nevertheless do well to remember the Framers' fears about the excessive concentration of power over war and peace. The question is not whether presidents should retain the initiative in leading the nation's foreign policy. Rather, it is whether other political actors will retain any meaningful capacity to constrain this initiative. Since securing their dominant position atop the modern national security state, presidents of both parties have stumbled into a range of blunders, from the quagmire in Southeast Asia to the war against Iraq and its phantom WMDs, from missteps in Beirut to Mogadishu, from the intelligence agency abuses of the 1960s and 1970s to contemporary intrusions into Americans' civil liberties in the name of national security. Even if a transformed security environment demands executive initiative, democratic accountability requires that other political actors be able to contest presidential policies and impose political costs on the executive for policy failures.

Establishing the post-1945 constitutional order

The National Security Act of 1947 and subsequent amendments played an important role in establishing the institutional framework for what legal scholar Stephen Griffin has called the "post-1945 constitutional order" in which the initiative to respond to and combat foreign threats resides firmly with the president.[12] While power plainly swung toward the executive branch, the shift was not absolute. Rather, both branches recognized the need for deliberation and continued engagement in shaping the nation's foreign and military affairs. Somewhat ironically, at the very time that the aphorism "politics stops at the water's edge" was coming into vogue, inter-branch politics driven by a healthy dose of partisan politics was crucial to establishing and rebalancing the constitutional authority of the branches over the nation's conduct of foreign affairs.

At a 1967 hearing before the Senate Foreign Relations Committee, Under Secretary of State Nicholas Katzenbach challenged notions of congressional supremacy in the field of war powers and instead contended that the relative silence of the constitutional text on key issues meant that ambiguities were to be resolved by later practice: "The Constitution left to the judgment and wisdom of the Executive and Congress the task of working out the details of their relationship."[13] A new wave of legal scholarship has forcefully echoed Katzenbach's interpretation. Rather than taking sides in a pitched battle between competing presidentialist and congressionalist camps, these legal scholars argue that when assessing constitutional fidelity we should look first and foremost to politics. Has the constitutional order produced genuine inter-branch deliberation that informed the course and content of foreign policy?[14]

The construction of the national security state did not resolve the constitutional "invitation to struggle."[15] However, it did weaken many of Congress' formal checks on presidential foreign policy power. The contrast between the serious constraints that shackled Franklin Roosevelt, who despite his best efforts to provide material aid to the Allies was unable to bring the United States directly into the fight before Pearl Harbor (much to Churchill's chagrin), and the independent initiative enjoyed by his immediate successors could not be more stark.

Of course, Congress retains the formal tools of influence that it sometimes wielded more effectively in the pre-1945 era. Most importantly, Congress still controls the federal purse strings. Moreover, the aftermath of Watergate was widely heralded by contemporary observers as an era of congressional resurgence, particularly in the foreign policy realm.[16] One of the crowning achievements of this resurgence was the enactment, over President Nixon's veto, of the War Powers Resolution (WPR) of 1973. Somewhat ironically, the WPR recognized (albeit unconstitutionally, its critics argued) the president's privileged position in directing the nation's military affairs in the nuclear era. It tacitly delegated to the commander in chief the authority to dispatch American forces anywhere around the world for up to 60 days (with another 30 days to bring them home) without requiring any prior congressional sanction. However, after that period the WPR was intended to provide Congress with another mechanism to compel withdrawal without having to cut off funds for troops in the field. The congressional resurgence was visible in other aspects of foreign policy, as well. For example, the lengthy mid-1970s investigations into intelligence abuses and the new legislation they precipitated were direct efforts to rein in the excesses of the intelligence community and covert operations directed by the White House – a direct legacy of the National Security Act of 1947, which created the Central Intelligence Agency and made it accountable only to the president.

However, in all but the rarest of cases Congress has been unable to use most of these tools to constrain the foreign policies, and particularly military policies, of the commander in chief. The institutional constraints that hinder efforts at legislative redress are well known.[17] In contrast to the unitary actor in the White House, Congress faces an intense collective action dilemma when endeavoring to mobilize to defend its institutional power stakes. When policy entrepreneurs in Congress do try to enact legislation checking the commander in chief, they confront a cumbersome legislative process riddled with transaction costs. And even if legislation succeeds in passing both chambers, it still confronts the most stubborn obstacle of all: a president wielding the veto pen.

The result is that most legislative efforts by Congress to invoke the War Powers Resolution's withdrawal clock, exercise the power of the purse to terminate military actions of which it disapproves, or otherwise legislatively mandate a change in foreign policy course have failed to become law.[18] Moreover, even when Congress does appear actively engaged in the international arena, some scholars argue that its influence over policymaking is often "less than meets the eye."[19]

However, Congress' repeated failure to compel presidents to change their preferred policy course through legislation does not mean that Congress has not played an important role in shaping the course and conduct of American military policy since 1945.[20] Rather, for most of this era Congress has exercised power and influence over the conduct of the nation's foreign affairs primarily through *informal* means. Rather than writing its policy preferences into law, Congress has ceded the initiative to the executive. However, it has sought to raise the political costs that the executive stands to pay should it pursue martial policies that deviate too far from congressional preferences.

Congressional influence through informal means

Throughout the post-1945 era, the most consistent and significant constraint that Congress has exercised on the president in the field of military policy has been political in nature. If the primary objective of opponents of the president's martial policies in Congress is to raise the political costs of noncompliance, then they need not overcome the steep institutional barriers to enacting legislation. One of the most important mechanisms through which congressional opponents of presidential policies have sought to impose political costs on the commander in chief is by mobilizing public opinion against the administration.[21] As early as 1917, Edward Corwin wrote in *The President's Control of Foreign Relations*, "For the president even in the exercise of his most unquestioned powers, cannot act in a vacuum. He must ultimately have the support of public sentiment."[22] Given the key role played by political elites, and particularly by members of Congress in shaping public opinion on major questions of foreign policy, turning public opinion against a president and his policies is a particularly potent tool through which congressional opponents can seek to bring political pressure to bear on the commander in chief.[23]

More generally, presidents are also mindful of the broader costs to their political capital that congressional opposition to their foreign policies can entail. Policy battles with Congress in the international arena – even if the administration carries the day – can have unintended consequences for presidential power in other realms.[24] These costs, too, may influence presidents' strategic calculus in foreign affairs, even when they know that Congress is all but powerless to enact legislation compelling a change in policy course.

To sway public opinion and generate broader political costs, Congress enjoys a number of tools in its strategic arsenal. For example, even ultimately unsuccessful legislative initiatives to constrain the president may be politically costly, provided that they attract significant attention in the media and thereby focus public scrutiny on the administration's policies. Roll call votes on legislation to overturn or curtail presidential policies may often represent the most dramatic challenges to presidential initiative in the international arena. However, another powerful weapon in Congress' quiver is its power to launch high-profile investigations into the executive branch's conduct of international affairs. More broadly, congressional opponents of administration policies have exploited a variety of even more informal opportunities, from press releases to making the rounds of the Sunday-morning talk shows to engage the foreign policy debate in the "public sphere."[25]

Empirical analyses of the most important military actions since World War II confirm that the frequency with which Congress exercises these tools significantly influences the expected duration of each military action.[26] When Congress takes action to raise the political costs of a military action, the predicted duration of the deployment decreases, even though none of these actions legislatively compelled such a change in course.

Equally if not more importantly, a wealth of empirical scholarship demonstrates that presidents *anticipate* the political costs that congressional opposition generates, and they adjust their conduct of the nation's foreign and military affairs accordingly. Presidents logically anticipate more pushback from a legislature that is dominated by strong majorities of opposition partisans than from a Congress where the opposition party's ranks are thin. Accordingly, presidents anticipate greater risk from using force when the opposing party controls Congress. Consistent with this, Howell and Pevehouse find that presidents facing a strong partisan opposition on Capitol Hill are less likely, all else being equal, to respond militarily to an international crisis than are presidents backed by stronger ranks of co-partisans in Congress.[27]

Yet, forgoing a military response to a foreign crisis altogether is but one potential option for a president who anticipates considerable opposition from Congress. In some situations, presidents may judge that the precipitating crisis all but compels military action; however, they may moderate the scale and scope of that response, in part to minimize the domestic costs of using force. Consistent with this, Kriner finds that presidents facing a strong opposition party in Congress choose military responses that are significantly smaller in scale and shorter in duration than do presidents who are backed by stronger co-partisan majorities in Congress, all else being equal.[28] Thus, in at least some political climates, particularly when the president has faced significant partisan opposition at the other end of Capitol Hill, the political constraint imposed on presidential conduct of foreign policy has been significant indeed.

Exogenous shocks to the post-1945 system

Over the past quarter-century, the post-1945 institutional order has been buffeted by two major exogenous shocks: first the end of the Cold War, and then the genesis of the global war on terror following the terrorist attacks of September 11, 2001. In key respects, the basic inter-branch dynamic remains mostly intact. Undoubtedly, presidents remain the predominant actor setting the nation's foreign and military policy course. If anything, both developments may have only increased presidential initiative in the military arena. By removing anticipations of a Soviet response from the president's calculations, the end of the Cold War may have lessened the external constraints on the president's freedom of action in the military arena. In the post-9/11 era, presidents may enjoy an even stronger position. Nevertheless, Congress remains relevant in the military arena through its capacity to impose political costs on the president through informal means.

Consider, for example, President Clinton's mixed record of military intervention in various peacekeeping and humanitarian missions throughout the 1990s. In Bosnia, Haiti, and Kosovo, among others, President Clinton ordered extensive and often lengthy commitments of American forces, sometimes in active combat roles, to advance key administration priorities. Often, Clinton committed American troops to battle or to extended peacekeeping missions with only limited support from Congress. However, Clinton's policy decisions also repeatedly demonstrated a keen sensitivity to the tenuous situation on Capitol Hill and the possibility of congressional pushback. In the case of the Rwandan genocide, the administration's unwillingness to go to battle with Congress over another humanitarian mission in sub-Saharan Africa so soon after the bruising inter-branch battle following the disastrous Battle of Mogadishu encouraged Clinton to forgo a military response to the mass killings entirely. "With the memory of Somalia just six months old, and with opposition in Congress to military deployments in faraway places not vital to our national interests," Clinton remembered, "neither I nor anyone on my foreign policy team adequately focused on sending troops to stop the slaughter."[29] In retrospect, Clinton labeled the failure to act in Rwanda one of the greatest regrets of his presidency. In the case of Kosovo, congressional reticence to authorize military action to stop the ethnic cleansing – and stinging criticisms that Clinton was endeavoring to "wag the dog" and distract the country from contemporaneous personal scandals at home – did not dissuade the administration from acting. However, concerns over Congress' response and its capacity to raise political costs may well have encouraged Clinton to mitigate significantly the scale and scope of the mission, even against the advice of his commanders.[30]

Congress has also remained relevant in the military arena in the post-9/11 era, even as its efforts to exercise formal legislative constraints on the commander in chief have failed. The limits on Congress' formal powers are perhaps most evident in the case of congressional efforts to mandate an end to the war in Iraq. For example, after a lengthy legislative battle to overcome a Republican filibuster in the Senate, the newly empowered Democratic congressional majority in 2007 passed a military appropriations bill that mandated a timeline for withdrawing American forces from Iraq. True to form, President Bush calmly vetoed the measure. Congressional Democrats blinked, and passed a "clean" appropriation without the withdrawal timeline.

However, it would be wrong to conclude that the staunch congressional opposition that the Bush administration encountered on the floor, in the hearing rooms, and over the airwaves, did not impose a political cost on the administration. Despite the considerable signs of progress on the ground in Iraq in the wake of the surge, President Bush failed to translate such gains into increased public support for the war and his conduct of it. The congressional counter-narrative emphasizing costs and wartime policy failings seriously undercut administration efforts to capitalize on signs of progress. Moreover, the political costs of this inter-branch battle were felt much more broadly. With the president severely weakened, his approval ratings at Truman-esque levels, and his political capital all but depleted, virtually every other item on the Bush agenda was brought to a screeching halt.[31]

Similarly, domestic political calculations almost certainly factored heavily into the decision calculus of President Obama in the first months of his presidency as he weighed the need for more resources to prosecute the war against the Taliban, which during the campaign he had called a "war of necessity" in contrast to the "war of choice" waged in Iraq, against the increasingly strident opposition to escalation in Congress primarily emanating from liberals in his own party.[32] Ultimately, the president struck a tenuous balance by first announcing in December 2009 a significant troop surge for Afghanistan to conduct counter-insurgency operations and then, in virtually the very next breath, outlining a timeline for the initial drawdown of these surge forces.[33]

Congress' continued capacity to influence presidential military decision-making in the post-9/11 era is perhaps most vividly on display in the case of President Obama's response, or lack thereof, to the use of chemical weapons by the Assad regime in Syria in August 2013. Confronted with compelling evidence that Assad had crossed the president's red line and used chemical weapons against his own people, President Obama met with his advisers and by all accounts settled on a military response.[34] The administration publicly released its official assessment that Assad had, indeed, used chemical weapons, and in an address on the evening of August 30, Secretary of State Kerry boldly made the case for a military response: "As previous storms in history have gathered, when unspeakable crimes were within our power to stop them, we have been warned against the temptations of looking the other way."[35] However, by the time President Obama strode into the Rose Garden to address the nation the next morning, he had changed his mind.[36] Obama began by declaring that he had determined that it was in the national interest to take military action against Assad to punish the regime for its violation of international norms and use of chemical weapons. However, Obama then proceeded to shock many when he announced that he would not order the strikes unilaterally, but would first seek congressional authorization.[37] Constitutional mores did not drive Obama's reversal. Indeed, Obama publicly maintained that he possessed sufficient constitutional authority to order the strikes unilaterally.[38] Rather, the forces driving the president's decision to first seek congressional authorization were primarily *political*.

At a press conference four days later President Obama frankly admitted that calculations concerning Congress' likely reaction to a unilateral response drove his reversal. If he acted unilaterally, "Congress will sit on the sidelines, snipe. If it works, the sniping will be a little less; if it doesn't, a little more."[39] Legislation constraining his freedom of action was not what Obama feared. Rather, public criticism of his policies, particularly if they should prove to be more costly or less immediately successful than expected, is what Obama hoped to avoid. By compelling members of Congress to vote to authorize military action against Syria, Obama hoped that he could tie members to the mission politically and thereby minimize the political costs downstream.[40] Thus, the dynamics of the Syrian case – involving the anticipated reactions of members of Congress, corresponding shifts in public opinion, and future political costs, which culminated in a dramatic policy reversal – largely mirror the politics of informal inter-institutional constraints on presidential war-making observed throughout the post-1945 period.[41]

Outside of the military arena, other scholars have also argued that the president, while plainly enjoying significant advantages in the transformed security environment of the post-Cold War, post-9/11 period, continues to exercise power under considerable constraint. For example, Harvard Law professor Jack Goldsmith describes "an accountable presidency after 9/11." As former head of the Office of Legal Counsel under President Bush, Goldsmith has firsthand experience of the bold assertions of executive power made in the aftermath of the 9/11 attacks. However, Goldsmith concludes that presidents can maintain such powers only with institutional and public support: "The president simply cannot exercise these war powers over an indefinite period unless Congress and the courts support him."[42] Public opinion, which a wealth of political science scholarship reminds us is significantly shaped by the reaction of congressional and other political elites on questions of foreign policy, serves as perhaps the ultimate constraint in Goldsmith's account.[43] "The Commander in Chief is constrained by law and politics," Goldsmith concludes, "even in this endless war."[44]

Similarly legal scholars Eric Posner and Adrian Vermeule turn the table on Arthur Schlesinger Jr.'s famous phrase and argue that "even an imperial president is constrained by politics and public opinion."[45] While Posner and Vermeule suggest that the old Madisonian ideal of institutional checks and balances is largely obsolete, they contend that it has been replaced by a more informal system that nonetheless imposes genuine constraint on the president. To be sure, times of crisis can weaken this constraint, for example by increasing the pressure for bipartisanship. However, Posner and Vermeule also argue that crises can, somewhat paradoxically, increase political constraints. Toward this end, they cite the political battle over the Authorization to Use Military Force (AUMF) passed by Congress just three days after the 9/11 attacks. Whereas the Bush administration requested incredibly broad authority to preempt and deter all future terror attacks in its draft legislation, Congress pushed back and denied it sweeping power.[46]

Three challenges to the system of informal constraints

This scholarship across disciplines makes clear that presidents do not exercise their heightened powers unchecked in the contemporary era. However, three developments – and their interaction – do threaten to erode the informal constraints that have limited presidential power for decades following the conclusion of World War II. First, increasing levels of partisan polarization in Washington not seen since the early 20th century have intensified the boom-bust cycle of inter-branch conflict that underlies much of the democratic constraint on presidential power in the international arena. Second, the fundamental informational asymmetry between the executive branch and other institutional actors seeking to exercise some constraint on its power has only been exacerbated by the demands for increased secrecy to prosecute the global war on terror. Finally, the extraordinary claims of unilateral executive authority articulated since 9/11 – indeed, claims that presidential power in the security realm is all but immune from congressional and judicial constraints – have far exceed Katzenbach's belief that the constitutional order is a product of practice determined by mutual dialogue between the branches. Many of these claims have been used to further strengthen the executive branch's informational advantages over would-be rivals, which undermine other actors' capacity to check the president through more informal, political means. These informal mechanisms, many of which rely on inter-branch contestation in the court of public opinion, cannot operate if presidential power is exerted clandestinely.

Partisan polarization

The National Security Act of 1947 was passed during a period of historically low partisan polarization (Figure 3.1). However, since its enactment, the parties in both chambers of Congress have steadily polarized, growing more ideologically distant from one another, to the point that the contemporary Congress is even more polarized than the bitterly divided and highly partisan congresses of the late 19th and early 20th centuries. This steady rise in polarization is often lamented as a source of gridlock in Washington and as the cancer that has undermined the search for bipartisan solutions to pressing questions of national import.[47] However, another oft-overlooked consequence of polarization is that it has made critical congressional oversight of the foreign policy president almost exclusively a feature of divided government.

Scholars, pundits, and average citizens alike often give Congress' investigative oversight function short shrift. However, it has historically been one of the most important tools through which Congress shines a light on the alleged shortcoming of presidential foreign policies and raises the political costs for

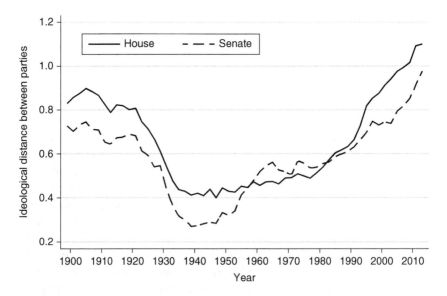

FIGURE 3.1 Partisan polarization in the House and Senate.

Note: Polarization is measured as the difference (absolute value) in the first-dimension DW NOMINATE score of the average Republican and the average Democrat of each chamber.

the president of noncompliance with congressional preferences. The very first congressional investigation during the Washington administration examined the circumstances surrounding the Indian massacre of American forces under St. Clair on the western frontier and the extent to which the tragedy was the result of failed policies by the War Department.[48] Many 19th-century investigations focused squarely on the president's actions as commander in chief.[49] Missouri Senator Harry S. Truman burst onto the national stage not for his prominence as a legislator, but as an investigator at the head of the Senate Special Committee to Investigate the National Defense Program during World War II. As committee chair, Truman frequently and publicly battled the Roosevelt administration over its coordination and management of the war effort on the home front.[50] And even as the modern national security state began to take shape and foreign policy power became increasingly concentrated in the president, Congress continued to use its investigative power aggressively to superintend the executive's conduct of foreign affairs.

Indeed, many of the most prominent foreign policy battles between the branches in the post-1945 era took place not on the floor, but in the committee room: the congressional inquest into who "lost" China to the Communists; the firing of MacArthur and the conduct of the Korean War; McCarthy and alleged Communist infiltration of the executive branch; the Fulbright hearings into first the military intervention in the Dominican Republic and then Vietnam; the Church Committee investigation into alleged abuses by the intelligence agencies; and a series of later inquests into scandals such as Iran-Contra, Abu Ghraib, and Benghazi. Writing in the aftermath of Watergate, Arthur Schlesinger Jr. argued that "the manner in which Congress exercises the investigative power will largely determine in years to come whether the problem posed in the *51st Federalist* can be satisfactorily answered – whether the constitutional order will in the end oblige the American government to control itself."[51]

In some cases, such as the Truman Committee, the primary goal of congressional overseers was primarily constructive, to force policy concessions from the White House. In others, the process was decidedly more adversarial with inflicting political damage on the president seeming to be the investigators' primary goal. However, regardless of the tack taken, again and again, investigative oversight proved a powerful weapon by which Congress influenced the strategic calculations of presidents in the international arena.[52]

There has always been a partisan dimension driving variation in investigative oversight. However, during the Cold War era – a period of relatively low partisan polarization – there are clear examples of important investigations of presidential conduct of foreign affairs launched and sustained in periods of unified government. Arkansas Democrat J. William Fulbright famously broke with his party to criticize President Johnson's 1965 military intervention in the Dominican Republic as a "grievous mistake" following a series of hearings in his Senate Foreign Relations Committee on the crisis.[53] The following year, Fulbright would again challenge his party leader's foreign policy, this time by taking aim at Johnson's conduct of the war in Vietnam. The Senate Foreign Relations Committee's scrutiny of the Vietnam War would continue and intensify during the Nixon administration.[54] Moreover, even in periods of divided government, while the president's co-partisans had incentives to blunt some of the worst critiques of administration policy, in less polarized decades they often participated in substantive, meaningful ways in the process, rather than simply playing an obstructing role. For example, during the Church Committee's lengthy inquest into alleged abuses by the intelligence agencies and covert operations, not only did the minority actively participate, but the ranking minority member John Tower chaired a number of the committee's 120 hearings, and each of the committee's fourteen final reports enjoyed bipartisan support.[55]

However, as partisan polarization in Washington has increased, investigations of even gross allegations of executive branch misconduct in foreign policy have become almost exclusively a function of divided government, particularly in the House of Representatives. Consider, for example, the congressional response to the revelations of the systematic abuse of Iraqi prisoners at Abu Ghraib. The Republican-controlled House all but refused to hold formal inquiries into the policy failures that led to the scandal at Abu Ghraib.[56] The Republican leadership's success in blocking damaging hearings led California Democrat Henry Waxman to lament that the House Armed Services Committee held only five hours of testimony on Abu Ghraib, compared to 140 hours of House testimony on whether Bill Clinton improperly used the White House Christmas card list.[57] Both the Senate Foreign Relations and Armed Services committees did, ultimately, hold a modest number of hearings on Abu Ghraib; however, they did so only after being attacked first by the House majority leader for disloyalty to the party and potentially harming President Bush's reelection prospects and then by their House counterparts for undermining popular support for the war effort.[58]

A more systematic analysis of variation in congressional oversight of the Iraq War as a whole similarly reveals evidence of a strong partisan dimension. For example, critical oversight of the Iraq War increased significantly following the Democratic victories in the 2006 midterm elections and the return of divided government in the 110th Congress. Indeed, the average level of oversight activity increased four-fold in 2007 and 2008 from that observed in the war's first four years during which Republicans controlled both the House and the Senate.[59] Narrowing the focus to congressional hearings that investigated an alleged instance of misconduct or abuse of power by the Bush administration in its conduct of the Iraq War reveals a similar pattern. Despite the widespread looting, collapse of civil order, and kindling of a deadly insurgency that threatened the American occupation of the country, congressional Republicans held no investigative hearings of the Iraq War during 2003. As the years dragged on, the situation in Iraq presented a myriad of targets for would-be investigators in Congress: the failure to find weapons of mass destruction; the abuse of Iraqi prisoners at Abu Ghraib; the inadequate provision of body armor and armored vehicles to protect American soldiers; the battle of Fallujah; the Haditha massacre; and the poor treatment of disabled war veterans at Walter Reed. Yet, an analysis of the data clearly shows that in a highly polarized polity which party controlled Congress was the most important predictor of the volume of investigative activity. The return of divided government in 2007 roughly doubled the average intensity of investigative activity.[60] When Republican chairs controlled the committee gavels, they routinely used their power of negative agenda control to either block altogether or seriously limit the scope of any investigation into the wartime failings of the commander in chief. By contrast, Democratic committee chairs proved much more zealous to use their investigative power to ratchet up the political costs on the Bush administration.

In an era of intense polarization, partisan political incentives usually overwhelm institutional incentives to defend the legislature's prerogatives in the foreign policy realm. In periods of unified government, the intense pressure to defend a co-partisan president often short-circuits the important investigative oversight mechanism by which members of Congress can engage the debate in the public sphere and raise the political costs for the president of pursuing extreme or unsuccessful policies. This is particularly true in the House, where investigations are almost exclusively a feature of divided government in polarized eras. Reflecting the greater rights of the minority and even of individual members, the Senate has historically been more willing to engage in critical oversight, even during unified government. However, partisan loyalties nonetheless often blunt the force of the resulting inquiries.

Consider the two chambers' responses to the first nine months of the Trump presidency. Republican committee chairs in both chambers largely eschewed calls to investigate a host of alleged improprieties, from charges of conflict of interest to allegations of sexual assault. However, the demand for an investigation into Russian interference in the 2016 election and potential collusion by the Trump campaign with these efforts proved impossible to ignore. Both chambers launched inquests into the Russia allegations. The House investigation quickly became bogged down in partisan rancor, and the committee has used its mandate to attack the Clinton campaign almost as much as it has to investigate Trump. The upper chamber's inquiries, particularly the Senate Intelligence Committee's investigation led by Richard Burr (R-NC) and Mark Warner (D-VA), have proceeded on a more bipartisan basis. However, whether the investigations will ultimately produce some legislative rebuke or energize congressional oversight on other issues remains to be seen.[61]

Presidents have always operated with greater leeway when their co-partisans control the institutional machinery in Congress. However, they may be even more insulated from the political constraints that congressional oversight and investigations can generate during periods of unified government in a highly polarized era. In such conditions, the potential for presidential mischief may be even greater than in earlier decades when the polity was less polarized along partisan lines.

Enhanced secrecy

One of the president's most important institutional advantages in foreign affairs has always been the information asymmetry the executive enjoys vis-à-vis other institutional actors.[62] At the very core of the "imperial presidency" was not just the increasing capacity of the president to effect change unilaterally, but also the dramatic increase in the resources at his disposal to keep such actions secret.[63] The National Security Act of 1947 played an important part in bolstering this institutional advantage of the executive branch. It centralized foreign policy expertise within the National Security Council. It also created the Central Intelligence Agency (CIA) and made it accountable to the president alone without a detailed charter or precise mechanisms of congressional oversight.[64] It was not until the Church and Pike Committee investigations of intelligence agency abuses that Congress learned the full extent of how great presidential capacity for covert activity absent any meaningful congressional oversight had become.

In response to the revelations, Congress endeavored to right the balance in the 1970s through a number of new laws including the Privacy Act of 1974; strengthening amendments to the Freedom of Information Act; the Presidential Records Act of 1978; and the Foreign Intelligence Surveillance Act of 1978. Congress also tried to bolster its own institutional capacity by creating permanent Select Intelligence committees in both chambers.

These and related efforts to restore the balance of power between the branches were widely interpreted at the time as evidence of a congressional resurgence. However, successive presidents quickly did all within their power to circumvent any strictures on the executive's ability to conduct various aspects of policy in secret, particularly in the foreign policy realm.[65] Perhaps the clearest example of Congress' failure to rein in clandestine presidential initiatives was the Iran-Contra scandal of the mid-1980s. Following the 1982 midterms, emboldened congressional Democrats passed a series of measures to restrict the Reagan administration's efforts to arm anti-communist rebels in Nicaragua. Between 1982 and 1986, Congress passed a series of measures known as the Boland Amendments, which first seriously restricted and then forbade altogether funding by the CIA or Department of Defense of the Nicaraguan Contras.[66] Undeterred, President Reagan directed his National Security Advisor Robert McFarlane "to do whatever you can to help these people [i.e. the Contras] keep body and soul together."[67] Toward this end, McFarlane spearheaded a secret arms-for-hostages deal with Iran, despite the arms embargo still in effect against the Iranian regime. Some of the proceeds from the sale were then clandestinely funneled to the Nicaraguan Contras in violation of the Boland Amendment prohibition.

The aftermath of the 9/11 attacks may have only intensified presidential incentives to demand and do all in their power to secure heightened secrecy for their unilateral initiatives in the international arena. The threat posed by global terrorism both at home and abroad has blurred the line between foreign and domestic intelligence gathering. Moreover, the prospect of a cyber attack against American financial and military institutions and the demonstrated power of cyber weapons, such as the Stuxnet worm employed with devastating effect against the Iranian nuclear program, have bolstered executive branch claims for absolute secrecy over an expanding range of activities and programs.[68] Finally, the sheer scale and scope of the electronic data collection programs at the heart of the government's anti-terrorism effort is exponentially greater than the programs that triggered the Church Committee and related investigations.[69]

If the president's incentives to insure maximum secrecy and to maintain or even strengthen the informational asymmetry they enjoy have grown considerably, Congress' capacity to check this presidential advantage may be even weaker than it was in the 1970s.[70] Consider, for example, the Bush administration's rebuttal to congressional objections to the Terrorist Surveillance Program, under which the Bush administration secretly authorized the National Security Agency (NSA) to violate the terms of existing statutes, namely the Foreign Intelligence and Surveillance Act of 1978 (a direct legacy of the Church Committee investigations), and eavesdrop on the international communications of American citizens without a warrant from the FISA court.[71] When the program's existence was leaked by the *New York Times* in 2005, the Bush administration scrambled to provide a legal justification for its action. Rejecting claims of constitutional overreach, the Department of Justice claimed that Congress had actually authorized the warrantless surveillance – when it passed the AUMF in October 2001.[72] Needless to say, many in Congress vehemently disagreed with the Justice Department's assessment.[73] However, even if one rejected the AUMF argument, the Department of Justice maintained that President Bush's actions to create unilaterally the warrantless surveillance program were well within his "inherent constitutional authority as Commander in Chief and sole organ for the Nation in foreign affairs."[74]

Under such logic, is the NSA program beyond the purview of Congress? Even noted presidentialist scholar John Yoo, who served in the Office of Legal Counsel under President Bush, argues that it is not. As Yoo notes, "Congress could easily eliminate the surveillance program … simply by cutting off funds for it" or by using other formal tools at its disposal.[75] However, as law professor Heidi Kitrosser observes, Yoo's argument overlooks the fact that the administration instituted and operated the program for years without the knowledge of most members of Congress and completely unbeknownst to the public.[76] More generally, executive privilege and related presidential claims of the right to limit what information can be shared even with Congress severely circumscribe the power of oversight. The heightened secrecy demanded and enforced by the executive negates both the formal constraints mentioned by Yoo and the more informal political constraints hailed by other scholars.

Extraordinary claims of presidential power

A third development that unfolded in the wake of the 9/11 attacks is a series of extraordinary claims of inherent executive power to act not just unilaterally in the foreign policy realm, but to act free from any legislative or judicial over-sight or constraint. Such arguments are not merely a departure from the legislative supremacy school of constitutional interpretation; presidents had long since abandoned that view. Rather, they even represent a significant departure from the view articulated by Undersecretary of State Katzenbach in 1967 that the balance of war powers is a product of interplay and dialogue between the branches. Under these new, extreme interpretations of executive branch foreign policy powers articulated with growing frequency since 9/11, the power of the unitary executive in the international arena is virtually limitless with other actors having no constitutional capacity to constrain it.

One of the first and most striking examples of such claims in the post-9/11 era concerns the Bush administration's legal response to the 2001 Authorization to Use Military Force. As discussed previously, Posner and Vermeule examine the creation and amendment of the AUMF as a test case of how Congress responds in a crisis scenario to a decision concerning how much power to delegate to the executive versus how much of a check to retain on that delegated power.[77] Congress considered the administration's legislative proposal just days after the worst attack on American soil since Pearl Harbor. Yet, even in these exigent circumstances Congress resisted giving the Bush administration a blank check to take any action it deemed necessary to preempt all future terrorist threats. Fearing that the administration's broad language could be construed as freeing the president from ever having to go to Congress to request authorization for the use of force against a future terrorist threat, Congress balked and struck the expansive language from the final version of the AUMF.

However, having been defeated in Congress, President Bush turned instead to the Office of Legal Counsel (OLC) for its opinion as to the scope of the president's powers to confront terrorism. In a memo to the White House Counsel's Office, the OLC argued that even though Congress had struck the White House's proposed sweeping language granting the president the power "to deter and preempt any future acts of terrorism or aggression against the United States" from the final legislation, this must not be construed as a legal constraint on the president's war powers as commander in chief.

Instead, the OLC concluded that the scope of the authorization afforded by AUMF was narrower than the president's independent authority under the Constitution. It acknowledged that the AUMF only authorized retaliatory strikes against those who had "planned, authorized, committed, or aided the [9/11] attacks, and those nations that harbored them." However, the OLC argued that the president also possessed "broad constitutional power to use military force to defend the Nation" that "would allow the President to take whatever actions he deems appropriate to pre-empt or respond to terrorist threats from new quarters." In other words, what Congress explicitly refused to grant the president, the OLC concluded he already possessed independently of the AUMF.

Not only did the president not need AUMF to delegate such power to him, the OLC memo also radically concluded that Congress could not exercise its constitutional powers to limit the president's exercise of this independent power in any way. "Neither statue [AUMF or the War Powers Resolution], however, can place any limits on the President's determinations as to any terrorist threat, the amount of military force to be used in response, or the method, timing, and nature of the response. *These decisions, under our Constitution, are for the President alone to make.*"[78]

The expansive vision of presidential war power articulated in John Yoo's OLC memo concerning AUMF, while one of the first post-9/11 assertions of all-but-unchecked executive authority in the international arena, was merely a harbinger of things to come. The past fifteen years have been replete with unprecedented claims of plenary executive power to prosecute the war on terror both at home and abroad. The undefined residuum of war power alleged to have been entrusted to the unitary executive has been cited to justify a wide range of presidential actions, from unilaterally determining that combatants captured on foreign battlefields will not be granted Geneva Convention rights, to defying congressional statutes banning torture during the interrogation of terror suspects, to authorizing the veritable execution of an American citizen abroad via drone strike absent any judicial proceeding or oversight.[79]

Perhaps equally important, if less well known, are the aggressive steps taken by the executive branch since 9/11 to prevent other actors from acquiring the information essential to overseeing key aspects of the executive's conduct of the war on terror and to activating the informal political constraints so vital to inter-branch politics for most of the post-1945 era. For example, many of President Bush's most controversial signing statements involved constitutional challenges to provisions of laws that required greater transparency from the executive branch. President Bush announced his intention not to be bound by statutory provisions requiring the administration to inform Congress before reprogramming funds to launch new secret operations, such as the creation of new "black sites" where terror suspects could be subject to enhanced interrogation techniques by friendly intelligence services. Following the media revelations and gruesome images of prisoner abuse at Abu Ghraib, the Republican-led Congress enacted a series of measures to tighten rules and regulations for military prisons. Indeed, this is one of the rare cases where a formal legislative constraint – new legislation compelling a change in policy course – appears, superficially at least, to have succeeded. However, while President Bush signed the bill, he effectively gutted it through a signing statement declaring that the administration and military would not be bound by its strictures.[80] More generally, on two separate occasions Congress created inspectors general for Iraq, first in 2003 during the early stages of the occupation, and then again in 2004 following the dissolution of the Coalition Provisional Authority. In his signing statement for the first bill, President Bush declared that the inspector general could not transmit to Congress any information without first receiving permission from the administration itself. In his signing statement for the second, Bush blunted the law's impact by directing the new inspector general to refrain from investigating any intelligence or national security issue that could result in the release of sensitive information.[81]

While the Bush administration was extraordinary for the sheer scope of the unilateral power it claimed for the presidency, subsequent administrations have also relied heavily on unilateral tools. While Barack Obama campaigned against what he deemed to be his predecessor's excessive unilateralism, as president he ultimately came to embrace unilateral powers. President Obama tripled the number of ground troops in Afghanistan and quietly ordered a massive intensification of the drone war without seeking any explicit approval from Congress. In 2011 he ordered extensive American air operations against the Qadaffi regime in Libya and continued them long beyond the War Powers Resolution's withdrawal clock without seeking any congressional approval. Meanwhile on the home front, President Obama continued and even expanded a Bush-era program allowing warrantless surveillance of many electronic communications involving American citizens.

The end result of such maneuvers is a mutually reinforcing vicious cycle. The executive branch's pursuit of heightened secrecy often makes it difficult to discover when presidents are making fantastic claims of presidential power, which can serve to strengthen even further the executive's monopoly on national security information. Absent access to such information, Congress' capacity to exercise an informal political constraint on a wayward commander in chief may be no greater than its admittedly limited capacity to place formal legislative constraints on the executive branch.

Conclusion

If polarization and increased demands for secrecy emanating from the executive branch – demands that are often bolstered by extraordinary claims of unilateral presidential power – threaten to erode the system of informal political constraints that have been at the core of inter-branch politics in the post-1945 national security state, are there any reforms that might reverse these trends and re-energize our separation of powers system in the realm of foreign affairs? While the pendulum of power has swung back and forth many times in American history and may well sway back toward the legislature again in the future, there are reasons to doubt whether piecemeal reform can significantly strengthen Congress' informal constraints over executive power in the short term.

The almost unprecedented levels of partisan polarization in the contemporary Congress are unlikely to abate soon. Congress will always suffer from a significant collective action problem when trying to defend and even claw back some of its institutional power from an ascendant executive. This basic problem is exacerbated during periods of unified government in a polarized era when partisan incentives to defend a co-partisan president will almost always trump institutional incentives to protect the legislature's own power prospects. In such conditions, the foundation of checks and balances articulated in *Federalist 51* – that "the interest of the man must be connected with the constitutional rights of the place" – falls apart. The ranks of those willing to perform what Mayhew called "institutional maintenance," always a rare commodity in Congress, are perhaps even thinner today.[82]

One possible path forward would be to re-energize both chambers' Foreign Relations/Affairs and Armed Services committees, which have historically spearheaded congressional oversight of the executive in the international arena. Recent research by Fowler demonstrates that changing patterns in congressional workload, the end of the Cold War, and a significant decrease in the media visibility of Congress' foreign policy committees (and of Senate Foreign Relations in particular), has seriously eroded the capacity of these committees to oversee and superintend the executive branch. To reverse this trend, Fowler proposes a number of possible reforms. For example, the committees themselves could change their *modus operandi* to attract more media coverage by regularly engaging in a spirited back-and-forth with administration officials by embracing something akin to Question Time in the British Parliament. To address the problem of complacency in a unified government, such sessions should guarantee sufficient time for minority members to aggressively query the administration on key policy questions. The increased potential for inter-branch conflict would significantly increase the newsworthiness of the hearings. Regularizing communications and discursive dialogue between the executive branch and congressional foreign policy leaders could also serve the broader goal of informing the public and strengthening popular constraints on executive initiative as well. Finally, any steps to increase the internal institutional prestige of service on these committees could encourage ambitious legislative entrepreneurs to increasingly value a position on a foreign oversight committee. In such cases, personal ambition for institutional power or higher office could also serve broader, institutional interests.[83] While reforms in this vein may strengthen congressional oversight at the margins, there are strong reasons to question whether they could overcome the strong partisan incentives blunting vigorous oversight during unified government in a polarized era.

Another option for building congressional capacity would be to strengthen the House and Senate Select Intelligence committees. These committees were created in the 1970s with the express purpose of enabling vigorous oversight of classified actions and programs. The committees (briefly united) enjoyed a surge in visibility and prestige after the 9/11 inquiry, and the Senate Intelligence Committee, in particular, has earned plaudits for its methodical and bipartisan approach to the Russian interference investigation through most of 2017. However, both intelligence committees remain under-resourced and dependent upon the executive branch for access to the requisite information.[84] Steps to bolster their oversight capacity and to insure that statutorily mandated information-sharing actually takes place are essential if the intelligence committees are to exercise any meaningful check on executive power.[85]

Heightened secrecy and the extraordinary informational asymmetry enjoyed by the president in the post-9/11 world pose a different, and perhaps equally intractable set of challenges. While acknowledging the steep barriers to successful reform, Kitrosser suggests a number of pathways through which reformers might strengthen what she labels a "substantive accountability framework" in which Congress and the courts can impose checks on the executive to insure both transparency and accountability. Among others, Kitrosser supports greater subpoena powers and budgets for congressional oversight committees, augmented protections for "whistleblowers" within the executive branch, and additional support for outside groups that use the Freedom of Information Act to keep a watchful eye trained on the executive.[86] However, as Howell and Zeisberg argue, such efforts would almost certainly encounter significant presidential resistance. For example, despite the restrictions passed by Congress in the 2015 Freedom Act, presidents retain multiple pathways to continue expanded surveillance programs and circumvent statutory strictures. More generally, there are reasons to doubt whether such efforts have any realistic hope of reining in executive branch secrecy given the extraordinary scope and scale of the contemporary data collection efforts at the forefront of the war on terror.[87]

Ultimately, the most powerful constraint on presidential excess in the contemporary polity may still be the electorate. If presidential policies – assuming that the public learns of them! – fail to produce positive results, the opposition party should be able to capitalize on public unrest. In a polarized world, opposition party gains should energize inter-branch contests and bolster congressional oversight and other informal checks on a wayward executive. And of course, the ultimate constraint on executive abuse of power, as articulated by Hamilton in *Federalist 72,* remains the president's own desire either for reelection or for a co-partisan successor who will defend the president's legacy.

Notes

1 For example, see Richard Beeman. 2009. *Plain, Honest Men: The Making of the American Constitution.* New York: Random House.
2 Quoted in David Gray Adler. 1996. "The Constitution and Presidential Warmaking." In David Gray Adler and Larry George, eds., *The Constitution and the Conduct of American Foreign Policy.* Lawrence: University of Kansas Press, p. 186.
3 Of course, presidents before Roosevelt, including most notably Polk and Lincoln, had pushed on the bounds of their wartime authority. Indeed, Polk deliberately provoked a Mexican attack to provide Congress a *fait accompli* and all but force it to declare war (the outcome of which he made even more certain by attaching the declaration as a preamble to an appropriations bill to fund the troops under fire in the field).
4 Arthur Schlesinger Jr. 1973. *The Imperial Presidency.* Boston: Houghton Mifflin; Andrew Rudalevige. 2005. *The New Imperial Presidency: Renewing Presidential Power After Watergate.* Ann Arbor: University of Michigan Press.
5 William Howell and Jon Pevehouse. 2007. *While Dangers Gather: Congressional Checks on Presidential War Powers.* Princeton, NJ: Princeton University Press; Douglas L. Kriner. 2010. *After the Rubicon: Congress, Presidents, and the Politics of Waging War.* 2010. University of Chicago Press.

6 For example, Douglas L. Kriner. 2014. "Obama's Authorization Paradox: Syria and Congress' Continued Relevance in Military Affairs." *Presidential Studies Quarterly* 44: 309–327; William Howell and Jon Pevehouse. 2007. "When Congress Stops Wars." *Foreign Affairs*, September/October 2007: 95–107.

7 Eric Posner and Adrian Vermeule. 2010. *The Executive Unbound: After the Madisonian Republic.* New York: Oxford University Press; Jack Goldsmith. 2012. *Power and Constraint: The Accountable Presidency after 9/11.* New York: WW Norton & Company.

8 Nolan McCarty, Keith Poole, and Howard Rosenthal. 2006. *Polarized America: The Dance of Political Ideology and Unequal Riches.* Cambridge, MA: MIT Press.

9 Thomas Mann and Norman Ornstein. 2006. *The Broken Branch: How Congress is Failing America and How to Get It Back on Track.* New York: Oxford University Press; Thomas Mann and Norman Ornstein. 2012. *It's Even Worse than It Looks: How the American Constitutional System Collided with the Politics of Extremism.* New York: Basic Books.

10 For a particularly forceful articulation of this view concerning policymaking writ large, see: William Howell and Terry Moe. 2016. *Relic: How Our Constitution Undermines Effective Government and Why We need a More Powerful Presidency.* New York: Basic Books.

11 William Howell, Saul Jackman, and Jon Rogowski. 2013. *The Wartime President: Executive Influence and the Nationalizing Politics of Threat.* Chicago: University of Chicago Press; Rebecca Thorpe. 2014. *The American Warfare State: The Domestic Politics of Military Spending.* Chicago: University of Chicago Press; Helen Milner and Dustin Tingley. 2015. *Sailing the Water's Edge: The Domestic Politics of American Foreign Policy.* Princeton: Princeton University Press. For a countervailing view questioning the extent to which presidents routinely eschew particularistic concerns in both domestic and foreign policy, see Douglas L. Kriner and Andrew Reeves. 2015. *The Particularistic President: Executive Branch Politics and Political Inequality.* New York: Cambridge University Press.

12 Stephen Griffin. 2013. *Long Wars and the Constitution.* Cambridge, MA: Harvard University Press, p. 29.

13 Quoted in Griffin, *Long Wars and the Constitution*, p. 33.

14 Mariah Zeisberg. 2013. *War Powers: The Politics of Constitutional Authority.* Princeton, NJ: Princeton University Press.

15 Edward Corwin. 1940. *The President: Office and Powers.* London: H. Milford, Oxford University Press, p. 200.

16 James Sundquist. 1981. *The Decline and Resurgence of Congress.* Washington, D.C.: Brookings Institution Press; Randall Ripley and James Lindsay. 1993. *Congress Resurgent: Foreign and Defense Policy on Capitol Hill.* Ann Arbor: University of Michigan Press.

17 Terry Moe. 1994. "The Presidency and the Bureaucracy: The Presidential Advantage." In Michael Nelson, ed., *The Presidency and the Political System.* Washington, DC: Congressional Quarterly Press; Terry Moe and Scott Wilson. 1994. "Presidents and the Politics of Structure." *Law and Contemporary Problems* 57: 1–44; Keith Krehbiel. 1998. *Pivotal Politics: A Theory of U.S. Lawmaking.* Chicago: University of Chicago Press; William Howell. 2003. *Power without Persuasion: The Politics of Direct Presidential Action.* Princeton: Princeton University Press.

18 James Meernik. 1995. "Congress, the President and the Commitment of the U.S. Military." *Legislative Studies Quarterly* 20: 377–392. There are, of course, several important exceptions. For example, in 1970 Congress enacted HR 19911 cutting off funds for President Nixon's clandestine expansion of the Vietnam War into Cambodia, but only after extensive negotiations with the administration and after the troops had been withdrawn. The 1975–1976 Tunney and Clark amendments barred U.S. covert assistance to paramilitary forces in Angola, and the Boland amendments of the 1980s (unsuccessfully) banned aid to the Nicaraguan Contras. For an overview, see Kriner, *After the Rubicon*, pp. 39–41.

19 Barbara Hinckley. 1994. *Less Than Meets the Eye: Foreign Policy Making and the Myth of the Assertive Congress.* Chicago: University of Chicago Press.

20 See, for example, Robert David Johnson. 2006. *Congress and the Cold War.* New York: Cambridge University Press; Ralph Carter and James Scott. 2009. *Choosing to Lead: Understanding Congressional Foreign Policy Entrepreneurship.* Durham, NC: Duke University Press.

21 Louis Klarevas. 2002. "The 'Essential Domino' of Military Operations: American Public Opinion and the Use of Force." *International Studies Perspectives* 3: 417–437; Howell and Pevehouse, *While Dangers Gather*; Kriner, *After the Rubicon.*

22 Edward Corwin. 1970 [1917]. *The President's Control of Foreign Relations.* Princeton, NJ: Princeton University Press, pp. 45–46. This sentiment was echoed by Secretary of Defense Caspar Weinberger in what became known as the Weinberg Doctrine: "Before the U.S. commits combat forces abroad, there must be some reasonable assurance we will have the support of the American people." Caspar Weinberger. "The Uses of Military Power: Remarks prepared for delivery by the Hon. Caspar W. Weinberger, Secretary of Defense, to the National Press Club, Washington, D.C. November 28, 1984."

23 Richard Brody. 1991. *Assessing the President: The Media, Elite Opinion, and Public Support.* Stanford, CA: Stanford University Press; John Zaller. 1992. *The Nature and Origins of Mass Opinion.* New York: Cambridge University Press; Eric Larson. 1996. *Casualties and Consensus: The Historical Role of Casualties in Domestic Support for U.S. Military Operations.* Santa Monica, CA: RAND; Adam Berinsky. 2009. *In Time of War: Understanding American Public Opinion from World War II to Iraq.* Chicago: University of Chicago Press; Douglas L. Kriner and Francis Shen. 2014. "Responding to War on Capitol Hill: Battlefield Casualties, Congressional Response, and Public Support for the War in Iraq." *American Journal of Political Science* 58: 157–174.

24 See, for example, Richard Neustadt. 1990 [1960]. *Presidential Power and the Modern Presidents.* New York: The Free Press.

25 David Mayhew. 2000. *America's Congress: Actions in the Public Sphere, James Madison through Newt Gingrich.* New Haven, CT: Yale University Press. Testifying to the reach of such efforts, an empirical analysis of 3,225 front-page *New York Times* articles on eighteen major uses of force from 1945 through 2004 revealed that 27 percent reported the views of Congress and 22 percent reported the policy views of individual members (see Kriner, *After the Rubicon*, pp. 160–166). Through such efforts, members can provide an important counter-frame to the narrative presented by the White House. See Robert Entman. 2004. *Projections of Power: Framing News, Public Opinion, and U.S. Foreign Policy.* Chicago, IL: University of Chicago Press.

26 Kriner, *After the Rubicon*, pp. 170–189.

27 Howell and Pevehouse, *While Dangers Gather.*

28 Kriner, *After the Rubicon.*

29 Bill Clinton. 2004. *My Life.* New York: Alfred A. Knopf. p. 593. In her memoirs, then Ambassador to the United Nations concurs; though she regrets not more forcefully advocating her belief that the United States should have intervened more forcefully to stop the killing, Albright notes that such a response never would have won support in Congress. Madeline Albright. 2003. *Madam Secretary.* New York: Miramax Books. p. 155.

30 Wesley Clark. 2002. *Waging Modern War.* New York: Public Affairs.

31 Kriner, *After the Rubicon*, pp. 276–283.

32 "Excerpts from the First Presidential Debate." *New York Times*, September 27, 2008, A14. Among the fiercest critics were Wisconsin Democrat Russ Feingold, who warned, "I and the American people cannot tolerate more troops without some commitment about when this perceived occupation will end," and House Appropriations Chair David Obey (D-WI), who openly lamented the war's steep financial costs, and noted that the Afghan surge could preclude action on other key priorities: "It is obvious to any but the most obtuse that that expenditure is killing our ability to finance a recovery of our own economy." Helene Cooper. "G.O.P. May Be Vital to Obama

in Afghan War Effort." *New York Times*, September 3, 2009, A1. David Herszenhorn. "House Democrats vs. White House." *New York Times*, July 3, 2010, A11.

33 Barack Obama, "Remarks by the President in Address to the Nation on the Way Forward in Afghanistan and Pakistan." December 1, 2009. www.whitehouse.gov/the-press-office/remarks-president-address-nation-way-forward-afghanistan-and-pakistan.

34 See, for example, Adam Entous and Carol Lee. "At the Last Minute, Obama Alone Made Call to Seek Congressional Approval: Change in President's Thinking Confounded White House Insiders." *Wall Street Journal*, September 1, 2013. http://online.wsj.com/articles/SB10001424127887324009304579047542466837078.

35 "Full Transcript: Secretary of State John Kerry's Remarks on Syria on August 30." *Washington Post*, August 30, 2013. www.washingtonpost.com/world/national-security/running-transcript-secretary-of-state-john-kerrys-remarks-on-syria-on-aug-30/2013/08/30/f3a63a1a-1193-11e3-85b6-d27422650fd5_story.html.

36 Adam Entous and Carol Lee. "At the Last Minute, Obama Alone Made Call to Seek Congressional Approval: Change in President's Thinking Confounded White House Insiders." *Wall Street Journal*, September 1, 2013. http://online.wsj.com/articles/SB10001424127887324009304579047542466837078.

37 "But having made my decision as Commander-in-Chief based on what I am convinced is our national security interests, I'm also mindful that I'm the President of the world's oldest constitutional democracy. I've long believed that our power is rooted not just in our military might, but in our example as a government of the people, by the people, and for the people. And that's why I've made a second decision: I will seek authorization for the use of force from the American people's representatives in Congress." Barack Obama. "Statement by the President on Syria." September 1, 2013, Office of the Press Secretary, www.whitehouse.gov/the-press-office/2013/08/31/statement-president-syria

38 Charlie Savage. "Obama Tests Limits of Power in Syrian Conflict." *New York Times*. September 9, 2013. www.nytimes.com/2013/09/09/world/middleeast/obama-tests-limits-of-power-in-syrian-conflict.html?pagewanted=all# (accessed October 7, 2014).

39 Barack Obama, "The President's News Conference with Prime Minister John Fredrik Reinfeldt of Sweden in Stockholm, Sweden," September 4, 2013. Online in Gerhard Peters and John T. Woolley, *The American Presidency Project*. www.presidency.ucsb.edu/ws/?pid=104040.

40 At the time of his decision, President Obama also seemed confident that he could secure the necessary votes in Congress. Chuck Todd. "The White House Walk-and-Talk that Changed Obama's Mind on Syria." *NBCNews.com*, August 31, 2013. http://firstread.nbcnews.com/_news/2013/08/31/20273128-the-white-house-walk-and-talk-that-changed-obamas-mind-on-syria.

41 For an extended discussion of this case, see Douglas L. Kriner. 2014. "Obama's Authorization Paradox: Syria and Congress' Continued Relevance in Military Affairs." *Presidential Studies Quarterly* 44: 309–327.

42 Goldsmith, *Power and Constraint*, p. 42.

43 Brody, *Assessing the President*; Zaller, *The Nature and Origins of Mass Opinion*; Berinsky, *In Time of War*.

44 Goldsmith, *Power and Constraint*, p. 48.

45 Posner and Vermeule, *Executive Unbound*, p. 12.

46 Posner and Vermeule, *Executive Unbound*, pp. 13, 45–46.

47 Sarah Binder. 1999. "The Dynamics of Legislative Gridlock, 1947–96." *American Political Science Review* 93: 519–533; Michael Barber and Nolan McCarty. 2015. "Causes and Consequences of Polarization." In Nathaniel Persily, ed., *Solutions to Political Polarization in America*. New York: Cambridge University Press.

48 Telford Taylor. 1955. *Grand Inquest: The Story of Congressional Investigations*. New York: Simon and Schuster; George Chalou. 1975. "St. Clair's Defeat, 1792." In Arthur Schlesinger Jr. and Roger Burns, eds., *Congress Investigates: A Documented History, 1792–1974*. New York: Chelsea House Publishers.

49 For example, Congress investigated General Andrew Jackson's unauthorized invasion of Spanish Florida, and the Monroe administration's knowledge of it, to attack Seminole Indians in 1818. The Mexican–American War and the Civil War were also targets of considerable congressional scrutiny. In fact, so great was the Joint Committee on the Conduct of the War's harassment and second-guessing of Lincoln and his commanding generals that Confederate Commander Robert E. Lee is alleged to have remarked that the committee was as valuable to his cause as two divisions of Confederate soldiers. David McCullough. 1992. *Truman*. New York: Simon and Schuster, p. 304. Ironically, given his future experience at the other end of a congressional investigation that would ultimately result in articles of impeachment, the third Senate seat was given to the sole southern Democrat to remain in office after secession, Tennessee Democrat Andrew Johnson.

50 Theodore Wilson. 1975. "The Truman Committee, 1941." In Schlesinger and Burns, eds., *Congress Investigates*; Alonzo Hamby. 1995. *Man of the People: A Life of Harry S. Truman*. New York: Oxford University Press.

51 Schlesinger and Burns, eds., *Congress Investigates*, p. xxvi.

52 Douglas L. Kriner and Eric Schickler. 2016. *Investigating the President: Congressional Checks on Presidential Power*. Princeton, NJ: Princeton University Press, pp. 172–209.

53 "U.S. Troops Sent to Dominican Republic." In *CQ Almanac* 1965, 21st ed.: 514–518.

54 Randall Bennett Woods. 1998. *J. William Fulbright, Vietnam, and the Search for a Cold War Foreign Policy*. New York: Cambridge University Press.

55 Carl Levin. "Church Committee Demonstrated Value of Bipartisan Oversight." *The Hill*, November 5, 2015. http://thehill.com/blogs/congress-blog/lawmaker-news/259134-church-committee-demonstrated-value-of-bipartisan-oversight.

56 Samuel Brenner. 2010. "'I am a Bit Sickened': Examining Archetypes of Congressional War Crimes Oversight After My Lai and Abu Ghraib." *Military Law Review* 205: 1–93.

57 151 CONG. REC. H4833 (daily ed. June 21, 2005) (statement of Rep. Waxman).

58 Linda Fowler. 2015. *Watchdogs on the Hill: The Decline of Congressional Oversight of U.S. Foreign Relations*. Princeton, NJ: Princeton University Press, p. 21.

59 Douglas L. Kriner. 2009. "Can Enhanced Oversight Repair the 'Broken Branch'?" *Boston University Law Review* 89: 765–793, pp. 776–782.

60 Kriner and Schickler, *Investigating the President*, pp. 62–65.

61 The pressure produced by the generations did help encourage both chambers to pass a new Russian sanctions bill, one that implicitly rebuked the White House by denying the president the power to unilaterally lift the new sanctions.

62 Aaron Wildavsky. 1966. "The Two Presidencies." *Trans-Action* 4: 7–14, p. 9.

63 Heidi Kitrosser. 2015. *Reclaiming Accountability: Transparency, Executive Power, and the U.S. Constitution*. Chicago, IL: University of Chicago Press, p. 3.

64 Griffin, *Long Wars and the Constitution*, p. 101.

65 Jason Ross Arnold. 2014. *Secrecy in the Sunshine Era: The Promise and Failure of U.S. Open Government Laws*. Lawrence: University of Kansas Press.

66 Joseph Maheady. "The Boland Amendments: A Chronology of Congressional Action." *CRS Report* 87-833A, October 13, 1987.

67 Quoted in John Ehrman and Michael W. Flamm. 2009. *Debating the Reagan Presidency*. New York: Rowman & Littlefield, p. 144.

68 Richard Clarke and Robert Knake. 2010. *Cyber War: The Next Threat to National Security and What to Do About It*. New York: Ecco.

69 Arnold, *Secrecy in the Sunshine Era*.

70 William Howell and Mariah Zeisberg. "Executive Secrecy." *Boston Review*, July 1, 2015. http://bostonreview.net/books-ideas/howell-zeisberg-executive-secrecy

71 Elizabeth Bazan and Jennifer Elsea. "Presidential Authority to Conduct Warrantless Electronic Surveillance to Gather Foreign Intelligence Information." *CRS Report*, January 5, 2006.

72 Department of Justice, "Legal Authorities Supporting the Activities of the National Security Agency Described by the President." January 19, 2006.

73 For example, Senators Leahy (D-VT) and Kennedy (D-MA) introduced in January 2006 S Res 350 to express the sense of the Senate that the AUMF did not authorize the NSA surveillance program.

74 Department of Justice, "Legal Authorities Supporting the Activities of the National Security Agency Described by the President." January 19, 2006, p. 1.

75 John Yoo. 2006. *War by Other Means: An Insider's Account of the War on Terror.* New York: Atlantic Monthly Press, p. 125.

76 Kitrosser, *Reclaiming Accountability,* p. 13.

77 Posner and Vermeule, *Executive Unbound.*

78 John Yoo. Memorandum for David S. Kris. "The President's Constitutional Authority to Conduct Military Operations Against Terrorists and Nations Supporting Them." September 25, 2001. Emphasis added.

79 For an overview, see Pfiffner 2008. See also, Charlie Savage. "Secret U.S. Memo Made Case to Kill a Citizen." *New York Times,* October 8, 2011. The Obama era memo authorizing drone strikes against American citizens is decidedly more circumspect in its claims about inherent executive authority. Rather, the OLC memo argues that the strikes fell within the bounds of actions authorized by Congress with the AUMF. David Barron. "Memorandum for the Attorney General." July 16, 2010, p. 20. www.washingtonpost.com/r/2010-2019/WashingtonPost/2014/06/23/National-Security/Graphics/memodrones.pdf?tid=a_inl.

80 Charlie Savage. 2007. *Takeover: The Return of the Imperial Presidency and the Subversion of American Democracy.* Boston: Back Bay Books, pp. 237–242. Dahlia Lithwick. "Look for the Sign: The Fallout from President Bush's Signing Statement Spree." *Slate.com,* June 19, 2007. www.slate.com/articles/news_and_politics/recycled/2007/06/look_for_the_sign.html. On Bush's use of signing statements to defend presidential secrecy and power in foreign affairs more generally, see Philip Cooper. 2005. "George W. Bush, Edgar Allan Poe, and the Use and Abuse of Presidential Signing Statements." *Presidential Studies Quarterly* 35: 515–532.

81 Charlie Savage. 2007. *Takeover: The Return of the Imperial Presidency and the Subversion of American Democracy.* Boston: Back Bay Books, p. 238. George W. Bush. "Statement on Signing the Ronald W. Reagan National Defense Authorization Act for Fiscal Year 2005." October 28, 2004. Online in Gerhard Peters and John T. Woolley, *The American Presidency Project.* www.presidency.ucsb.edu/ws/?pid=72803

82 David Mayhew. 1974. *Congress: The Electoral Connection.* New Haven, CT: Yale University Press.

83 Fowler, *Watchdogs on the Hill,* pp. 193–201.

84 For example, in a 2017 op-ed former Senate Intelligence Chairman Bob Graham warned that the contemporary intelligence committees are woefully understaffed; their resources are simply not commensurate with what is required to complete the wide-ranging investigation into Russian interference in the 2016 elections. Bob Graham. "I Ran Congress' 9/11 Investigation. The Intelligence Committees Today Can't Handle Russia." *Washington Post,* September 1, 2017.

85 For a discussion of presidential failures to provide the intelligence committees with information that is mandated by statute, see Heidi Kitrosser. 2010. "National Security and the Article II Shell Game." *Constitutional Commentary* 26: 483–521.

86 Kitrosser, *Reclaiming Accountability,* pp. 198–204.

87 Howell and Zeisberg, "Executive Secrecy."

4

CONTRADICTIONS IN U.S. SECURITY PLANNING FOR A GLOBAL ENVIRONMENT AND A PROCESS APPROACH TO SOLVING THEM

Deborah Avant

Global security challenges – from violent extremism to cyber threats, migration, transnational crime, epidemics, and natural disasters – exist alongside state structures that are challenged by globalization. As Philip Cerny noted decades ago, increased global connection has generated a growing array of concerns on scales that do not match the scale of the nation state. The unfolding of what Cerny and others predicted has generated contradictory pressures leading "not to the supersession of the state by a homogenous world order" but to increasing differentiation of political orders.[1] Indeed, though the political arrangements we see in the world go far beyond what Cerny imagined in 1995, his overall prediction – that there would be a growing disjuncture between the legitimating structures of social action (within the framework of territorial states presumed to be sovereign) and collective action and collective problems increasingly outside the nation state framework – has proved prescient.

This disjuncture has generated a number of contradictions in how the U.S. talks about and plans for security, on the one hand, and what would actually meet security challenges, on the other. At the least, these contradictions produce a drag on the U.S. ability to meet its challenges. At the most, they actually exacerbate rather than ameliorate challenges. I focus on three: (1) the U.S. discusses security challenges as if they were a war for which military force will be decisive when in fact it seeks governance for which less-violent means are more useful; (2) the U.S. focuses its preparations for security on national military forces even though it consistently deploys more contractors than troops and works through a wide variety of commercial, civil society, and governmental organizations in solving security problems; and, building on the first two, (3) though the U.S. has taken promising steps towards more effective policies – that do work toward governance and in tandem with relevant other organizations – they remain outside the political discussion. Leaders have not developed procedures that would evaluate these new steps, integrate successful policies, or build a political follow-ing around them.

One might be tempted to propose a fundamental restructuring of the U.S. for-eign policy machinery to resolve these contradictions. Given the contemporary setting, though, this is both unlikely and unwise. The fraught political conversa-tion (that has only become more acute since Donald J. Trump was elected presi-dent) makes it unlikely and the dynamism of change means that a new structure could be obsolete by the time it is in place. More promising would be more open talk about these contradictions as *problems*. This is not only a 12-step program truism. Studies of relational dynamics – from pragmatic philosophy in the 19th and 20th centuries to contemporary network theory – have held that acknowl-edging problems and gathering around them can be a first step toward more productive interactions.[2] Gathering around problems can engender the discov-ery of common concerns and often leads to new connections. New connections can generate innovative ideas about solutions and also the potential for different coalitions to support them.[3] Innovative ideas can be a way around stuck politics when they generate new potential that creates win–win situations or causes indi-viduals to reimagine their situations and concerns. Fresh connections are most likely to lead to innovation when participants are open to new information and attentive to the workability of different options. Openness to information allows ongoing evaluation. And focus on workability can direct attention and resources accordingly in ways that can lead to integration and institutionalization.

Open conversations addressing these contradictions as problems are the most productive way the U.S. could begin to move toward such a process.[4] More open conversations, new interactions, openness to information, attention to the work-ability of policy, and flexibility in directing resources are the most useful tools for moving the U.S. toward a more productive process for responding to an uncer-tain and rapidly changing environment. Below, I describe each contradiction. I then entertain a brief discussion of steps that might move toward generating, acknowledging and building upon workable governance efforts. I conclude by suggesting that the turbulent character of the current U.S. political scene makes these efforts both more challenging and more necessary.

Contradiction 1: Preparing for war when the security challenge requires governance

U.S. policy continues to focus on security challenges as threats in war-like sce-narios. This orientation generates attention to violent capacities. It also maintains our attention on the military as the primary agency for meeting these challenges. The military is an institution designed to deliver violence. It is very good at breaking things and killing people. But most of what the U.S. wants in the world is, effectively, governance. In the best case, this means processes through which disputes can be solved without violence. Even when that is not possible, evidence suggests that it is the most limited violence that is most useful for changing political behavior. Though violence can be effective for destroying or disrupting others' control, it is less useful for generating productive social behavior. Governance is often best accomplished by appeals to the collective benefits to be had through cooperation and self-interest in conjunction with coercion. The most consequential uses of coercion, self-interest, or the two together, also rely on appeals to legitimacy.[5] This is true even assuming a system of highly independent states; it is even more consequential in the interconnected contemporary order. By talking about security challenges in a war-like frame, we privilege a less useful tool.

A 2016 report on 'the Future of War' by the New America Foundation provides a useful example. It summarizes 15 insights from an event held at Arizona State University involving top military leadership and security scholars. The insights include: profound uncertainty over what threats will be; small wars (and ineffective U.S. response) are likely to continue; there will be increasing use of unmanned and autonomous weapon systems; cyberspace will be a key domain of conflict; security capacity will be dependent on integrating multiple capabilities and adapting to change; armed conflicts will involve hybrids of state and non-state adversaries and, increasingly, the private sector; existing legal and political systems will be unprepared; cities and megacities will play a growing role in defining global security threats; the invasion of Iraq will continue to loom large in the United States' strategic thinking; viruses and diseases will challenge international security; civil/military relations may stress the United States' capacity to address threats; climate change will shape the future of war; and big data and mass surveillance will threaten civil liberties and human rights and play a growing role in future conflicts. The final insight is that interstate war will remain rare and elements of global violence may decline, but "armed conflict will *retain many of its core qualities*."[6]

This report does little to reflect on the source of threats or insecurity. But almost all of its insights suggest that the core assumptions associated with war – particularly that threats come from other territorially based entities and government-issued violence is effective for meeting them – are not relevant to these threats. The report also relays a consensus questioning the effectiveness of current policies. Thus the conclusion that many core qualities of armed conflict will remain the same is puzzling.

It could be that the participants in this conference – along with the U.S. policy community more generally – have not noticed this contradiction because it has grown slowly over the years. The U.S. military has taken on insurgent threats that (by definition) seek to influence populations rather than win on the battlefield ever since Vietnam. Though some saw even in Vietnam that successful counterinsurgency would require a close integration of violence with political goals as well as the integration of military forces with police, civilian agencies, and populations,[7] others were less sure that this was not just a lesser form of war. The revision of the counterinsurgency field manual FM 3-24 moved toward a more political strategy and has gained widespread traction.[8] But this document devotes more attention to adding incentives to sanctions than to integrating them or tying them to some common purpose. Even if one buys the argument that coercion and elite deal-making are more important than good governance,[9] unrestrained force is not what leads to counterinsurgency; it is the close connection between coercion and political strategies such as elite deal-making.

But battling insurgents is only one example. As threats have diversified so have the missions that the U.S. military undertakes. This is perhaps best illustrated by Rosa Brooks' book, *How Everything Became War and the Military Became Everything*. From anti-piracy to humanitarian assistance to stability operations to anti-terrorism, the U.S. military has taken on tasks that fit uneasily with the more destructive aims of war. As it has, these tasks have become part of the "war" frame even if they sit there uneasily. Among the many poignant examples in Brooks' book is the one she begins with – a drone strike on a young man linked (in an undetailed way) to elaborately detailed terrorist activities.[10] This effort to take out dangerous personalities is fraught in many ways, but among the most important for the contradiction between requirements to meet threats and U.S. preparations is that such strikes not only kill particular people who may be part of "enemy" forces, they also can grow enemy forces by playing into their recruiting strategies. This argument has been advanced by journalists[11] and intelligence experts, including General Michael Flynn, President Trump's first National Security Advisor.[12] Perhaps more important, however, is the argument that tactics are driving the strategy.[13] Once one thinks of "terrorists" (often quite loosely discovered by their associations) as "enemies," one also assumes that they must be killed. This leads the U.S. to look only at which tactics are easiest (or least dangerous to U.S. service people) to kill them. Broader strategic thinking would ask how the U.S. could best dampen terrorist recruitment or violence rather than assuming it should kill terrorists. It would then ask whether drone strikes are working – not just to kill terrorists but to dampen violence. These questions, however, are rarely part of the conversation.

There is burgeoning academic literature that is relevant to this contradiction. For instance, Lyall and Wilson explore why states have become less effective at countering insurgencies over time and find that mechanization is closely associated with failure.[14] They deduce that mechanization removes the necessity of working with the population. In other words, the separation of violence from interactions with the population reduces the chance that its use will lead to greater stability. Counterinsurgency efforts in Iraq and Afghanistan provide further evidence for the importance of strategies that privilege engaging with relevant local and national authorities rather than only focusing on destroying enemy forces.[15] Violent efforts that created civilian harm in Afghanistan reduced support for ISAF and increased support for the Taliban.[16]

These arguments fit into a larger literature on the micro-dynamics of violence. In situations of intra-state war this literature finds that treating "sides" as static, as we often do, is problematic. Violence often escalates as individuals or sub-groups take advantage of conflictual settings to settle scores or pursue personal gains that have little to do with the narrative on which the conflict is based. Increased violence, even for opportunistic reasons, is often nonetheless justified by the macro narrative and thus drives counter-reaction cycles that intensify violence overall.[17]

A government's reaction to violence is particularly important but the government can be represented by police and local officials as well as the broader leadership.[18] When police, military personnel, or other state representatives take sides with one or another extremist element they often accelerate violence.[19] When they remain true to their role as law enforcers, this is less likely to be the case. This dynamic has been demonstrated in case studies[20] and its logic is also supported in experimental settings.[21] Rhetoric based on an "us versus them" frame produces less compromising attitudes by the targeted "others" – generating greater approval for risk-prone leadership strategies.[22]

A similar dynamic has also been found in studies that compare the effectiveness of different counter-terrorism strategies. Dugan and Chenoweth find that deterrence or punishment by the Israeli government, often carried out with violence, is either unassociated with or increases violence by Palestinians.[23] Only conciliatory strategies that promise some benefit for less violent behavior are associated with decreases in violence by Palestinians.

The enemy language plays into thinking of "terrorists" as bad individuals, violent actors no matter what the situation or circumstance. In this thinking the key to ending violence is capturing – or killing – them. It leads to a focus on such tactics as sting operations and drone strikes. But a wide range of studies shows that becoming a terrorist is not predetermined. Rather, it is a response to situations.[24] People may be drawn into, *but also away from*, these kinds of strategies. This implies that strategies to counter terrorists as "enemies" may actually produce them.[25] Indeed Abdul Razak, a Somali student as Ohio State University, showed no terrorist tendencies when interviewed by a student newspaper in August 2016. He was worried, though, about negative portrayals of Muslims in the media and by then presidential candidate Donald Trump as enemies.[26] In a Facebook post shortly before he drove his brother's car into pedestrians and lashed out at them with a knife, he expressed outrage at the treatment of Muslims. Though it is unknowable whether a more conciliatory atmosphere toward Muslims could have avoided the attack, his behavior is consistent with the argument that situational circumstances matter for whether people behave violently or not.

Thus even in the most intrinsically violent of emerging challenges, violent extremism, there is evidence that thinking in a traditional war frame can exacerbate rather than ameliorate the problem. The most effective strategies for reducing violence focus on restraint in rhetoric and actions that project fairness, along with savvy use of coercion.[27] These strategies are, in effect, governance efforts rather than war. They use a combination of coercion, appeals to self-interest, and legitimating claims to convince people that non-violent avenues are most useful for resolving conflict and to offer other options. This is not to deny the difficulty of generating such governance – nor is it to suggest that there is no role for coercion or violence. But it does suggest that treating the current context as a war is likely to backfire and exacerbate rather than ameliorate violent extremism.

Furthermore, most of the emerging challenges are not inherently violent. Thinking in terms of war and violent strategies is likely to be even less useful for preventing cyber threats and transnational crime or dealing effectively with migration, epidemics, and natural disasters. Enduring challenges, such as competition with China, should aim not to destroy the Chinese or their economy (as that would also be disruptive to the U.S.) but to better manage interactions with the Chinese and work to facilitate the rise of more moderate leaders.

Contradiction 2: Who the U.S. plans to use for operations versus who it actually joins with in its efforts

The second contradiction is between how the U.S. talks about and plans for security focused on military forces versus who it actually uses to conduct operations. Over the past 25 years, contractors have routinely made up half or more of the personnel the U.S. deploys in contingency operations.[28] The numbers are even greater if one looks at the foreign policy apparatus more generally.[29] The October 2015 census in the USCENTCOM Area of Responsibility counted 44,824 contractors.[30] By comparison, at that time roughly 10,000 U.S. troops remained in Afghanistan and 3,500 in Iraq. As of March 2016 contractors represented 77 percent of DoD presence in Afghanistan and 38 percent of its presence in Iraq.[31] And yet, contractors are not a meaningful part of overall defense or foreign policy planning.

Just focusing on defense, contractors are not mentioned on DoD 101.[32] Although Title 10 of the United States Code lists contractors as part of the "Total Force", contractors remain almost absent in any discussion of that force. The Army talks about the reserve and the National Guard, but not about contractors on its website. Former Secretary of Defense Ash Carter's "Force of the Future" mentions "military" interaction with technology and other companies but not the companies that provide military and security services. Serious management planning for contracted services goes beyond simply assessing the required capabilities that can or must be met by contractors and how to access them. Using contractors changes the way the U.S. military, the State Department, USAID, and others do their work. This is true in logistics, it is true in training, it is true in armed protective services – it is likely to be true in many other areas.[33]

The Trump administration has elevated the potential for using contractors. It reportedly considered a proposal Erik Prince aired in a *Wall Street Journal* op-ed to install a viceroy, move from a focus on population control to resource control, and do the bulk of the work with contractors.[34] But it has not addressed the need to plan for contractors and how they change the impact of U.S. policy.

From the literature on contracting and privatization more generally we know that the change contractors bring is most likely to be disruptive or problematic at moments when contractors are operating in new circumstances and contexts in which they need to make judgements.[35] And this is precisely where contractors are most likely to be used. Contractors are a tool for responding to *unexpected* shortages in capacity.[36] The flexibility of contractors and their usefulness as a tool to fill in makes them very likely to be used in situations for which there are not clearly developed plans. If contractors are most likely to be disruptive in new circumstances and are also most likely to be used in new circumstances it suggests that contractors are highly likely to be disruptive. Thus far, this has frequently been the case. Though contractors have been a crucial part of U.S. efforts in virtually every part of the world in the last 25 years, their use has also often been accompanied by controversy.[37]

Relying on contractors has caused three primary types of complication: misbehavior by the U.S. government, misbehavior by contractors, and reductions in military effectiveness. To begin, because they work through different channels, their availability has allowed poor judgements or misbehavior on the part of U.S. leaders or U.S. agencies. This poor judgement can influence the effectiveness or legality of foreign policy. For example, members of the executive branch used contractors as a way of getting around congressionally mandated restrictions on the use of U.S. forces in Colombia.[38] Contractors were also licensed to provide training for Equatorial Guinea's Coast Guard – a decision some claim to have been poor judgement. Many in the international community see U.S. use of contractors as a way of evading its commitments under international law. Some countries have criticized the U.S. for this kind of behavior but others have emulated it. Russia, for instance, has relaxed restrictions on the use of its firms in ways that would allow it to work toward national interests without involving, or implicating, the government.[39]

These poor judgements can also be detrimental to the personnel that work for the U.S. Thinking of using "only contractors" can cause U.S. officials to create policy that takes undue advantage of the individuals who will carry out the work. For instance, one of the reasons for opening more opportunities for contractors in the drone program is to address problems filling the ranks with Air Force personnel stressed and exhausted by the pace of expansion and the inability of the Air Force to train up an adequate force. But contractors are likely to feel similar levels of stress. And there is no reason to believe that private sector training will be easier. So using contractors will not solve this problem, it will only shift it from Air Force personnel to contractors. Why would the U.S. owe contractors any less than service people who operate drones?

Second, contractors can issue poor judgements or misbehavior themselves. This could be because individuals working in private security are motivated by profit rather than service – though the research is divided on this.[40] Regardless of motivation, however, private security providers often have *different backgrounds* (including vetting and training) than their public counterparts. Private security pulls from a broader pool of individuals than do public security organizations and companies generally rely on whatever training individuals received elsewhere.

In Iraq private security teams had retired U.S. special operations personnel working alongside individuals trained in South Africa or Uganda or Fijian forces.[41] They also work under *different rules*. The rules that guide private forces are the terms of the *contract*, rather than a broader set of institutional rules and norms that public forces attend to. Differences in training can affect the degree to which private security providers know general standards for behavior; the rules affect their incentives to comply with them.

The most notorious case of misbehavior is when Blackwater personnel working for the State Department opened fire on civilians in Nisour Square, Iraq. But there have been many others, including the child-trafficking scandal in the Balkans during the 1990s depicted in the film, *The Whistleblower*.[42] And then there have been hundreds of cases of waste and fraud – including an unfinished $40-million prison facility, cash laundering, and inflated pricing. A good summary of such cases in Iraq can be found in the Special Inspector General for Iraq's final report.[43] And misbehavior is not limited to those who work for the DoD, it is also apparent among contractors for diplomatic security.[44]

Sometimes it is hard to know just where the misbehavior is coming from because contracting can diffuse responsibility. For example, consider Special Inspector General for Afghanistan Reconstruction, John F. Sopko's 15 April 2016 testimony before the House Armed Services' Subcommittee on Oversight and Investigations on the DoD Task Force for Business and Sustainability Operations (TFBSO). The TFBSO is a DoD program to use private-sector strategies to foster sustainable growth in Iraq and Afghanistan. One could ask a variety of questions about its wisdom and execution.[45] The particular $6.1 million TFBSO program John Sopko testified about on the 15th was one to bolster the cashmere goat industry in Afghanistan. It was was unrealistic (the farm was too small to achieve what it undertook and the timeline too constrained) and it was poorly staffed (TFBSO personnel had no idea what they were doing and CSU staff determined what the project should cost, despite no one at CSU having any experience with cashmere). Also, it was mismanaged by TFBSO (leadership rented specially furnished, privately owned "villas" and hired contractors to provide 24-hour building security, food services, and bodyguards for TFBSO staff and visitors traveling in country, on which it spent nearly $150 million (almost 20 percent of its budget). Had TFBSO employees instead lived at DoD facilities in Afghanistan, where housing, security, and food service are routinely provided at little or no extra charge to DoD organizations, it would have saved tens of millions of dollars).[46]

The final complication raised by contractors is the chance that they can reduce military effectiveness. Contractors often generate a greater number of personnel. This can yield effective policy when contractors are well differentiated from other forces and perform tasks that do not require integration. When they operate in close proximity to regular forces and perform similar tasks, however, their different rules frequently lead to friction that impedes integration and decreases effectiveness.[47]

The Commission on Wartime Contracting and the Special Inspectors General for Iraq and Afghanistan – along with the Congressional Research Service (CRS)[48] have focused on uncovering waste, fraud and abuse. As useful as this has been, the U.S. also needs a more strategic understanding of how a system reliant on contracting can get around some of these problems. By addressing some of the issues pointed out in many CRS reports[49] the U.S. could position itself to think more systematically about the services contractors might provide for a wide variety of purposes, the potential complications that might arise, and what could stabilize their use. If the U.S. continues to rely on contractors for the vast majority of its operations, but only makes plans for military forces, however, it can expect problems to continue – and even escalate.

Contradiction 3: The U.S. has taken promising small steps toward addressing portions of these contradictions but struggles to explain, implement, and evaluate them, or to institutionalize those that work

Policy analysts and policy makers in and out of government have come up with innovative thinking on how the U.S. might use various tools to achieve its goals and be more restrained in its use of violence – and how the U.S. might more productively rein in the problems that using contractors introduces. Some of this thinking has been translated into particular promising programs. The first contradiction led to the revision of the U.S. counterinsurgency doctrine and various related programs, including efforts toward countering violent extremism abroad. The second led the U.S. to engage with various stakeholders to construct a nascent transnational regulatory structure. These programs, though, have been hampered by the lack of evaluation tools with which to tell if they are gaining traction, as well as unclear paths for implementation and institutionalization of those policies that do gain traction.

Counterinsurgency and CVE

Counterinsurgency thinking was spurred by push-back from the world in Iraq.[50] Worse-than-expected outcomes led people to identify a problem with the U.S. approach to the conflict. While the response was familiar in some ways, and some had been advocating a change in its approach to insurgency since Vietnam, the process demonstrated some openness, new connections, and innovative thinking.

The U.S. Army's Combined Arms Center led the effort. It tapped not only innovative military leaders but also less usual suspects, including human rights activists focused on civilian protection.[51] The product was new doctrine: Field Manual 3-24, *Counterinsurgency*.[52] This new counterinsurgency doctrine was the most publicized product, but alongside it were various innovative ideas for the war in Iraq as well as other new programs, such as the Task Force for Business and Stability Operations (TFBSO) that sought to foster development in ways that would work toward what was presumed to be a stability-enhancing interaction between economic growth and dampening support for the insurgency.

Whether these programs worked in Iraq, and then Afghanistan, is subject to debate.[53] In Iraq it is clearly the case that there was a drop in violence accompanying the change in strategy. Some have argued that it was the Sunni awakening rather than the surge, its counterinsurgency orientation that led to a drop in violence, or other innovative programming.[54] Parsing the relative impact of the counterinsurgency strategy and local allies, though, is unproductive for evaluating why violence dropped, as both were clearly important.[55] This kind of causal dicing violates the history of the Iraq war, as well as the logic of counterinsurgency as a strategy that puts politics at its core and uses violence sparingly and in tight coordination with rewards and a logic of legitimacy. The interaction between local politics and violence should be fundamental to a serious counterinsurgency policy – not only in Iraq[56] but in general.

In Afghanistan, questions about the effectiveness of U.S. counterinsurgency are more pressing because it was not accompanied by a similar change in the levels of violence. Some attribute this to less reliable local partners than the Sunni tribal leaders. It is also the case that counterinsurgency efforts in Afghanistan operated alongside an American counter-terrorism campaign that often worked at odds with the counterinsurgency logic. Some thus question whether the U.S. ever had a serious counterinsurgency strategy for Afghanistan.[57]

Another way to think about the problem was to imagine ways to head off violent extremism before it became an insurgency. Complementary efforts led by the State Department aimed to do just this. Sarah Sewall, one of those consulted in the process of drafting the new counterinsurgency manual, was appointed Under Secretary for Civilian Security, Human Rights and Democracy during the Obama administration. In this role she devoted much effort to countering violent extremism. This effort took three tracks. First was engaging with others at the UN and in other countries focused on countering (or preventing) violent extremism (CVE and PVE, respectively). Second, the State Department identified areas prone to violent extremism so as to engage with local governments, civil society, and other actors on changes that might head off violence. Third, the State Department office explicitly coordinated in some cases with anti-terrorism efforts at the Department of Defense. By connecting disparate issues (human rights and terrorism) and linking people across the world coming from very different perspectives, the CVE logic built on some practical experience and social science research to foster inclusive governance models that address concerns and violence before they become insurgencies. The CVE/PVE programs had some promising results.[58]

This policy, though, was pursued in quite different ways within the U.S. and abroad. Abroad, the State Department actively engaged with a variety of stakeholders: other governments, the United Nations, and various elements of civil society. Their goal was to move beyond a military response and take a citizen-centered approach to threat that protects rights, provides economic opportunity, mentors youth, holds security forces accountable, and supports families.[59] In the U.S., however, Justice Department efforts generally focused on American Muslims[60] and based their logic on more widely contested theories of radicalization. This execution of policy both alienated many in American Muslim communities and ignored white nationalism and other far-right movements that, before the Orlando shooting in 2016, were responsible for a greater number of domestic terrorism deaths.[61] Some wondered whether these efforts at home did more harm than good.[62] It is somewhat ironic that the State Department preaches a more inclusive approach abroad while the Justice Department has employed a more exclusionary approach at home – one might expect the reverse. Existing research (though not conclusive) suggests that an inclusive approach is more likely to be successful.[63] More importantly, there are few mechanisms to evaluate the effectiveness of these two approaches – or even put them in comparative perspective.

At the end of the Obama administration, many questions remained about the effectiveness of both counterinsurgency and CVE/PVE but most involved argued that each had some successes and was here to stay. They both responded to important needs for the U.S. to rein in both the extremism that leads to violence and violence itself when it arises in pursuit of more stable governance – at home and abroad. Assessment and implementation, though, were often problematic and there was little effort to demonstrate the successes and build political constituencies for them, particularly in the U.S.

Months into the Trump administration, the U.S. government's commitment to these programs appears much more fraught. Even critics of Trump have also suggested that counterinsurgency success does not hinge on restraint but on escalation of violence.[64] A crass reading of these arguments is likely to be appealing to the Trump administration. I would argue that the evidence underpinning these arguments suggests that it is more the political strategy than the escalation of violence that is important to counterinsurgency success, but this nuance is downplayed. CVE, even its harsher variants, has also been resoundingly criticized by the administration – and Trump himself. The administration has cut funding for CVE uses except for those focused on Islamic extremism.[65] While other governments, along with the UN and civil society groups, continue to focus on CVE abroad and local governments and others continue to pursue it at home, the U.S. national government's voice in these programs is likely to be absent.[66]

A transnational governance framework for private military and security services

A sense that contracting was not working well (in Iraq, particularly, but also in many other parts of the world) led the Swiss government and the International Committee of the Red Cross to launch the Swiss Initiative in 2006. Like the efforts to revise the U.S. counterinsurgency doctrine and create a program to counter violent extremism, this process drew together states with different relationships to the health service industry, industry groups and companies, and prominent civil society members, including human rights organizations.[67] Initial hopes were actually quite low given extreme disagreements and concerns on the part of many in the U.S. government that any transnational framework would limit the flexibility of U.S. policy. Small agreements yielded steps toward progress, though, and within two years the process had led to an agreement – the Montreux Document – that spelled out the responsibilities of contracting states, home states and host states vis-à-vis this industry under international law and also various best practices they should follow. Many of the best practices for contracting states and home states drew from nascent U.S. regulations or responded to problems the U.S. had faced in Iraq and Afghanistan.

The Montreux Document was followed by a related process to develop an International Code of Conduct (ICoC) for private security providers (those parts of the industry that provide armed and unarmed protection). The ICoC was issued in 2010 and an association to oversee its implementation was then negotiated among similar stakeholders and launched in 2013. Related processes by both the American National Standards Institute (ANSI) and then the International Standards Institute (ISO) developed standards for private security providers explicitly based on the Montreux Document and ICoC.[68] When these standards are written into contracts they make the best practices associated with the Montreux Document and ICoC legally enforceable.

The U.S. DoD and DoS became enthusiastic supporters of the Montreux Document and the ICoC, and the DoD made a variety of changes in keeping with this new framework. The U.S. now keeps track of contractors in named contingencies, has instructions to better coordinate between military commanders and contractors in their area of operations, and keeps track of incidents relating to contractors, among other things. These are small steps toward making contractors less invisible in the public discourse. The DoD also requires that those companies it contracts with for security services be compliant with the new standards and the DoS requires that companies be members of the International Code of Conduct Association (ICoCA) in order to be eligible for its Worldwide Protective Services contracts.[69] Continued efforts to increase awareness of who contractors are, what they do, and what they should (and should not) do could both make it more difficult for U.S. leaders to use them in illegal ways – thus responding to the first complication that the use of contractors poses – and reassure others (states, NGOs, and the public at large) that the U.S. is not trying to evade its responsibilities when it uses contractors. The ICoC and the standards based on it limit the kinds of activities that private security providers can engage in and thus the potential that they could be used for the purpose of skirting international law.

The ICoC and standards also have begun to address the second complication – contractor misbehavior. The ICoC is the first step toward extending military and security professionalism to the private sector. It develops a conception of what a "professional" private security contractor will look like in keeping with international humanitarian law. It can make it more likely that in new circumstances, when contractors need to make judgements, they will have a basis on which to make them. The ICoCA has developed certification and monitoring mechanisms.[70]

This code of conduct could be extended to behavior associated with a professional military trainer, a professional drone operator, and others. Indeed, those involved in the process initially expected that this would be the case. Extension would require thinking through what issues might come up in the provision of each kind of service. How do military and police trainers typically operate? What kinds of judgements do they need to make to avoid the potential that their training might be used for purposes that violate international law? Similarly, what does contractor-driven drone information gathering look like? How important is the information to targeting? What kinds of judgements would we want contractors to make in order to reduce the potential for information to generate an erroneous strike (as was the case in the Uruzgan Province, central Afghanistan, in 2010 when contractor-provided information led to a strike on a convoy that killed 15 civilians). Clearer standards for behavior and training that reflects professional norms could lead contractors to make better judgements.

Despite the promise of this system of regulation, however, its implementation has been more haphazard. Knowledge of the system does not extend adequately beyond those offices involved in its creation. For instance, in an attempt to streamline the International Transfer of Arms Regulations (ITAR), proposed changes remove the requirement that private military and security contractors (PMSCs) must get a license from the U.S. government to sell law-enforcement training, physical security, personal protective services, and even combat training abroad unless the sale also involves a defense article.[71] This not only undercuts one of the "best practices" for home states in the Montreux Document, but this best practice was actually drawn from the U.S. ITAR rules. Though the ITAR rules were not designed for the kinds of military services PMSCs sell, they provided a very useful regulatory frame as the industry grew. The office that issues the license, however, is not even aware of the degree to which this regulation has become an important part of the regulatory structure over PMSCs.

Also the various multi-stakeholder bodies – from the ICoCA to the ISO committees that oversee some of these instruments – require continued participation by knowledgeable government representatives in order to ensure they work as intended. But even garnering the travel budget for participation on the part of members of the Program Support Office (under the Assistant Secretary of Defense for Logistics and Material Readiness) has been difficult.[72] This could prove problematic for both the functioning of these instruments and the ability to ensure that the right people in the U.S. government know about how they work.

And these initiatives have very little public visibility. In the absence of information about these programs, the media and pundits continue to claim that the industry is virtually unregulated. This actually threatens the potential value of ICoCA membership and standards certification.

As congressional demand for action on contractors has ebbed, so has support for those interested in further developing this system. Many recommendations from the Commission on Wartime Contracting have not been acted on, requirements for different parts of the U.S. government to have similar methodologies to keep track of contractors have not been met, and legislation to create a Civilian Extraterritorial Jurisdiction Act to ensure that contractors working for any U.S. agency could be prosecuted in U.S. courts for criminal wrongdoing has not been passed.[73] Beyond that, there is no impetus to continue to build on the successes of this framework to extend the ICoC.

Though the Special Inspectors General for Iraq and Afghanistan have been important tools for uncovering wrongdoings, only focusing on uncovering wrongdoings without attention to the conditions under which contractors work well has fostered dismissive (or worse) attitudes about the very people the U.S. relies on to do its work.[74] If contractors are inherently problematic, the U.S. should not use them at all. If the U.S. is going to use them, it should invest in developing the best ways of using them. Oversight should highlight positive as well as negative outcomes. The U.S. should fund and otherwise enable the offices working to set transnational standards for particular services. And there should be tools for evaluating what works and what does not that inform future policy.[75]

None of these steps are likely under the Trump administration. Indeed, the plans it purportedly discussed with Erik Prince and others included uses of contractors that would be in violation of the Montreux Document and the ICoC.[76] Those who understand the problematic consequences that moving outside this framework could spell have been working hard to make this more widely known in the administration, but with unclear success. Those outside the U.S., however, have found the governance framework useful and are continuing to push it forward with governmental as well as commercial clients of PSMCs. Again, to the extent that the U.S. is not a part of these efforts, the efforts will lose U.S. support but also the U.S. will lose a voice in them.

How might the U.S. move beyond these contradictions?

The argument that there is a disjuncture between U.S. goals and U.S. tools has been made by many.[77] I have focused on three contradictions but there are many others. What to do about them, however, is often more puzzling. Many aim for clarity and suggest very specific reforms. Political realities have often laid waste to these, though, and are even more likely to do so given current levels of political polarization. Even if that were not true, the pace of global change is so great that specific reforms are often obsolete before they are even agreed upon.

I suggest instead a more process-based approach. The first step is open talk about these contradictions as *problems*. Even acknowledging problems can lead to more productive discussion, and potential action. Focusing on problems often leads to connections between otherwise unconnected people and their associated networks. It also is more likely to involve those directly implicated in the problem.

Interaction among those involved in a problem, particularly when it connects those who were previously unconnected, can be a productive way to generate innovative ideas about solutions.[78] And innovative ideas can get around disagreement by changing perspectives or offering ways to avoid sensitive trade-offs. Instead of debates over solutions, then, I suggest the U.S. begin with discussions of the problems. In the public realm these kinds of discussions are rare but there are a few examples.[79]

In order for this approach to work, though, interactions should also be relatively open to new information. And they should pay attention to whether solutions work. The segmented media environment and arguments about "fake" news join the polarized political situation to make these requirements difficult to meet. Historically, though, even particularly problematic moments have nonetheless led to greater openness under some circumstances. And there is evidence that processes focused on problems, generating new connections, open to information and attentive to workability, often do lead to innovations. This is clearly the case for the innovations in private security governance I outline above[80] but one could make a similar case for the process in generating the beginnings of innovative change on counterinsurgency and CVE as well.

In the bureaucratic trenches, many in the U.S. government have already been engaged with these sorts of processes. On a wide variety of issues, U.S. officials engage with different stakeholders to solve specific problems. In many instances, it has led to progress – the Proliferation Security Initiative is a particularly useful example on a difficult issue.[81] Those in the trenches rarely create processes of ongoing evaluation and adjustment, though. And they are ill-equipped to put in place mechanisms to engender attention, or resources to those innovations that work. Finally, there has not been high-level or public attention to either the results of these processes or the potential that problem-solving processes hold for generating useful responses to rapidly changing environments.

A more public conversation about these and other contradictions the U.S. faces – as a set of problems – could engender more attention to ongoing evaluation, and generate the requisite resources and institutionalization for workable solutions. This kind of conversation could also be politically useful – bringing public attention to the instances of governance success. At a moment where public satisfaction with governmental institutions is at appallingly low levels one might think agency and congressional members would welcome this.[82] A greater focus on the potential for process-based reform could also lead the U.S. to attend more to similar examples elsewhere, such as "experimentalist" modes of governance in other parts of the world.[83] More attention to how to evaluate policy results, sustain the relationships that work, and diffuse successful policies to other relevant parts of the U.S. government and its governmental and non-governmental partners would allow the U.S. to slowly build on successful efforts and make incremental changes to improve policy.

Thoughts about the cost of violence and the usefulness of policy tools that focus on a mix of coercion, self-interest, and legitimacy should be fundamental to policy development to prevent extremism and tamp down violence. And it should be impossible to talk about U.S. foreign policy capacity without acknowledging that contractors (along with various other partners) will comprise a significant portion of the workforce. Discussions of policy implementation should be openly attentive to the likelihood of using contractors and the complications their use is likely to cause. Keeping these problems at the center of policy makers' minds is the first step toward generating the kind of thinking necessary to solve them.

Conclusion

The contradictions I have examined were of fundamental concern even before the 2016 campaign and election. They are of even greater concern after. The campaign demonstrated that while many in the U.S. are frustrated with politics as it is, many fewer understand the varied dynamics behind these politics. Furthermore, different segments of the population have fundamentally different inclinations as to how to make Americans safe, and different opinions of the degree to which information provided by experts is of any use in evaluating their inclinations. These different leanings will undoubtedly make a process-based approach, and particularly one that relies on openness to new information, difficult.

However, the divisive political environment also makes it all the more important to undertake such a process. And process-based tools are often a useful way to generate agreement where there is little to start with. Pushing in this direction will require, though, some commitment on behalf of politicians to publicly recognize that they and their opponents begin from different predispositions. It will also be important to lay out alternatives and the evidence that supports them, and to commit to evaluating their workability. If the new administration is willing to entertain fresh thinking about the wisdom of threats versus rapprochement with the Russian leadership, it should also be open to fresh thinking about how to best characterize extremism to limit rather than heighten its appeal. And it should be willing to say how we might evaluate the success of each.

Notes

1 Cerny, Philip. "Globalization and the Changing Nature of Collective Action," *International Organization* 49, no. 4 (1995): 595–625.
2 See, for example, Dewey, John. *The Public and Its Problems*. Athens, OH: Swallow Press, 1927; Joas, Hans. *The Creativity of Action*. Chicago: University of Chicago Press, 1996; White, Harrison C. *Identity and Control: How Social Formations Emerge*. Princeton: Princeton University Press, 2008.
3 Many network analyses suggest that new connections are a fundamental way through which innovation is generated. Burt, Ronald S. *Brokerage and Closure: An Introduction to Social Capital*. New York: Oxford University Press, 2005; Granovetter, Mark S. "The Strength of Weak Ties," *American Journal of Sociology* 78 (1973); Padgett, John and Walter W. Powell. *The Emergence of Organizations and Markets*. Princeton: Princeton University Press, 2012.
4 Zegart, Amy. "Trump isn't the only Problem with Trump's Foreign Policy," *The Atlantic*. (October 2017). Available at: https://www.theatlantic.com/international/archive/2017/10/the-complexities-of-foreign-policy/543891/ is an example of the kind of intervention I am calling for.

5 Hurd, Ian. "Legitimacy and Authority in International Politics," *International Organization* 53, no. 2 (1999). This logic also animates arguments about effective civil control of the military. See Avant, Deborah. "Conflicting Indicators of 'Crisis' in American Civil-Military Relations," *Armed Forces and Society* 24, no. 4 (1998): 375–388 and Avant, Deborah. *The Market for Force: the Implications of Privatizing Security*. Cambridge: Cambridge University Press, 2005: 54–57.

6 Bergen, Peter L., Daniel Rothenberg, David Sterman, and Emily Schneider. *Reflections from the first annual conference on the future of war*. New America Foundation and Arizona State University, 2015. Available at: https://www.newamerica.org/international-security/future-war/policy-papers/reflections-from-the-first-annual-conference-on-the-future-of-war/.

7 Dewar, Michael. *Brush Fire Wars: Minor Campaigns of the British Army since 1945*. New York: St. Martins, 1984; Komer, Robert. *The Malayan Emergency in Retrospect: Organization of a Successful Counterinsurgency Effort*. Santa Monica: Rand, 1972; Stubbs, Richard. *Hearts and Minds in Guerilla Warfare: The Malayan Emergency, 1948–1960*. Singapore: Oxford University Press, 1989; Krepinevich, Andrew F. *The Army in Vietnam*. Baltimore: Johns Hopkins, 1986; West, F. J. The Village. Madison: University of Wisconsin Press, 1985; Nagl, John. *Learning to Eat Soup with a Knife: Lessons from Malaya and Vietnam*. Chicago: University of Chicago Press, 2002.

8 Nagl, John. *The U.S. Army/Marine Corps Counterinsurgency Field Manual*. Chicago: University of Chicago Press, 2007.

9 Hazelton, Jacqueline. "The Hearts and Minds Fallacy: Violence, Coercion, and Success in Counterinsrugency Warfare," *International Security* 42, no. 1 (2017).

10 Brooks, Rosa. *How Everything Became War and the Military Became Everything: Tales from the Pentagon*. New York: Simon and Schuster, 2016.

11 Abbas, Hassan. "How Drones Create More Terrorists," *The Atlantic* (August 23, 2013).

12 https://theintercept.com/2015/07/16/retired-general-drones-create-terrorists-kill-iraq-war-helped-create-isis.

13 Cronin, Audrey Kurth. "Why Drones Fail: when tactics drive strategy," *Foreign Affairs* (July/August 2013).

14 Lyall, Jason and Wilson, Isaiah. 2Rage against the Machines: Explaining Outcomes in Counterinsurgency Wars," *International Organization* 63 (2009): 67–106.

15 Kilcullen, Rory. "Counterinsurgency Redux," *Survival* 48, no. 4 (2006).

16 Lyall, Jason, Graeme Blair and Kosuke Imai. "Explaining Support for Combatants during Wartime: A Survey Experiment During Wartime," *American Political Science Review* (2013).

17 Kalyvas, Stathis. *The Logic of Violence in Civil War*. Cambridge: Cambridge University Press, 2006.

18 Grubb, Amy. *The Microdynamics of Violence and Order: Variations in Community Security Processes*. Dissertation, University of California Irvine, 2014; Grubb, Amy. "Microlevel Dynamics of Violence: Explaining Variation in Violence among Rural Districts during Northern Ireland's Troubles," *Security Studies* 25, no. 3 (2016): 460–487.

19 First, they allow one side to access the violent resources of the state, which increases violence. Second, they cause those targeted by the violence to feel unfairly treated and less able to use state institutions for non-violent resolution of their claims. This then increases the likelihood of a counter-reaction.

20 Grubb, Amy. *The Microdynamics of Violence and Order: Variations in Community Security Processes*. Dissertation, University of California Irvine, 2014; Grubb, "Microlevel Dynamics of Violence."

21 Gottfried, Matthew S. and Robert F. Trager. "A Preference for War: How Fairness and Rhetoric Influence Leadership Incentives in Crises," *International Studies Quarterly* (2016).

22 Gottfried, Matthew S. and Robert F. Trager. "A Preference for War: How Fairness and Rhetoric Influence Leadership Incentives in Crises," *International Studies Quarterly* (2016).

23 Dugan, Laura and Erica Chenoweth. "Moving Beyond Deterrence: The Effectiveness of Raising the Expected Utility of Abstaining from Violence in Israel," *American Sociological Review* 77, no. 4 (2012).

24 Apuzzo, Matt. "Who will become a terrorist? Research yields few clues," *New York Times* (March 27, 2016); Sageman, Marc. "The Stagnation in Terrorism Research," *Terrorism and Political Violence* 26, no. 4 (2014); National Counterterrorism Center. *2011 Report on Terrorism*. 2012. Available at: https://fas.org/irp/threat/nctc2011.pdf.

25 See for instance, Jalal, Malik. "I am on the kill list. This is what it feels like to be hunted by drones," *The Independent* (April 12, 2016).

26 Smith, Mitch and Adam Goldman. "From Somalia to U.S.: Ohio State Attacker's Path to Violence". *The New York Times*, December 1, 2016. www.nytimes.com/2016/12/01/us/from-somalia-to-us-ohio-state-attackers-path-to-violence.html. Retrieved December 1, 2016.

27 See, for instance: http://blogs.cfr.org/davidson/2014/09/08/we-learned-the-hard-way-the-value-of-restraint-in-iraq-we-cant-forget-it-now-against-isis.

28 Avant, Deborah and Renee de Nevers. "Military Contractors and the American Way of War," *Daedalus* 140, no. 3 (2011): 88–99.

29 Stanger, Allison. *One Nation Under Contract: the Outsourcing of American Power and the Future of Foreign Policy*. New Haven: Yale University Press, 2009.

30 www.acq.osd.mil/log/ps/.CENTCOM_reports.html/5A_October2015_Final.pdf.

31 Peters, Schwartz, and Kapp 2016, 3–4. These are the best figures we have available but analysts have critiqued their reliability. For an analysis of contractors and U.S. forces in historical context, see Schwartz, Moshe and Joyprada Swain. *Department of Defense Contractors in Afghanistan and Iraq: Background and Analysis*. Washington, DC: Congressional Research Service, (May 16, 2011).

32 www.defense.gov/About-DoD/DoD-101#How%20We're%20Organize.

33 Avant, Deborah. "Contracting for Services in US Military Operations," *PS: Political Science and Politics* 50, no. 3 (2007): 457–460.

34 The *New York Times* first reported on this consideration here: www.nytimes.com/2017/07/10/world/asia/trump-afghanistan-policy-erik-prince-stephen-feinberg.html?hp&action=click&pgtype=Homepage&clickSource=story-heading&module=first-column-region&region=top-news&WT.nav=top-news&_r=1. The op-ed by Erik Prince can be found here: www.wsj.com/articles/the-macarthur-model-for-afghanistan-1496269058.

35 Donahue, John. *The Privatization Decision: Public Ends, Private Means*. Basic Books, 1989.

36 Avant, Deborah. "The Mobilization of Private Forces after 9/11: Ad hoc Response to Inadequate Planning." In James Burk, ed. *How 9/11 Changes Our Ways of War*. Stanford: Stanford University Press, 2013.

37 Singer, Peter F. *Corporate Warriors: The Rise of the Privatized Military Industry*. Ithaca: Cornell University Press, 2003; Avant, Deborah. *The Market for Force: the Implications of Privatizing Security*. Cambridge: Cambridge University Press, 2005; Dunigan, Molly. *Victory for Hire: Private Security Companies' Impact on Military Effectiveness*. Stanford, CA: Stanford University Press, 2011; Dunigan, Molly and Ulrich Petersohn, eds. *The Markets for Force: Global Variation in the Trade of Military and Security Services*. Philadelphia: University of Pennsylvania Press, 2015.

38 Lumpe, Lora. "US Foreign Military Training: Global Reach, Global Power, and Oversight Issues," *Foreign Policy in Focus Special Report* (May 2002).

39 See http://sputniknews.com/analysis/20120413/172789099.html; and https://inmoscowsshadows.wordpress.com/2013/06/16/russia-and-elastic-power-will-the-burgeoning-private-security-industry-lead-to-private-military-companies-too/.

40 Krahmann, Elke. *States, Citizens, and the Privatization of Security*. Cambridge: Cambridge University Press, 2010; Franke, Volker. "Guns for Hire: Motivations and Attitudes of Private Security Contractors," *Armed Forces & Society* 37, no. 4 (2011).

41 Fainaru, Steve. *Big Boy Rules: America's Mercenaries Working in Iraq*. Philadelphia: Da Capo Press, 2008.

42 See the summary in Lynch, Colum. "The Whistleblower: the movie the U.N. would prefer you didn't see," *Foreign Policy* (June 29, 2011).

43 http://cybercemetery.unt.edu/archive/sigir/20131001092420/http://www.sigir. mil/files/quarterlyreports/September2013/Report_-_September_2013.pdf#view= fit. See also Watkins, Ali. "Final report on Iraq reconstruction says fraud, waste cost U.S. $1.5 billion," *McClatchky DC* (July 9, 2013).

44 Cusumano, Eugenio. "Diplomatic Security for Hire: The Causes and Implications of Outsourcing Embassy Protection," *The Hague Journal of Diplomacy* 12 (2016).

45 Zimmerman, S. Rebecca, Daniel Egel, and Ilana Blum. *Task Force for Business and Stability Operations: Lessons from Afghanistan.* Washington, DC: RAND, 2016.

46 www.sigar.mil/pdf/testimony/SIGAR-16-29-TY.pdf

47 Avant, "Contracting for Services in US Military Operations"; Avant and de Nevers, "Military Contractors and the American Way of War"; Dunigan, Molly. *Victory for Hire: Private Security Companies' Impact on Military Effectiveness.* Stanford, CA: Stanford University Press, 2011.

48 e.g. Belasco, Amy. *The Cost of Iraq, Afghanistan, and Other Global War on Terror Operations Since 9/11.* Washington, DC: Congressional Research Service, December 2014.

49 e.g. Schwartz, Moshe and Jennifer Church. *The Department of Defense's Use of Contractors to Support Military Operations: Background, Analysis, and Issues for Congress.* Washington, DC: Congressional Research Service, May 2013.

50 The story of earlier push-back in Vietnam and its results is told in Krepinevich 1985. See Avant, Deborah. *Political Institutions and Military Change: Lessons from Peripheral Wars.* Ithaca: Cornell University Press, 1994 for one argument about why these adaptations were not successful.

51 See Sarah Sewell's introduction in Nagl, John. *The U.S. Army/Marine Corps Counterinsurgency Field Manual.* Chicago: University of Chicago Press, 2007.

52 Nagl, John A. United States Department of the Army. U.S. Army Field Manual No. 3–24, Counterinsurgency. 2007. Available from https://usacac.army.mil/cac2/ Repository/Materials/COIN-FM3-24.pdf.

53 Gventer, Celeste Ward. "Counterinsurgency: A Debate Far from Over," *Foreign Policy* (June 15, 2012).

54 Long, Austin. "The Anbar Awakening," *Survival* 50, no. 2 (2008): 67–94.

55 Biddle, Stephen, Jeffrey A. Friedman, and Jacob N. Shapiro. "Testing the Surge: Why did Violence Decline in Iraq in 2007?" *International Security* 37, no. 1 (2012).

56 Green, Daniel R. "The Fallujah Awakening: A case study in successful counterinsurgency," *Small Wars and Insurgencies* 21, no. 4 (2010).

57 Sewall, Sarah. Introduction. In *The U.S. Army/Marine Corps Counterinsurgency Field Manual.* Chicago: University of Chicago Press, 2007.

58 www.lawfareblog.com/it-all-over-cve

59 Sewall, Sarah. Remarks by Sarah B. Sewall U.S. Under Secretary For Civilian Security, Democracy, And Human Rights on Democratic Values and Violent Extremism. 2007. Available from https://in.usembassy.gov/democratic-values-and-violent-extremism-remarks-by-sarah-b-sewall-u-s-under-secretary-for-civilian-security-democracy-and-human-rights/.

60 McKenzie, Robert. *Countering Violent Extremism in America: Recommendations for the Next President.* Washington, DC: Brookings Report, 2016.

61 Bergen, Peter, Albert Ford, Alyssa Sims, and David Sterman. *Terrorism in America after 9/11. Part IV: What Is the Threat to the US Today?* Washington, DC: New America Foundation Report, 2016.

62 McCants, Will and Clinton Watts. "U.S. Strategy for Countering Violent Extremism: An Assessment," *Foreign Policy Research Institute e-notes* (December 2012).

63 Nasser-Eddine, Minerva, Bridget Garnham, Katerina Agostino and Gilbert Caluya. Countering Violent Extremism Literature Review. Counter Terrorism and Security Technology Centre Defense Science and Technology Organisation. Australian Government Department of Defense.

64 Metz, Steven. "Is the Afghanistan Debate the Beginning of the End for US Counterinsurgency," *World Politics Review* (August 11, 2017); Hazelton, Jacqueline L.

"The 'Hearts and Minds' Fallacy: Violence, Coercion, and Success in Counterinsurgency Warfare," *International Security* 42, no. 1 (2017): 80–113.

65 www.cnn.com/2017/07/01/politics/cve-funding-changes/index.html.

66 www.lawfareblog.com/it-all-over-cve.

67 Much of the following draws from Avant, Deborah. "Pragmatic Networks and Global Governance: Explaining Governance Gains in Private Military and Security Services," *International Studies Quarterly* 60, no. 2 (June 2016).

68 Avant, Deborah. "Pragmatic Networks and Global Governance: Explaining Governance Gains in Private Military and Security Services," *International Studies Quarterly* 60, no. 2 (June 2016).

69 Avant, Deborah. "US Progress Toward PSC Regulation: Promising but Potentially Stalled," *Korbel Quickfacts in Peace and Security* (September 2015).

70 https://icoca.ch/en/certification; https://icoca.ch/en/monitoring.

71 Avant, Deborah and Colby Goodman. "Enhanced interrogation could become a new US export under revised regulations," *Foreign Policy* (October 26, 2015).

72 Personal email correspondence with member of this office, 15 April 2016.

73 Avant, Deborah. "US Progress Toward PSC Regulation: Promising but Potentially Stalled," *Korbel Quickfacts in Peace and Security* (September 2015).

74 Mayer, Christopher T., Charles, F. Maurer, James Lariviere, Tara Lee, and Deborah Avant. "Contracting Support to Military Operations during the Global War on Terrorism," Paper prepared for *The Conference on American Use of Strategic Landpower Since 9/11, US Army War College* (December 15, 2015).

75 As an aside, in an echo to the discussion of CVE, while private security personnel working for the Pentagon in contingency operations must abide by standards respecting human rights, there is no such standard for private security provided in the U.S. A hodgepodge of regulations works in different states and some states have none at all (Bergal, Jenni. "In Many States Security Guards Get Scant Training, Oversight," *The Pew Charitable Trusts Stateline* (blog) (November 10, 2015)).

76 Lander, Mark, Eric Schmitt, and Michael Gordon. 2017. "Trump Aides Recruited Businessmen to Devise Options for Afghanistan." *New York Times.* 10 July. Available at: https://www.nytimes.com/2017/07/10/world/asia/trump-afghanistan-policy-erik-prince-stephen-feinberg.html?hp&action=click&pgtype=Homepage&clickSource=story-heading&module=first-column-region&region=top-news&WT.nav=top-news&_r=1.

77 Most recently, see Brooks, *How Everything Became War and the Military Became Everything.*

78 Many network analyses suggest that new connections are a fundamental way through which innovation is generated. Burt, Ronald S. *Brokerage and Closure: An Introduction to Social Capital.* New York: Oxford University Press, 2005; Granovetter, Mark S. "The Strength of Weak Ties," *American Journal of Sociology* 78 (1973); Padgett, John and Walter W. Powell. *The Emergence of Organizations and Markets.* Princeton: Princeton University Press, 2012.

79 See, for instance, Zegart, Amy. "Trump Isn't the only Problem with Trump's Foreign Policy," *The Atlantic* (October 2017). Available at: https://www.theatlantic.com/international/archive/2017/10/the-complexities-of-foreign-policy/543891/.

80 Avant, Deborah. "Pragmatic Networks and Global Governance: Explaining Governance Gains in Private Military and Security Services," *International Studies Quarterly* 60, no. 2 (June 2016).

81 www.psi-online.info.

82 See Pew analysis of trust in government here: www.people-press.org/2015/11/23/1-trust-in-government-1958-2015.

83 De Búrca, Gráinne, Robert O. Keohane and Charles F. Sabel. "New Modes of Pluralist Global Governance," *New York University Journal of International Law and Politics* 45, no. 3 (2013).

5

WHAT HAVE WE LEARNED ABOUT HOW PRESIDENTS ORGANIZE FOR NATIONAL SECURITY DECISION MAKING, 1947–2017?

Meena Bose

The National Security Act of 1947 institutionalized foreign-policy direction and leadership in the executive branch. By creating the Central Intelligence Agency (CIA), Department of Defense (DoD), Joint Chiefs of Staff (JCS), and National Security Council (NSC), all with direct lines of responsibility to the president, the law was intended to provide presidents with the necessary resources to protect expanding U.S. interests in the world. With the rise of the United States as a global superpower after World War II, as well as the growing conflict – soon to be the Cold War – with the Soviet Union, the need for centralized information gathering and analysis, and more unified military decision making was evident. Presidents would be better equipped to set national security policy with intelligence and military resources at their disposal.[1]

More than seventy years later, the 1947 law has reshaped national security decision making in significant, and sometimes unexpected, ways. The original NSC, for example, had just a few statutory members (including the secretary of state and secretary of defense), was chaired by the president, and did not have an independent staff. In 1953, President Dwight D. Eisenhower appointed a special assistant for national security affairs to manage the NSC process. Starting with the John F. Kennedy administration, this person assumed a policy advocacy role in addition to managerial responsibilities, and became known as the national security advisor. Today, the national security advisor is the top White House aide to the president in the policy area, oversees a large NSC staff, and is responsible for running NSC meetings with the president, as well as "Principals" meetings that do not include the president. Depending on the president, either the national security advisor or the secretary of state will be the primary spokesperson in foreign policy, which can create conflict between the State Department, the NSC, and the White House.[2]

This chapter examines the evolution of presidential leadership in foreign policy with a specific focus on how presidents organize their decision-making processes with the NSC. Understanding how presidents structure their national security decision making is essential to determining how well the 1947 law meets the needs of executive information collection and assessment in the twenty-first century. While each president's needs will vary according to personality, expertise, and the issues that an administration faces, the extensive scholarship on presidential organization demonstrates that certain features in decision making contribute to a more informed, deliberative process.[3] How the 1947 law facilitates that process, and how it might be adapted to address contemporary challenges, merits scholarly attention for policy-making recommendations.

To evaluate presidential leadership in foreign policy across administrations, this chapter contains three paired case studies that illustrate contrasting approaches to national security policy making, with important lessons for the future. It starts with a comparison of Cold War decision making by Presidents Eisenhower and Kennedy, who employed almost diametrically opposed advisory processes for gathering and evaluating information. It then compares the decision-making processes of Presidents Ronald Reagan and George H.W. Bush (Bush 41)[4], whose administrations witnessed the historic transition from the Cold War to the post-Cold War era. Finally, the chapter undertakes a comparison of national security decision making in the George W. Bush (Bush 43) and Barack Obama presidencies, focusing on how White House organization influenced decisions on combating terrorism in the post-9/11 world. The paucity of information about national security policy making in the first year of the Trump White House makes a current case study difficult, but a few preliminary observations are discussed.

The chapter concludes with a discussion of lessons learned from the six case studies and implications for how the National Security Act of 1947 may require adaptation to meet executive needs for information gathering and assessment in the twenty-first century. It finds that each presidency provides both positive and cautionary lessons for national security policy making, and that models of structured, systematic deliberation are most instructive for current policy-making expectations.

The cold war decision making of Eisenhower and Kennedy

While President Harry S. Truman signed the National Security Act of 1947, the institutionalization of the NSC's role in decision making took place largely in the Eisenhower and Kennedy administrations. With very different professional backgrounds and personalities, the two presidents contrasted sharply in their approach to decision making; Kennedy's initial method of White House governance in fact was explicitly designed to counter perceived defects in his predecessor's system. Nevertheless, the Eisenhower and Kennedy presidencies made the

NSC a central resource for information and advice on national security policy, a responsibility that has endured, albeit in varying forms, ever since.[5]

Eisenhower's NSC

Eisenhower's national security decision-making process reflected his extensive and wide-ranging military expertise. A career officer who graduated from West Point in 1915, Eisenhower held several demanding and important assignments working for senior officers such as General Fox Conner, General John J. Pershing, and General Douglas MacArthur in the first two decades of his career. He rose quickly during World War II to serve as Supreme Commander of the Allied Expeditionary Force, overseeing the historic D-Day invasion of Normandy on June 6, 1944. After World War II, Eisenhower also served as the first Supreme Allied Commander of the North Atlantic Treaty Organization (NATO) before running successfully for president in 1952.[6]

In his military career, Eisenhower developed several leadership lessons that he applied skillfully to politics. During World War II, Eisenhower decided that a cheerful public image at all times was necessary to build and maintain troop morale. As president, he did the same, purposely maintaining a public image of being above, even disinterested in, politics. He once famously told reporters, "The word 'politics' … . I have no great liking for that." Behind the scenes, though, Eisenhower actively engaged in political leadership, directing policy and personnel choices, particularly in national security, and demonstrating an astute understanding of both substantive and personality conflicts. Presidential scholar Fred I. Greenstein found extensive evidence of this conscious, deliberate strategy in the archival record at the Dwight D. Eisenhower Presidential Library in Abilene, Kansas, and identified it as the "hidden-hand presidency."[7]

Upon taking office, Eisenhower immediately established a carefully structured national security decision-making system that endured throughout his presidency. To manage NSC meetings, Eisenhower created the position of special assistant to the president for national security affairs. Under Eisenhower, the special assistant's responsibilities were procedural, not advisory; the position was created to oversee planning and implementation for weekly NSC meetings, as well as coordinate the flow of discussion in the actual sessions. To develop NSC agendas, the special assistant presided over a Planning Board, composed of principals from the NSC agencies. To implement NSC decisions, the special assistant led an Operations Coordinating Board. Together, the two boards became known as "policy hill" in the Eisenhower administration.[8]

The careful preparation for weekly NSC meetings ensured organized and systematic discussion of policy issues. Eisenhower attended NSC meetings and engaged in discussion, pressing advisers to defend their positions and periodically directing the conversation. The organization and attention to detail in the NSC created a textbook example of "multiple advocacy," a decision-making model developed by political scientist Alexander L. George that focuses on thorough review of policy options, active participation by the decision maker, i.e., the president, and sufficient time for deliberation before decision making.[9]

One of the most significant examples of multiple advocacy in Eisenhower's national security decision making is the 1953 "Project Solarium" exercise that produced the administration's "New Look" national security strategy. Named after the room in the White House where the exercise took place, Project Solarium brought together three teams of political and military leaders to examine and advocate for three strategic options: continuing containment; drawing a line between communist and non-communist countries and threatening "massive retaliation," with the possible use of nuclear weapons, if Soviet aggression crossed the line; and promoting "liberation" of Eastern European countries behind the Iron Curtain. After the presentation of each option and discussion, Eisenhower proposed a combination of the three approaches that ultimately became the foundation of his New Look strategy. In retrospect, the archival record suggests that this may have been Eisenhower's plan from the outset, and that Project Solarium served more to bring key national security leaders together in support of the strategy than to change the president's views. Nevertheless, Project Solarium served important substantive and teamwork-building purposes, and illustrated the merits of Eisenhower's highly structured approach to national security planning.[10]

Kennedy's NSC

Although Eisenhower enjoyed great public popularity during his presidency, his leadership was not viewed favorably at the time. Because Eisenhower purposely maintained a public image of disinterest in politics, critics said his awareness of U.S. prestige and interests in the Cold War was lacking. After the Soviet Union launched the artificial satellite Sputnik in October 1957, charges of a looming "missile gap" for the United States prompted further criticism of Eisenhower's national security policies.[11] In the 1960 presidential campaign, Democratic candidate John F. Kennedy focused on the perceived weaknesses of the Eisenhower administration's defense posture, particularly reliance on the threat of using nuclear weapons to deter Soviet aggression.[12]

As president, Kennedy aimed to change Eisenhower's decision-making processes as much as his policies. Just as Democrats had criticized Eisenhower's national security policies after Sputnik, so, too, did they identify problems with staffing and planning. Kennedy wrote in 1957 that "the massive paper work and the clearance procedure, the compulsion to achieve agreement among departments and agencies, often produce policy statements which are only a mongrelization of views."[13] The Senate Subcommittee on National Policy Machinery, chaired by Senator Henry M. Jackson (D-WA) and popularly known as the Jackson Committee, held hearings on the subject toward the end of the Eisenhower administration, marking the first major review of national security planning since the 1947 law. The Jackson Committee issued a series of staff reports that recommended many procedural changes in national security decision making.[14]

Such changes were consistent with Kennedy's professional background and personality. The youngest person ever elected U.S. president, Kennedy entered the White House with a legislative background, having served for six years in the U.S. House of Representatives and eight years in the U.S. Senate. His political experiences led him to favor more fluid organizational procedures than Eisenhower, with less structure and multiple venues for acquiring information. Kennedy's views also were influenced by presidential scholar Richard E. Neustadt's book *Presidential Power*, which praised Franklin D. Roosevelt's active governance as a model of presidential leadership, and presented Eisenhower's perceived passiveness as weakness in the White House. Kennedy read Neustadt's book in page proofs in the fall of 1960, just before it was published, and found that the proposed model for presidential governance matched his own instincts and expertise.

Consequently, Kennedy had little interest in the "policy hill" that Eisenhower had developed for the NSC, nor did he want to have regular NSC meetings. Upon taking office, Kennedy abolished the NSC Planning Board and Operations Coordinating Board (as the Jackson Committee had recommended), as well as other staff positions, including chief of staff to the president. As Kennedy's close adviser and chief speechwriter (whose formal title was Counsel to the President) Theodore C. Sorensen later wrote, Kennedy "abolished the pyramid structure of the White House staff ... all of which imposed, in his view, needless paperwork and machinery between the president and his responsible officers."[15]

In Kennedy's view, a president's advisors should function as the spokes of a wheel, all with access to the president, who serves as the hub. Instead of having regular NSC meetings, Kennedy met informally with advisors, often initiating those discussions with queries based on his exhaustive reading of reports as well as the daily news. Kennedy also created special task forces as needed to examine pressing international concerns. During the 1960–61 transition period, Neustadt, who had served as an informal advisor to Kennedy during the campaign, introduced incoming national security advisor (the "special assistant" position from the Eisenhower administration) McGeorge Bundy in the White House as the person who would replace five people on Eisenhower's NSC staff.[16]

Kennedy made some organizational adjustments after the disastrous Bay of Pigs invasion in April 1961. Initial planning for the invasion, which was developed as a covert U.S. operation to assist Cuban exiles in overthrowing communist leader Fidel Castro, began in the Eisenhower administration, and Kennedy began to receive intelligence briefings about the plans after his election in November 1960. After the invasion, which ended disastrously with the capture of more than 1,000 exiles (and more than a hundred deaths) and Castro's hold on power intact, Kennedy's decision-making procedures faced extensive scrutiny. Critics said the president failed to review options thoroughly, particularly when deciding to change the landing site for rebels to a place that was considered less conspicuous, but also made retreat more difficult.[17]

Furthermore, Kennedy's top advisors focused on unanimity of support for the new president over voicing concerns about the invasion plans, a situation that social psychologist Irving Janis later identified as "groupthink."[18] Eisenhower's staffing system likely would have prompted airing and discussion of such concerns in national security deliberations, a point that Neustadt noted after the invasion when, in describing the dismantling of Eisenhower's NSC system, he said, "We aimed at Eisenhower and hit Kennedy. We did away with the old and didn't put anything in its place."[19]

Kennedy did not reinstate the staffing system from the Eisenhower administration, but he did take steps to ensure more systematic decision making, particularly during the 1962 Cuban missile crisis. During the thirteen days that the White House debated how to respond to the Soviet placement of nuclear missiles in Cuba, Kennedy established a special Executive Committee (known as the "ExComm") to examine policy options. Kennedy's brother, Attorney General Robert F. Kennedy, was responsible for making sure that proposals were vetted thoroughly, and President Kennedy at times purposely left meetings to ensure that participants would raise questions that they might hesitate to do in the president's presence. After the Soviet Union agreed to withdraw the missiles, the ExComm was widely praised as a textbook model of decision making. Still, the change from the Eisenhower system was significant, not just in staffing, but also in the role of the national security advisor, which became a position of policy advocacy as well as organization.[20]

By the mid-1960s, then, the NSC was an established source of information and analysis for presidents, but with considerable variation in how it was used. Eisenhower's "policy hill" staffing model did not endure, but the position of special assistant to the president for national security affairs did. Beginning with the Kennedy administration, though, the special assistant became a policy advocate as well as process manager, and eventually became known as "national security advisor." By the late 1980s, with the ending of the Cold War, the role of the organization and the position would change again.

Ending the Cold War in the Reagan and Bush administrations

The 1980s marked a turning point in the Cold War, with five U.S.-Soviet summit meetings, the first U.S.-Soviet treaty to reduce nuclear forces, the fall of the Berlin Wall, the downfall of communism in Eastern Europe, and much more.[21] By the early 1990s, the Cold War had ended, and countries around the world were shifting from dictatorship to democracy. Many factors contributed to this global transformation, including U.S. presidential leadership. And how Presidents Reagan and Bush 41 organized their national security decision making influenced their Cold War leadership in important ways. Reagan's heavy reliance on delegation complicated the policy process for his national security team, while Bush's extensive engagement in deliberations fostered a collegial process that promoted closely coordinated decision making.[22]

Reagan's NSC

Reagan came to the White House with little experience in foreign policy but strong, consistent convictions about U.S. interests that he maintained throughout his presidency. These convictions dated back to his days as president of the Screen Actors Guild after World War II, when many people in Hollywood faced accusations of communist ties. Initially a New Deal Democrat, Reagan switched to the Republican party in 1962, and he campaigned vigorously for Barry Goldwater in the 1964 presidential campaign, criticizing the rise of communism around the globe.[23] After serving as governor of California for two terms, Reagan began to communicate his views regularly to the American public through speeches, newspaper columns, and weekly radio addresses. These addresses, which Reagan drafted himself, frequently presented critiques of American foreign policy in the 1970s, and called for the United States to build up its defenses to wage the Cold War more effectively.[24]

In his advisory system, Reagan favored delegating responsibilities, protecting his personal time, and avoiding staff dissension. Reagan evinced little interest in the day-to-day tasks of the presidency and was more than willing to let his staff manage White House operations. His self-described leadership philosophy was, "Surround yourself with the best people you can find, delegate authority, and don't interfere as long as the policy you've decided upon is being carried out."[25]

For much of his eight years as president, Reagan had a national security team in which at least two key officials could not reach agreement on U.S. strategy toward the Soviet Union, and this dissension created severe strains on the policy-making process. Such divisions served to distract advisors from Reagan's policy agenda, and at times contributed to tensions in the already volatile political climate surrounding U.S.-Soviet negotiations in Reagan's second term. While Reagan ultimately signed a path-breaking arms control agreement with Gorbachev in 1987, advisory disputes overshadowed those negotiations throughout Reagan's presidency.

Reagan's willingness to delegate authority to his advisors meant they had ample opportunity to promote their own views, which frequently caused conflict in foreign policy. In eight years, he had two secretaries of state, two secretaries of defense and six national security advisers. Secretary of State George P. Shultz took office in the summer of 1982 and advocated efforts to reduce Cold War tensions with the Soviet Union, but faced strong resistance from his counterparts at Defense and the NSC. By mid-1983, Shultz offered Reagan his resignation, concluding that "the process of managing foreign policy has gone completely off the track."[26] Reagan asked Shultz to stay, and began to hold weekly meetings with him, but Shultz offered to resign again after Reagan's reelection in 1984, telling the president that his other advisers and Shultz "just don't see things the same way."[27]

For a brief period, Shultz initiated periodic White House lunches (at Reagan's suggestion) with the principal members of the president's national security team, but conflicts continued. As one observer notes, "There was just no getting over the deep substantive differences and the personal chemistry wasn't there."[28] National Security Adviser Robert McFarlane reflects that "the trouble was they [the lunches] weren't regular enough. We just didn't insist that there be a pattern or discipline to them."[29] Reagan's reluctance to address these substantive differences exacerbated tensions among his advisors. As Chairman of the Joint Chiefs of Staff William J. Crowe, Jr., later said, "As long as Weinberger and Shultz were arguing, there wasn't a consensus on anything. And I could never find – the President never, as far as I could tell, arbitrated any of those disputes. He just let the water seek its own well, which seemed to me a funny way to run a railroad."[30]

Ultimately, news of the Iran-contra affair – in which the United States sold arms to Iran in exchange for Iran's help in seeking the release of U.S. hostages in the Middle East, and then used some of the profits from the arms sales to support the contras in Nicaragua, in specific violation of a congressional prohibition on doing so – prompted changes in Reagan's national security organization. Army officer Colin Powell, who joined the NSC staff after the Iran-contra affair was revealed, concluded that the fiasco came about at least partly because of Reagan's aloof style: "Under [the NSC leadership of] McFarlane, Poindexter, North, and company, the NSC had gone off the rails. The situation was not entirely their fault. They worked for a President who did not like to step between his powerful cabinet members and make hard choices."[31]

In the fall of 1987, Powell became national security advisor, and his predecessor, Frank Carlucci, became defense secretary. As national security advisor, Carlucci had experienced conflict with Shultz over the responsibilities of their respective organizations, but ultimately, common interests overrode their differences. When Reagan and Soviet leader Mikhail Gorbachev signed the Intermediate-Range Nuclear Forces Treaty at their third summit meeting, which took place in Washington, D.C., in December 1987, the president's national security advisors finally were a team. As Shultz recalls, "Frank Carlucci, Colin Powell, and I had really clicked at the Washington summit. We had confidence and trust in each other. We tossed the ball around and used our comparative advantages effectively. President Reagan could see this for himself and gave us his full support."[32]

Bush 41's NSC

Unlike Reagan, Bush 41 became president with a diverse and extensive resume in foreign affairs, including U.S. ambassador to the United Nations in the Richard M. Nixon administration, U.S. liaison to China and director of the Central Intelligence Agency in the Gerald R. Ford administration, and of course, vice president during Reagan's eight years in the White House. Each of these positions helped Bush to appreciate the intricacies of American diplomacy without adhering to a uniform ideology, particularly given the policy differences of the presidencies in which he served. Bush's foreign policy record served primarily to develop his ability to pursue diplomatic channels behind the scenes and to interact with foreign officials whom he would meet again as president. As one former administration official notes, "Over the 20 years before [Bush] became president of the United States, the number of relationships he developed with leaders throughout the world was extraordinary." The official goes on to explain:

President Bush knew not just the prime ministers or the presidents, but the education ministers, the finance ministers, the defense ministers. He'd known them for 20 years. He knew their spouses, he knew their kids, he knew who was going to which school, who was in trouble, and who was doing well. These were extraordinary relationships that he had carefully built and cultivated and that I think many of his foreign policy successes were based on.[33]

Upon succeeding Reagan as president in 1989, Bush had a clear vision of how he would manage his foreign policy-making process, namely, that he would involve himself in the process much more than his predecessor. Bush was determined to work closely with his foreign policy team to understand, and engage in, policy debates. As he writes:

I intended to be a "hands-on" president. I wanted the key foreign policy players to know that I was going to involve myself in many of the details of defense, international trade, and foreign affairs policies, yet I would not try to master all the details and complexities of policy matters. I planned to learn enough so I could make informed decisions without micromanaging. I would rely heavily on department experts and, in the final analysis, on my cabinet secretaries and the national security advisor for more studied advice. A president must surround himself with strong people and then not be afraid to delegate.[34]

Bush also took great care to appoint a foreign policy team that would work well together. As vice president, he had witnessed the conflicts in the Reagan administration, and was "determined to make our decision-making structures and procedures in the new Administration so well defined that we would minimize the chances of such problems."[35] In selecting James A. Baker III to be secretary of state and Brent Scowcroft to be national security advisor, Bush chose people he had known for many years professionally and personally. Baker, Scowcroft, and Bush had all worked together in the Ford administration – Bush as director of central intelligence, Scowcroft as national security advisor, and Baker as campaign chairman in 1976 – so they had collective experience in policy coordination and decision making. The other key members of Bush's national security team, Defense Secretary Richard B. Cheney and Chairman of the Joint Chiefs of Staff (JCS) Colin L. Powell, also knew their colleagues through previous political experience. Baker describes the team as "a group of experienced, collegial peers who liked and respected one another."[36]

The NSC process operated smoothly from the beginning in the Bush administration, due to participants' collective expertise and interest. The president himself served as the model here – as Oberdorfer notes, "In dramatic contrast to the detached, chairmanlike Reagan, Bush was knowledgeable and very interested in foreign policy."[37] Powell similarly says, "President Bush was much more involved than President Reagan. He wanted to hear the fights; he wanted to hear the debates."[38] Bush gave his advisors full authority to manage the foreign policy-making process, which enabled them to resolve lower-level policy debates while still bringing issues of major importance to the president's attention. For example, the Bush administration began the practice of Principals Committee meetings, in which senior national security officials would meet regularly without the president to discuss policy concerns. As Bush describes the process:

Sometimes cabinet members might still have deep differences of opinion, or rival departments would feel strongly about an issue. Brent always made sure the views of every "player" were understood by him and by me. If he could not resolve the impasse separately, then the principals would sort it out with me. Even then Brent would have to knock heads before he let them in my door. He took a lot of the pressure off me by keeping an open, honest approach to the NSC job. He was one of the reasons why we had a really cohesive and sound policy-making process: key decisions were well vetted ahead of time. It was an imperfect system at times, but it worked.[39]

The collegiality within Bush's national security team did not always extend, however, to officials who had not worked closely with these advisors. Oberdorfer finds that "under Bush, the circle was so tight that people were concerned about the lack of diversity and absence of challenging voices to the policy consensus."[40] Jack Matlock, who served as U.S. ambassador to the Soviet Union from 1987 to 1991, describes the Bush transition period as "a hostile takeover," saying Bush's national security team did not even try to learn about developments in the Soviet Union from Reagan administration officials. Although Matlock visited Washington twice during the transition, he was not able to meet with any members of Bush's incoming foreign policy team. He later described an initial mixed impression of Bush's advisors: "They were all experienced and well informed in general but could not have been fully aware of many things that were then occurring in the Soviet Union, and – in particular – the growing potential for American influence on developments there. I was frustrated not to have an opportunity to discuss these matters with the incoming policy makers.[41]

In comparing the last two Cold War presidents, then, Reagan's unwillingness to address advisory disputes that repeatedly were brought to his attention permitted conflict between the State and Defense Departments to continue without any prospect of resolution. This hands-off approach to organization may have slowed progress in U.S.-Soviet negotiations. As Carlucci recalls, "Had the whole thing been much better coordinated and had we come up with positions that we were able to come up with in the last two years, sure, I think you could have accelerated the process."[42] Bush, in contrast, developed a more cohesive national security team from the beginning, which produced more consistency – though certainly not complete agreement – in policy making. Bush's advisers were able to work together in debating U.S. policy toward the Soviet Union, with a president who was willing, indeed determined, to mediate disputes.

At the same time, an important learning curve on presidential advising took place in the Reagan administration. Reagan chose not to take many opportunities in the first six years of his administration to address ongoing conflicts within his foreign policy team, but he did make key personnel changes in the aftermath of the Iran-contra affair. Although Reagan's approach to foreign policy making did not change drastically, the team he instituted toward the end of his presidency was able to work together much more effectively than previous ones.

Combating terrorism in the Bush (43) and Obama administrations

In the early post-Cold War era, policy makers wrestled with identifying the new U.S. role in the world. After several contentious debates about humanitarian intervention – including a swift withdrawal of military forces from Somalia, originally sent to assist with famine relief, after a disastrous attack on U.S. soldiers there, and a subsequent U.S. decision not to intervene in a civil war in Rwanda that took more than 800,000 lives – economic policy seemed the most likely guide to advancing American interests abroad. But after the terrorist attacks on September 11, 2001, national security concerns became the number one priority for policy makers and the public alike. To protect the United States at home, the Homeland Security Act of 2002 brought twenty-two federal agencies into the new Cabinet-level Department of Homeland Security. The NSC was not part of that reorganization, but national security decision making was central to presidential policy making, and Presidents Bush (43) and Obama employed very different approaches in those deliberations. For both presidents, though, lack of expertise in national security policy affected decision making, either through heavy reliance on administration officials with such expertise, or through a lengthy process that did not always encourage resolution. Both cases illustrate the challenges of establishing a structured decision-making process if the president is not fully engaged in that effort.[43]

Bush (43)'s NSC

George W. Bush entered the White House in 2001 with no professional experience in national security policy or foreign affairs.[44] A two-term governor, Bush had focused on domestic issues in his 2000 presidential campaign, including education and creating opportunities for religious organizations to provide social services, such as after-school programs, with public funding. In a presidential debate, Bush explicitly rejected an active role for the United States in world affairs, saying, "I don't think our troops ought to be used for what's called nation building."[45] His top adviser in foreign affairs, future national security advisor and secretary of state Condoleezza Rice, famously wrote during the campaign that the United States should not become "the world's '911.'"[46] By selecting seasoned foreign-policy experts such as Rice for national security advisor, retired General Colin Powell as secretary of state, former Ford administration defense secretary Donald Rumsfeld for the same position, and former Bush 41 defense secretary Richard B. Cheney for vice president, Bush ensured that his national security team would have the knowledge and political skill to provide the information he would need for decision making.

As the nation's only president with a Master's of Business Administration degree, Bush not surprisingly adopted a business model in policy making. As one scholar writes, Bush "set a bold direction and delegate[d] administrative matters to his executive team, led by his chief operating officer, Vice President Richard Cheney."[47] National Security Advisor Rice (and later Stephen Hadley) led NSC meetings as well as Principals meetings, but this was no easy task; one assessment of the Bush 43 presidency notes that Rice "had her hands full managing the case of experienced and powerful leaders of the Bush 43 team, who as a group reflected important differences that had not been fully aired since the end of the Cold War."[48] While Bush did give Rice the formal authority to direct the NSC, Vice President Cheney had his own national security staff, which was bigger than his predecessor's and had greater participation in NSC meetings. Due to Cheney's vast influence in policy making, political scientist Shirley Anne Warshaw describes the administration as a "co-presidency," and concludes that the vice president "undermined the president's established structure for receiving national security advice."[49]

Bush initially held regular NSC meetings, particularly in the weeks following the 9/11 attacks, and actively engaged in those deliberations, which quickly reached consensus to wage war in Afghanistan to destroy the terrorist network that had executed the attacks. But with the far more contentious debate over whether to invade Iraq, Bush's decision making lacked structure and sustained analysis of opposing views. James Pfiffner finds that the NSC did not deliberate in person at any time about all of the options on Iraq, including the major decision over whether to go to war. Bush acknowledges the tensions in his *Decision Points* memoir, referring to the "growing discord within the national security team" by 2004, and attributing it primarily to strong personalities who could not resolve their disagreements. But structural lapses created problems as well, particularly having Rice focus on communicating the president's views to the NSC, rather than airing and addressing divergent views from participants.[50]

Furthermore, many key national security decisions took place outside the NSC system. President Bush authorized the indefinite detention and interrogation of suspected terrorists at Guantanamo Bay, Cuba, via executive order, with no formal group evaluation of goals and implementation. President Bush also used an executive order to authorize bypassing special judicial warrants for surveillance of international phone calls and e-mails by American citizens with suspected terrorist connections. When public criticism of detainee treatment at the Abu Ghraib prison in Iraq in the spring of 2004 prompted inquiries into conditions at Guantanamo Bay, the Bush administration said national security interests required that these decisions be closely guarded. A similar case was made for surveillance when the program was revealed in late 2005. But subsequent judicial rulings requiring more procedures for detainee hearings, and congressional decisions on wiretapping, suggest that a fuller assessment of the programs before enactment might have addressed some of these concerns.[51]

While the credentials of Bush's national security team demonstrated both breadth and depth in policy analysis, then, the NSC process lacked the necessary structure for systematic review of policy options. The outsize role of the vice president's office overshadowed the national security advisor's role, and conflict between leading officials, particularly the secretaries of state and defense, could not be resolved. This may have been in part due to personalities and substantive policy differences, but the president's heavy reliance on delegation, as well as the national security advisor's responsibilities as policy communicator rather than process manager, made resolution especially difficult. Some of the problems were addressed in Bush's second term with the departure of some advisors and a rebalancing of authority from the vice president's office and Defense Department to the State Department and NSC. Still, by then, many of the president's foundational decisions in foreign policy were in place, with limited opportunities for change.[52]

Obama's NSC

Like Bush, Obama had a slim political resume before the White House, with limited professional experience in American foreign policy or national security. Both Bush and Obama came to the presidency with statewide political experience, Bush as a two-term governor of Texas, and Obama as an Illinois state senator for ten years. Obama won election to the U.S. Senate in 2004, where he chaired the Senate Foreign Relations Subcommittee on European Affairs. By 2006, though, Obama started to consider a presidential run, and he announced his candidacy early the following year. Although Obama had traveled extensively throughout his life, from his birth in Hawaii to childhood years in Indonesia to travel to Africa to meet his father's family, he had little governing experience in foreign and national security affairs before entering the Oval Office.[53]

Obama made clear the primary importance of the secretary of state in his administration by asking his former competitor for the Democratic presidential nomination, Hillary Rodham Clinton, to take the position. While Clinton had not practiced foreign policy, she had traveled the world as First Lady in the 1990s, and then served on the U.S. Senate Armed Services Committee for six years. Obama asked Bush's secretary of defense, Robert Gates, to continue in the position, which he did until mid-2011. Vice President Joe Biden had served on the U.S. Senate Foreign Relations Committee for many years, serving as ranking minority member or committee chair for a decade. For national security advisor, Obama selected retired U.S. Marine Corps General James L. Jones, who had served in the military for forty years and then held leadership positions in foreign policy, including special envoy for Middle East security, before joining Obama's national security team.[54]

Within weeks of taking office, the Obama administration announced a broad expansion of the NSC's authority, with attention to a wider range of issues, both domestic and international, with strategic implications, and broader participation by Cabinet members and other agency directors, depending on the topic. National Security Advisor Jones said he would have primary responsibility for conveying ideas to the president, including conflicting views on topics, and that he would present his own views when asked. But Obama and Jones did not have a prior working relationship; in fact, the two had met just a few times before Jones's appointment. Obama instead turned frequently to NSC deputies whom he had worked with since his 2008 presidential campaign, including Tom Donilon, Denis McDonough, and Ben Rhodes.[55]

In late 2010, Jones stepped down and was replaced by Donilon, who served through Obama's first term. Defense Secretary Gates also departed midway through the presidency and was replaced by CIA Director (and former Congressman, Director of the Office of Management and Budget, and White House Chief of Staff) Leon Panetta. In Obama's second term, U.S. Senator John Kerry became secretary of state, U.S. Senator Chuck Hagel became secretary of defense (until early 2015, when he was replaced by Ashton B. Carter), and U.S. Permanent Representative to the United Nations Susan B. Rice became national security advisor (after Obama unsuccessfully nominated her as secretary of state; she withdrew her nomination after strong resistance from Republican senators, who criticized her initial public remarks about the September 12, 2012 terrorist attack on the U.S. consulate in Benghazi, Libya).[56]

In addition to having many transitions in his national security team, Obama also had to contend with sharply divergent views among top advisors over how to proceed on major U.S. commitments such as the wars in Afghanistan and Iraq. While Obama won praise for acting decisively in crisis situations, such as the successful military mission to kill terrorist leader Osama bin Laden in May 2011, he faced criticism for inaction, or insufficient action, in other places. In December 2009, for example, Obama announced that he would send 30,000 additional troops to Afghanistan to bring stability to the region, which was less than the military had requested, but more than advisers such as Vice President Biden had recommended. In the summer of 2011, Obama followed through on his campaign promise to withdraw U.S. military forces from Iraq, but the subsequent rise of the Islamic State of Iraq and Syria (ISIS) terrorist network raised questions about whether the U.S. had withdrawn troops precipitously. In 2013, one year after declaring that the United States likely would take military action if Syria used chemical weapons in its civil war, Obama did not follow through when Syria used a nerve gas that killed more than 1,400 people, saying he would not act without congressional authorization, which he knew would not be forthcoming.[57]

Given Obama's limited experience in foreign policy, as well as his commitment as presidential candidate to reduce U.S. military involvement abroad and act multilaterally whenever possible, his resistance to the use of force was unsurprising. But problems with Obama's national security decision-making process complicated policy enactment and implementation. Since the Clinton years, the NSC staff had increased fourfold, to about 400 people (the staff doubled regularly in each presidency since the ending of the Cold War, from 50 in the Bush 41 administration, to 100 in the Clinton administration, to 200 in the Bush 43 administration.) A 2015 news article wrote that the large staff "had come to symbolize an overbearing and paranoid White House that insists on controlling even the smallest policy details, often at the expense of timely and effective decisions."[58] Centralization of policy making in the White House created conflicts between the NSC and other executive agencies and departments, and Obama did little to address those conflicts.

Initial observations of the Trump presidency

As with his surprising candidacy and unexpected election, President Donald J. Trump did not follow precedent in setting up his national security decision-making process. His first national security advisor, LTG (R) Michael T. Flynn, had sparked controversy during the campaign for his Republican National Convention speech, in which he joined the crowd's chant of "Lock her up!" during his critique of Democratic candidate Hillary Rodham Clinton. Flynn then resigned after just three weeks for providing misleading accounts to Vice President Mike Pence and White House officials of conversations with the Russian ambassador to the United States during the transition period between Trump's election and inauguration.[59] In late 2017, Flynn pleaded guilty to lying to the FBI about those communications, and he agreed to cooperate with special counsel Robert S. Mueller III's investigation into possible Russian efforts to influence the 2016 presidential election.[60]

Trump's second national security adviser, LTG H.R. McMaster, brought a more conventional management approach to the NSC, bringing in more staff directors with traditional policy and governing expertise, and pressing successfully for the removal of some contentious participants. At McMaster's recommendation, Trump removed White House political strategist Steve Bannon, whom he initially had appointed to serve on the NSC Principals Committee (and who left the White House a few months later) from the NSC, and McMaster also dismissed other staffers brought in by Flynn and Bannon.[61] But apart from personnel changes, little information about the workings of the NSC, or the president's involvement, was evident; indeed, nearly one year into the presidency, the NSC website still said, "Check back soon for more information."[62]

Conclusion

What lessons do the six case studies provide for presidents and national security decision making? First, while presidents may count on their national security advisors for policy advice, the primary responsibility of the position needs to be managing the NSC process to ensure that all policy options are reviewed thoroughly, and that the president's national security team has sufficient opportunity to state their views and engage with each other about policy disagreements. Bush 41's national security advisor, Brent Scowcroft, has been described as "the gold standard" for the job, and his leadership provides a model for future presidents, while the Kennedy, Reagan, Bush 43, and Obama case studies present more cautionary experiences. While Eisenhower set the foundation for a systematic NSC process, the Bush 41 case may provide more practical guidance for today, particularly given how the NSC has evolved since its creation.[63]

Second, regular, face-to-face meetings of the NSC are essential for policy debate and consensus building. For NSC meetings to be productive, they needed to be held in tandem with regular Principals and Deputies sessions as well. The expansion of the NSC and centralization of policy making in the White House have made these meetings less productive, as seen in the Obama administration. While major organizational changes are unlikely, the national security advisor needs to put this process in place and then ensure that it remains active.

Third, and perhaps most important, for the national security advisor to manage an NSC system that provides substantive policy analysis and advice to the president, strong and sustained executive leadership is essential for the process to work. Eisenhower and Bush 41 illustrate how active presidential participation can direct national security policy making productively, and Kennedy and Reagan do the same at certain points in their presidencies. Bush 43 and Obama illustrate the difficulties of having overlapping lines of authority for policy making and sometimes insufficient guidance from the Oval Office on managing conflicts.

In implementation, all of these recommendations will have some variation depending on the personality and leadership style of presidents and their advisers. Therefore, formal incorporation into the 1947 law is neither needed nor feasible. Instead, the importance of precedent – both positive and cautionary – will be essential for future presidents to examine as they develop and manage their national security teams. Just as policy issues merit substantial attention from presidents, so, too, do organizational plans. As Eisenhower said, "disorganization … can easily lead to disaster. … Organization helps the responsible individual make the necessary decision, and helps assure that it is satisfactorily carried out."[64]

Notes

1 The history behind and enactment of the National Security Act of 1947 is examined in Douglas T. Stuart, *Creating the National Security State: A History of the Law That Transformed America* (Princeton, NJ: Princeton University Press, 2009). Also see

David Rothkopf, *Running the World: The Inside Story of the National Security Council and the Architects of American Power* (New York: Public Affairs, 2005).

2 United States Department of State, Bureau of Public Affairs, Office of the Historian, "History of the National Security Council, 1947–1997" (August 1997). Available at http://fas.org/irp/offdocs/NSChistory.htm. For an analysis of the evolution of the national security advisor position, see John P. Burke, *Honest Broker? The National Security Adviser and Presidential Decision Making* (College Station, TX: Texas A&M University Press, 2009).

3 A systematic model for evaluating how presidents' personality, advisory system, and political environment influence their decision-making processes is in John P. Burke and Fred I. Greenstein (with Larry Berman and Richard Immerman), *How Presidents Test Reality: Decisions on Vietnam 1954 and 1965* (New York: Russell Sage Foundation, 1989). Patrick J. Haney examines how presidents organize their advisers to make decisions in foreign-policy crises in *Organizing for Foreign Policy Crises: Presidents, Advisers, and the Management of Decision Making* (Ann Arbor, MI: University of Michigan Press, 1997). Daniel J. Ponder examines how presidents assess advice and information in domestic policy in *Good Advice: Information and Policy Making in the White House* (College Station, TX: Texas A&M University Press, 2000).

4 "Bush 41" and "Bush 43" are used periodically in this essay to distinguish the two Bush presidencies. When an extended discussion of one president makes clear who is the subject, the presidency number is not used.

5 Much of the analysis in the Eisenhower and Kennedy case studies is drawn from a more extended study of the subject in Meena Bose, *Shaping and Signaling Presidential Policy: The National Security Decision Making of Eisenhower and Kennedy* (College Station, TX: Texas A&M University Press, 1998).

6 For a summary of Eisenhower's biography, see University of Virginia Miller Center, "Dwight D. Eisenhower (1890–1969)," at http://millercenter.org/president/eisenhower.

7 Bose, *Shaping and Signaling Presidential Policy*, p. 10; Fred I. Greenstein, "The President Who Led by Seeming Not to: A Centennial View of Dwight Eisenhower," *Antioch Review* 49 (Winter 1991): 39–44; Greenstein, *The Hidden-Hand Presidency: Eisenhower as Leader* (New York: Basic Books, 1982).

8 Anna Kasten Nelson, "The 'Top of Policy Hill': President Eisenhower and the National Security Council," *Diplomatic History* 7 (1983): 307–26.

9 Alexander L. George, "The Case for Multiple Advocacy in Making Foreign Policy," *American Political Science Review* 66 (September 1972): 751–85.

10 The Project Solarium exercise is discussed in several studies of Eisenhower's national security policy making, including Bose, *Shaping and Signaling Presidential Policy*; Robert R. Bowie and Richard H. Immerman, *Waging Peace: How Eisenhower Shaped an Enduring Cold War Strategy* (New York: Oxford University Press, 1998); and Saki Dockrill, *Eisenhower's New-Look National Security Policy, 1953–61* (New York: Palgrave Macmillan, 1996). For a comparison of Eisenhower's national security planning with that of his successors in the White House, see Meena Bose, "Eisenhower's 'Strategic Hand': Developing and Executing a Foreign Policy Vision," in *The Eisenhower Presidency: Lessons for the Twenty-First Century*, ed. Andrew J. Polsky (Lanham, MD: Lexington Books, 2015).

11 Peter J. Roman, *Eisenhower and the Missile Gap* (Ithaca, NY: Cornell University Press, 1996).

12 See, for example, John F. Kennedy, "A Democrat Looks at Foreign Policy," *Foreign Affairs* 36 (October 1957): 44–59; Kennedy, *The Strategy of Peace*, ed. Allan Nevins (New York: Harper & Brothers, 1960); Kennedy, *The Speeches of Senator John F. Kennedy: Presidential Campaign of 1960*, ed. Senate Committee on Commerce (Washington, DC: U.S. Government Printing Office, 1961).

13 Kennedy, "A Democrat Looks at Foreign Policy."

14 Senator Henry M. Jackson, ed., *The National Security Council: Jackson Subcommittee Papers on Policy Making at the Presidential Level* (New York: Praeger, 1965).
15 Theodore C. Sorensen, *Kennedy* (New York: Harper & Row, 1965), p. 281.
16 Arthur M. Schlesinger, Jr., *A Thousand Days: John F. Kennedy in the White House* (Boston, MA: Houghton Mifflin, 1965), 210. Neustadt's role in the 1960 campaign and transition is discussed on pp. 122–24.
17 Trumbull Higgins, *The Perfect Failure: Kennedy, Eisenhower, and the CIA at the Bay of Pigs* (New York: W.W. Norton, 1987). On the changing of the landing site, see Don Bohning, "Site Change Called Fatal to Invasion," *Miami Herald*, January 5, 1997.
18 Irving L. Janis, *Groupthink: Psychological Studies of Policy Decisions and Fiascoes* (2nd ed. Boston: Houghton Mifflin, 1982).
19 Office of the Secretary of Defense, Historical Office, *The Ascendancy of the Secretary of Defense: Robert S. McNamara, 1961–1963* (Cold War Foreign Policy Series: Special Study 4, July 2013), p. 5.
20 President Kennedy secretly recorded the ExComm meetings, and the transcripts are available in Ernest May and Philip D. Zelikow, eds., *The Kennedy Tapes: Inside the White House During the Cuban Missile Crisis* (New York: W.W. Norton, 2002).
21 Don Oberdorfer, *The Turn: From the Cold War to a New Era: The United States and the Soviet Union, 1983–1990* (New York: Poseidon Press, 1991).
22 Much of the analysis in the Reagan and Bush 41 case studies is drawn from Meena Bose, "Bringing the Cold War to Closure: A Comparison of Presidential Leadership in the Reagan and Bush Administrations," essay prepared for the James MacGregor Burns Academy of Leadership, University of Maryland, January 2001. Special thanks to the Burns Academy for a Leadership Fellow award to complete this project.
23 Fred I. Greenstein, *The Presidential Difference: Leadership Style from FDR to Clinton* (New York: The Free Press, 2000), pp. 147–48.
24 Kiron K. Skinner, Annelise Anderson, and Martin Anderson, eds., *Reagan in His Own Hand: The Writings of Ronald Reagan that Reveal His Revolutionary Vision for America* (New York: Touchstone, 2001).
25 James P. Pfiffner, *The Modern Presidency,* (3rd ed., New York: Bedford/St. Martin's Press, 2000), p. 65.
26 George P. Shultz, *Turmoil and Triumph: Diplomacy, Power, and the Victory of the American Ideal* (New York: Charles Scribner's Sons, 1993), p. 312.
27 Shultz, *Turmoil and Triumph*, p. 497.
28 Quotation is in Interview of Michael Armacost by Don Oberdorfer, 20 April 1989, Box 2, Oberdorfer Papers, Mudd Library, Princeton University, p. 11. For more details on the luncheons, see Interview of George Shultz by Don Oberdorfer (Segment III–IV), 13 July 1989, Box 2, Oberdorfer Papers, Mudd Library, Princeton University, pp. 21–22.
29 Center for International and Security Studies at Maryland and the Brookings Institution, "The Role of the National Security Adviser," National Security Council Project Oral History Roundtables, 25 October 1999, p. 43.
30 Interview of Adm. William J. Crowe, Jr. by Don Oberdorfer, 16 November 1989, Box 2, Oberdorfer Papers, Mudd Library, Princeton University, p. 1.
31 Colin L. Powell and Joseph E. Persico, *My American Journey* (New York: Random House, 1995), p. 332.
32 Shultz, *Turmoil and Triumph*, p. 1080.
33 Meena Bose and Rosanna Perotti, eds., *From Cold War to New World Order: The Foreign Policy World of George Bush* (Westport, CT: Greenwood Publishing Group, 2002), pp. 156–57.
34 George Bush and Brent Scowcroft, *A World Transformed* (New York: Alfred A. Knopf, 1998; reprint, New York: Vintage Books, 1999), pp. 17–18.
35 Ibid.
36 James A. Baker III, *The Politics of Diplomacy: Revolution, War, & Peace, 1989–1992* (New York: G.P. Putnam's Sons, 1995), p. 21.

37 Oberdorfer, *From the Cold War to a New Era*, p. 332.
38 "The Role of the National Security Adviser," National Security Council Project Oral History Roundtables, p. 57.
39 Bush and Scowcroft, *A World Transformed*, p. 35.
40 Oberdorfer, *From the Cold War to a New Era*, p. 332.
41 Jack F. Matlock, *Autopsy on an Empire: The American Ambassador's Account of the Collapse of the Soviet Union* (New York: Random House, 1995), p. 185.
42 Interview of Carlucci by Oberdorfer, 5 March 1990, p. 14.
43 David Rothkopf examines national security policy making in the Bush 43 and Obama presidencies in *National Insecurity: American Leadership in an Age of Fear* (New York: Public Affairs, 2014).
44 Information on Bush's political background draws from Meena Bose, "Leadership Challenges in National Security," in *Rethinking Madam President*, ed. Lori Cox Han and Caroline Heldman (Boulder, CO: Lynne Rienner, 2007), pp. 169–83.
45 Commission on Presidential Debates, "The Second Gore-Bush Presidential Debate," Wake Forest University, Winston-Salem, NC, 11 October 2000.
46 Condoleezza Rice, "Promoting the National Interest," *Foreign Affairs* (January–February 2000): 45–62. Quotation on p. 54.
47 James P. Pfiffner, "The First MBA President: George W. Bush as Public Administrator," *Public Administration Review* (January/February 2007): 6–20. Quotation on p. 6.
48 Richard K. Herrmann with Michael J. Reese, "George W. Bush's Foreign Policy," in *The George W. Bush Presidency: Appraisals and Prospects,* ed. Colin Campbell and Bert A. Rockman (Washington, DC: CQ Press, 2004), p. 199. On Bush's decision to have Rice lead NSC meetings, see Jane Perlez, "Directive Says Rice, Bush Aide, Won't Be Upstaged by Cheney," *New York Times,* 16 February 2001.
49 Shirley Anne Warshaw, *The Co-Presidency of Bush and Cheney* (Stanford, CA: Stanford University Press, 2009), pp. 66–67, 237.
50 James P. Pfiffner, "President Bush as Chief Executive," in *Judging Bush*, eds. Robert Maranto, Tom Lansford, and Jeremy Johnson (Stanford, CA: Stanford University Press, 2009), pp. 58–74; George W. Bush, *Decision Points* (New York: Crown Publishers, 2010), pp. 87–94; Fred I. Greenstein, *The Presidential Difference: Leadership Style from FDR to Barack Obama*, (3rd ed., Princeton, NJ: Princeton University Press, 2009), pp. 198, 203. On Rice's role as NSC adviser, see Burke, *Honest Broker?*, ch. 6. Bob Woodward's three volumes on the Bush 43 presidency – *Bush at War* (New York: Simon & Schuster, 2002), *Plan of Attack* (New York: Simon & Schuster, 2004), and *State of Denial* (New York: Simon & Schuster, 2006) – provide highly informative and engaging assessments of Bush's national security decision making, based on extensive interviews with many participants.
51 Pfiffner, "President Bush as Chief Executive," pp. 61–62, 65–71; Pfiffner, *Power Play: The Bush Presidency and the Constitution* (Washington, DC: Brookings Institution Press, 2008); James Risen and Eric Lichtbau, "Bush Lets U.S. Spy on Callers Without Courts," *New York Times*, 16 December 2005; "Bush Says He Signed NSA Wiretap Order," www.cnn.com, 17 December 2005; Eric Lichtbau, "The Education of a 9/11 Reporter," www.slate.com, 26 March 2008; Constitutional Rights Foundation, "The Rule of Law in Dangerous Times," *Bill of Rights in Action* 22:3 (Fall 2006).
52 For a comprehensive assessment of Bush's foreign-policy decision making, particularly the influence of Vice President Cheney, see Peter Baker, *Days of Fire: Bush and Cheney in the White House* (New York: Doubleday, 2013).
53 For a summary biography of Barack Obama's life and political career, see University of Virginia Miller Center, "Essays about Barack Obama," at http://millercenter.org/president/obama.
54 Laura Rozen and Ben Smith, "Scoring Obama's Nat'l Security Team," *Politico*, 13 December 2009.
55 Karen DeYoung, "Obama's NSC Will Get New Power," *Washington Post*, 8 February 2009; Michael Gordon Jackson, "A Dramatically Different NSC? President Obama's

Use of the National Security Council," Paper presentation, Annual Meeting of the Western Political Science Association, Portland, Oregon, March 22–24, 2012; Scott Wilson, "James Jones to Step Down as National Security Adviser," *Washington Post*, 8 October 2010.

56 I.M. Destler, "Donilon to the Rescue?" *Foreign Affairs*, 13 October 2010; Linda Feldmann, "Why Susan Rice Withdrew Her Name as Secretary of State," *Christian Science Monitor*, at https://www.csmonitor.com/USA/Politics/2012/1213/Why-Susan-Rice-withdrew-her-name-as-secretary-of-State, 13 December 2012.

57 Mark Bowden examines how the Obama administration hunted down bin Laden in *The Finish: The Killing of Osama bin Laden* (New York: Atlantic Monthly Press, 2012). Bob Woodward explains Obama's decision making on Afghanistan in *Obama's Wars* (New York: Simon & Schuster, 2011). On the debate about Obama's decision to withdraw U.S. forces from Iraq, see Alice Fordham, "Fact Check: Did Obama Withdraw from Iraq Too Soon, Allowing ISIS to Grow?" National Public Radio *Morning Edition,* 19 December 2015. On Obama's reticence to take military action in Syria, see Patrice Taddonio, "'The President Blinked': Why Obama Changed Course on the 'Red Line' in Syria," *Frontline*, 25 May 2015.

58 Karen DeYoung, "How the Obama White House Runs Foreign Policy," *Washington Post*, 4 August 2015. Also see Jeffrey Goldberg, "A Withering Critique of Obama's National Security Council," *The Atlantic,* 12 November 2014; and Stephen M. Walt, "Barack Obama Was a Foreign Policy Failure," *Foreign Policy*, 18 January 2017.

59 Maggie Haberman, Matthew Rosenberg, Matt Apuzzo, and Glenn Thrush, "Michael Flynn Resigns as National Security Adviser," *New York Times*, 13 February 2017.

60 Carol D. Leonnig, Adam Entous, Devlin Barrett, and Matt Zapotosky, "Michael Flynn Pleads Guilty to Lying to FBI on Contacts with Russian Ambassador," *Washington Post*, 1 December 2017; Gregory Krieg, "From 'Lock Her Up' to (Maybe) Locked Up," *CNNPolitics.com*, 1 December 2017.

61 Robert Costa, Abby Phillip, and Karen DeYoung, "Bannon Removed from Security Council as McMaster Asserts Control," *Washington Post*, 5 April 2017; Rosie Gray, "H.R. McMaster Cleans House at the National Security Council," *The Atlantic*, 2 August 2017.

62 www.whitehouse.gov/nsc, early December 2017.

63 Rothkopf's description of Scowcroft is in Goldberg, "A Withering Critique of Obama's National Security Council." For more specifics of Scowcroft's leadership at the NSC, see Burke, *Honest Broker*, and Bartholomew Sparrow, *The Strategist: Brent Scowcroft and the Call of National Security* (New York: Public Affairs, 2015).

64 Dwight D. Eisenhower, *The White House Years: Mandate for Change, 1953–1956* (Garden City, NY: Doubleday, 1963), p. 114.

6

TOWARD A SMALLER WHITE HOUSE NATIONAL SECURITY STAFF

A look at the present in historical perspective

I. M. (Mac) Destler

In November 2000, Ivo Daalder and I published a twelve-page "Brookings Policy Brief" on the National Security Council. In it we tracked the growth of the NSC policy staff over a 40-year period, from an activist ten or so under John F. Kennedy to around a hundred at the end of the Clinton administration. We found this staff growth excessive. We particularly decried the Council's expansion in the 1990s, which "made the NSC more like a government agency— preoccupied with the many details of foreign policy—and less like a presidential staff focused on managing a competitive policy process."[1]

That essay was released one day after the November 7th election. We had planned to address it to the president-elect by name, but his identity had not yet been determined, so we labeled our product "A New NSC for a New Administration." We pointed to various "pitfalls" in prior regimes, noted that growth in staff size was the "default position" in past Council experience as successive leaders yielded to "the natural temptation to take on new tasks" and "to broaden the focus of their work," and urged "professional restraint" to resist these pressures. The staff, we said, "should be *no more than 40–45 substantive professionals* (emphasis added)." This would make it "akin to the late Reagan, Bush and early Clinton administrations."[2]

Daalder had served on Tony Lake's NSC staff under President Bill Clinton. A bit over eight years later, President Obama would name him the United States Representative to the NATO Alliance. I had been writing about the NSC for roughly thirty years. Yet it would be hard to find a recommendation that was less vindicated by subsequent practice.

Fast-forward to 2015. The Obama administration was moving to "fine-tune" or "right-size" the National Security Council staff.[3] So said its head, presidential national security adviser Susan Rice and her chief of staff, Suzy George. As part of this effort, they were "reversing the trend of growth across successive

Administrations of both parties ... gradually right-sizing the NSC staff."[4] But the base from which they began working was now, by common estimates, a staff of four hundred, which would be double that of the George W. Bush administration, quadruple the peak under Clinton, and nine to ten times the Reagan-Bush-early Clinton level that we recommended. By mid-summer 2015, Rice told *Washington Post* correspondent Karen DeYoung, "the staff had been cut by 6 percent,"[5] which would make it around 375.

These numbers are likely on the high side. The staff counts that Daalder and I reported in 2000 included solely policy professionals, not cable-sorters and other operational staff in the White House Situation Room. The Obama White House was not at all eager to provide precise numbers. But DeYoung, who has tracked the NSC as much as any contemporary analyst, reported that "slightly more than half of today's NSC personnel are what Rice calls 'policy people.'"[6] This would put the core staff's size at around 225–250. And one significant contributor to staff growth was Obama's decision back in 2009, defensible in substance, to incorporate the formerly separate Homeland Security Council staff of about 35 professionals.

Putting all this together, NSC staff growth under Obama does not seem quite so egregious. Still, the enhanced size clearly generated serious problems. The administration acknowledged the need for "fewer, more focused meetings, less paper to produce and consume, and more communication ..."[7] Others were harsher, arguing that the size and scope of the NSC has led to micro-management, pulling far too many issues into the White House orbit, and simultaneously clogging the process of decision as meeting after meeting ends in irresolution. One prescient analysis summarized a key problem as "Too Many Meetings, Too Little Seniority and Decisions."[8] According to one staff listing, there were recently no fewer than 22 NSC people with the title, "Special Assistant to the President."[9] ("Special Assistant to the President for National Security Affairs" was, of course, the title inaugurated by Eisenhower and held by Kennedy's McGeorge Bundy, who was the first in this job to manage day-to-day presidential business, essentially inventing the modern national security adviser position. Chief Nixon aide H.R. Haldeman removed the word "special" from the title because, he recounted, no one could tell him what it meant. It is not clear that anybody can explain it today!)

This chapter will argue that in recent years NSC staff growth has truly gotten out of hand, that late Obama "right-sizing" efforts only scratched the surface, and that the time has come for truly radical down-sizing. It is not, the author must admit, the product of the sort of detailed empirical research that supported many of his previous writings on the topic.[10] It is appropriate here, however, to put forward in general terms some of the reasons why the staff has grown. Then we will set forth some reasons why that growth needs to be reversed. Finally, we will suggest what principles might guide a genuine "right-sizing" of the NSC staff, and suggest, tentatively, how we might get there from here.

Explanations for staff growth

The most frequently cited reason for NSC staff growth is enhanced responsibilities. The world has become more complex, it is said. The issue agenda has broadened, engaging more agencies. This broadening has made it ever more unlikely that cabinet agencies will be able to apply the comprehensive perspective to these issues that presidents require.

There is clearly some truth in this assessment. The number of independent nations continues to grow. The rise of Asia renders insufficient the longstanding U.S. priority to Europe and the Middle East. Economic challenges have risen to rival security threats. Most dramatic of all, perhaps, is the post-9/11 rise of terrorism to top-tier policy status, exemplified in recent years by the emergence of the "Islamic State of Iraq and the Levant" (ISIL), aka *Daesh*. As noted above, Obama's decision to bring the formerly separate homeland security staff into the NSC has been a significant contributor to staff growth.

Moreover, over the decades policy staffs linked to top officials have been growing across the government. Upon assuming the position of secretary of state in 1949, Dean Acheson recalled that "a vitally important step within the Department was the selection from among the young officers of a personal assistant for me"—someone who was "a bachelor, bright, pleasant, knowledgeable about the Department, energetic, and responsible."[11] Young Luke Battle, pulled from the Canada desk, was apparently all this historic Secretary needed for personal policy and operational support. Contrast that with the plethora of aides today on the personal staffs of the Secretary of State, the Deputy Secretary, the Under Secretaries, etc. And there are parallels in the other lead national security agencies—in the international security affairs offices of the Pentagon, for example.

So staffs generally have grown. So, as noted, has the policy agenda. But the challenges of today do not seem orders of magnitude different from those of the forties—or the sixties. Truman, Acheson, and Acheson's predecessor, George Marshall, faced a desperate Europe threatened with economic and political collapse, an incipient Cold War with Russia, Russia going nuclear, a surging independence movement in India and other longtime colonies, and a communist revolution in China, not to mention the creation of new policy institutions both domestic and international—DoD, CIA, NATO, IMF, World Bank, GATT. Like the Obama administration, the leaders of the first postwar decade also faced sustained political attack, particularly on China policy.

The Kennedy-Johnson sixties brought recurrent crises over Berlin, China going nuclear, an emerging common market in Europe, the Cuban missile crisis, war between China and India, war between Pakistan and India, and—of course—what became our all-consuming war in Vietnam.

Are today's challenges really greater? Doubtful. More numerous? Maybe. More politically contested? To some degree: the depth and bitterness of partisan polarization on foreign policy today is probably unique in the postwar period, though the Joseph McCarthy period of the late forties/early fifties must be rated a close second. But surely the present challenges are not ten or fifteen times as great as those faced by predecessors.

So important causes of staff growth must lie elsewhere.

A key driver is the fact that NSC aides are always overloaded with work—managing voluminous information flows, keeping on top of multiple issues, cultivating relationships across the government—and find it relatively easy to acquire help in handling this work. As one good recent study puts it,

> the NSC relies quite heavily on detailed civil servants, foreign service officers, and uniformed military who are placed at the White House for one-to-two-year rotations, even as their home agencies pay their salaries during this time. These "detailees" make up more than two-thirds of the NSC staff. The availability of this "free" labor pool—often highly talented, motivated mid-career staff who see service at the NSC as critical to career enhancement—has been attractive for the NSC leadership.[12]

This labor pool is also attractive, it should be added, to second- or third-tier NSC aides who seek help with *their* heavy workloads.

Problems with staff growth

Around the summer of 1978, I was working as a senior associate at the Carnegie Endowment for International Peace, running a project on Executive-Congressional Relations in Foreign Policy. As I was wandering somewhere on the top floor of the Eleven Dupont Circle Building, an excited secretary came running, saying something like: "Mac, Mac, the White House is calling!" Inured to Washington ways, I had the presence of mind to respond, *"Who* in the White House?" It turned out to be a summer intern. Perhaps seeking payback for the multiple interviews he had granted me on selling the Panama Canal treaties to Congress, a senior congressional liaison aide had tasked his short-term helper with writing a quasi-official history of the successful ratification campaign, and told him that I would be a good source!

I did, of course, talk to that intern. And I would be the last to criticize either him, his boss, or the work that he did. But as a longtime fan of Richard Neustadt, I recalled what that Presidential studies guru had said years before: "'This is the White House calling' means less every decade." For as White House staff expands, the proportion of those with White House titles who can actually speak for the president must shrink. We will never have more than one president, and that person will have trusting relationships with only a limited number of senior aides.[13]

The same principle holds, of course, for the aides of those aides. Henry Kissinger, whose NSC policy staff in 1970 numbered "only" in the thirties, found it necessary to create a *de facto* inner staff of assistants privy to his real thoughts and priorities (and not to all of those either). Kissinger was, of course, notorious for his secret mode of operation, but the principle still holds more generally—beyond a certain relatively low point, the accumulation of staff to a senior official means that most are no longer "staff" to her or him in any real sense. They cannot act for their leader in any direct sense, for they lack reliable connection to what s/he thinks and what s/he wants.

But these aides are typically talented, knowledgeable, and motivated individuals. They are where they are because of this talent and because of their ambition: they want to help shape the world. In the absence of direct relationships with top leaders, they inevitably search for ways to have impact. This will involve invoking the White House or NSC name. It will involve convening meetings to "get on top of" issues large and not-so-large. They can occasionally, of course, do great damage to a president—witness one Colonel Oliver North in the second Reagan administration.

But more often, in their genuine efforts to do good, they just clog the process.

The more staff aides there are, the larger the number of talented people who have to pull or push issues upward, to compete for the time and attention of top leadership, and to tax the time of those in the agencies. The more they will, intentionally or not, tie the hands of those agency officials. And since the number of top officials cannot, by its nature, increase, their demands will generate a bottleneck at the top. The result will be more NSC deputies' committee meetings, more meetings feeding into those meetings, etc. And because too many issues are being driven upward, an unintended result will be greater frustration at all levels of government.

What staff should be doing

So there is a problem. One "solution" would be to eliminate the NSC policy staff entirely, returning the Council to the role intended in the 1940s by its primary initial conceptualizer, James Forrestal. Policy would be the province of the great Cabinet departments, State above all. The Council would embody the Cabinet heads working collectively. Not a few foreign service officers have dreamed of such a change; so have some defense military and civilian officials across the river. This author once put forward a moderate version of this reform, calling for abolition not of the staff but of its head.[14] Concerned about the process-distorting impact of several assistants to the president for national security affairs, I urged in 1980 that this post be eliminated and that the staff be headed by the sole NSC official actually named in the statute, the Executive Secretary.

Ronald Reagan actually launched his administration with a variant of this reform, keeping the title but subordinating its first holder, Richard Allen, to his primary policy adviser, Edwin Meese. Secretary of State Alexander Haig moved aggressively to fill the leadership vacuum, but his demanding style provoked a backlash among his Cabinet and White House colleagues. Within a year, the

President had brought on a new, truly senior national security adviser, longtime Reagan associate William Clark. Within eighteen months, Haig was out of a job.

This was just one of many demonstrations over the period since World War II that presidents want, and feel they need, a senior, personal foreign policy adviser with a supporting staff. That, in practice, certainly decides the matter. But beyond the important question of presidential preference, there are matters of management principle that argue for effective policy staff aides at the White House level. So it is useful to step back at this point and reflect on what roles staff aides ought to play.

If a president depends solely on his "line" officers (Cabinet secretaries, agency heads) he[15] will limit the information flow to himself and become victim to least-common-denominator compromises among his senior subordinates, often reached without his knowledge or input. He needs staff to inform him, to help him shape real options for decision, to communicate decisions he makes, and to oversee implementation. He needs them to manage his substantial personal, day-to-day role in making foreign policy, including dealings with foreign counterparts. He needs them to protect him—from actions in "his" government that entail serious substantive or political risk.

But the president also needs supportive strong officials elsewhere in the foreign policy government—the secretaries of state and defense, but also their subordinates, down at least to the assistant secretary level. Without them empowered to do *his* work, the policy capacity of his administration will be severely limited. As I wrote decades ago, there need therefore to be "lines of confidence" stretching from the president to these officials.[16] Staff needs to nurture these lines. McGeorge Bundy commented in 1980 that the national security adviser should see himself (more recently, herself) as working for the secretary of state as well as the president, facilitating communication between these two busy, heavily scheduled individuals.[17] Steve Hadley, George W. Bush's second-term national security adviser, has made a similar argument on more than one occasion. And this point can be generalized to the relations of NSC senior directors (with those misleading "Special Assistant" titles) to, say, assistant secretaries of state and defense.

Presidential staff needs, of course, to assure that responsible officials are acting in accord with presidential and administration policy. But assuming agency officials are doing so, that staff needs not to dominate or overpower them but to *empower* them, to work with them, to link them to presidential authority so they can be effective in doing the president's work. Staff aides need to be strong and purposive, but also subtle, enticing cooperation. Their aim should not be to command a top-down process through their roles as chairs of interagency committees, but to build policy allies across the government and connect them to what senior officials want and need. They should enforce fidelity to policy *ends* but allow some leeway on implementation *means*.

It is useful to cite two examples of this being accomplished. Carter administration policy making is best remembered for the substantive, stylistic, and personal conflict between National Security Adviser Zbigniew Brzezinski and Secretary of State Cyrus R. Vance, particularly concerning relations with the Soviet Union. But from the time that Egyptian President Anwar Sadat made his historic visit to Jerusalem in November 1977, NSC aide William Quandt worked hand-in-glove with Assistant Secretary of State Harold Saunders to build the policy and political foundation for what became the Camp David Accords between Egypt and Israel. And they worked in particular in support of Secretary Vance, whose role was critical to the talks' success[18] (It helped that Saunders had served on the NSC staffs of several prior administrations, and Quandt had had previous NSC experience under Henry Kissinger.)

What was the exception under Carter was very much the rule under President George H. W. Bush and his exemplary national security adviser, Brent Scowcroft. Their administration, of course, saw the collapse of the Warsaw Pact, the unification of Germany, and the reversal of Iraqi dictator Sadaam Hussein's conquest of Kuwait. U.S. policy making across this range of historic events featured continuous collaboration among, for example, senior staff aides Robert Gates, Richard Haass and Condoleezza Rice at the NSC; Robert Kimmitt, Philip Zelikow, and Robert Zoellick at State; and Arnold Kanter, who played important roles in both locations. They provided the operational and substantive underpinning for the uniquely productive and collegial policy process at Cabinet level under Bush, Scowcroft, and Secretary of State James Baker. As NSC aide Peter Rodman noted, "[T]he Bush administration … consisted of grown-ups working together in a civilized way, and a president who made sure of it."[19]

In both of these administration cases, the cooperation involved a small group of people who grew to trust one another. This reinforces, in this author's mind, the central argument of this essay—that policy management staffs work best when they are relatively small. When, say, two or three NSC people are working an issue area (Europe, the Middle East), they cannot hope to handle issues themselves and so must engage departmental officials. If that number grows to six or more under a senior director, however, with a score or more of such subdivisions, this type of constructive, informal cooperation is less likely to emerge. For the NSC staff is then transformed into a bureaucracy with its inevitable rigidities, jurisdictional lines and likely turf conflicts.

So lacking persuasive counter-argument, this analyst must return to the Daalder–Destler recommendation of sixteen years ago: an NSC staff of 40–45, augmented perhaps by ten at most to cover homeland security.

This would mean, in turn, cutting back sharply on the number of organizational subdivisions. A useful rule of thumb might be to have no more NSC senior directors than the National Security Adviser and his principal deputy could work with continuously and productively on a daily basis, building strong relationships of mutual trust.

How do we get there from here? By far the best person to accomplish this is the president, of course, and by far the best time is the beginning of an administration. When Jimmy Carter came to office in 1977, he decided immediately to cut back sharply on the size of presidential staff, including the NSC. Seeing this handwriting on the wall, newly designated national security assistant Zbigniew Brzezinski recruited a staff numbering in the thirties, about 20 percent smaller than that of his predecessor. This did not prevent him from emerging, over time, as Carter's primary foreign policy adviser.

Whatever the size of the staff, it will be composed of very busy people. And their subordinates will be hyper-busy as well. The temptation will be to bring in more men and women to help. As one modest counter, however, we could do worse than reach back once again into that frenetic period in the aftermath of World War II.

About eighteen months after taking office, President Harry S Truman turned to George C. Marshall, architect of victory in that war, to serve as his secretary of state. In late April 1947, Marshall called in foreign service officer George Kennan and asked him to head a new staff to engage in policy planning. The immediate need? How to respond to a Europe on the verge of collapse. The younger man asked for instructions. The response? "Avoid trivia."

As Kennan recounted in his memoirs, he had, "on no notice at all, to scratch together something in the nature of a staff." It was clear, he continued, "that we would have to draw on people whose greatest qualifications, as in my own case, were simply that they were favorably known, and available." The staff was formally established within a week, and Kennan quickly recruited *five* men of varied backgrounds and specialties. Within a month of Marshall's mandate, the staff delivered him a paper with their findings and recommendations. The main elements of the paper found their way into Marshall's historic commencement address at Harvard, one month to the day from the staff's creation. There followed the Marshall Plan which saved Europe.[20]

Kennan plus five people. And they were very busy that month!

Epilogue: Beginnings with Trump

When the least-prepared President-elect in American history speaks (without much knowledge) of abandoning the pillars of post-World War II U.S. foreign policy (NATO, free trade, etc.), questions like the size of the NSC staff pale in significance. The question becomes, rather, will he assemble an at least minimally competent foreign policy team possessing the background and prudence that he lacks, and will he listen to their advice and proceed with due caution as he learns on the job?

The initial signs were not promising. From his deeply protectionist Inaugural Address to his designation of Michael Flynn as national security adviser and alt-right advocate Steve Bannon as chief White House planner, Trump entered office seeming ready to practice what he preached.

But reality intruded early. Less than a month into his tenure, Flynn was out, having discussed economic sanctions with the Russian ambassador during the transition and then lied about the conversation with the Vice President. He won the distinction of serving a shorter period of time in that position than any of his 22 predecessors, and he seemed destined to spend the next portion of his life as a target of multiple investigations into Russian interference in the 2016 presidential election.

His successor, General H. R. McMaster, was greeted with relief by the Washington policy community. He was a respected defense intellectual who immediately began sending reassuring messages at home and abroad. Together with Defense Secretary James Mattis, he acted to counter some of the President's impulsive Twitter messages. So, with perhaps less effectiveness, did Secretary of State Rex Tillerson, who failed to build a strong supporting team in his department.

McMaster did not, however, quickly establish the sort of close relationship with the President which has, in the past, been a prerequisite for long and effective service in the national security adviser job.[21] Nor was he always able to prevail on staffing decisions. He could only have gained, however, when Bannon was first removed from the NSC Principals Committee, and then left the White House staff in August to pursue his far-right agenda from the outside.

Thus, as this is written in fall 2017, the President has implemented some of his promised changes: withdrawal from the Trans-Pacific Partnership (TPP) trade agreement and the Paris climate accords—but not most. There have been ongoing, fractious efforts to renegotiate the North American Free Trade Agreement (NAFTA). But Trump's reported determination to withdraw from the Korea–U.S. FTA (in the midst of growing tensions with North Korea over nuclear weapons, no less) was reportedly overcome by the united opposition of his foreign policy advisers. Whether this point-counterpoint pattern would continue was anybody's guess.

Notes

1 Ivo H. Daalder and I. M. Destler, "A New NSC for a New Administration," Brookings Institution Policy Brief no. 68, November 2000, pp. 3–4.
2 Ibid., p. 10.
3 Suzy George, "Fine-Tuning NSC Staff Processes and Procedures," White House website, June 22, 2015.
4 Ibid.
5 Karen DeYoung, "How the Obama White House Runs Foreign Policy," *Washington Post*, August 4, 2015.
6 Ibid.
7 George, "Fine-Tuning NSC Staff."
8 Shawn Brimley, Dr. Dafna H. Rand, Julianne Smith, and Jacob Stokes, "Enabling Decision: Shaping the National Security Council for the Next President," Center for a New American Security, June 2015, p. 5.
9 Wikipedia, "The US National Security Council," unsourced.
10 See, for example, *President, Bureaucrats, and Foreign Policy: The Politics of Organizational Reform* (Princeton University Press, 1972 and 1974); "National Security Advice to U.S. Presidents: Some Lessons from Thirty Years" (*World Politics,* January 1977); "National Security Management: What Presidents Have Wrought" (*Political Science Quarterly,* Winter 1980–1981); *Our Own Worst Enemy The Unmaking of American*

Foreign Policy (Simon and Schuster, 1984 and 1985, with Leslie Gelb and Anthony Lake); Oral History Roundtables on the National Security Council (seven in number), Brookings Institution and University of Maryland, 1998–2000, co-edited with Ivo H. Daalder; and most recently, *In the Shadow of the Oval Office* (Simon and Schuster, 2009, with Daalder).

11 Dean Acheson, *Present at the Creation: My Years in the State Department* (New York: W.W. Norton & Company, 1969), p. 256.

12 Brimley et al., "Enabling Decision," p. 3.

13 Of course some, like Kennedy, will have a respectable number of such relationships; others, like Nixon, will have very, very few.

14 "A Job That Doesn't Work," *Foreign Policy*, Spring 1980.

15 I use the male pronoun for convenience, recognizing the distinct possibility that the next president may be a "she."

16 *Presidents, Bureaucrats, and Foreign Policy*, esp. chap. 9.

17 See, for example, McGeorge Bundy, "Mr. Reagan's Security Aide," *New York Times*, November 16, 1980.

18 William B. Quandt, *Peace Process: American Diplomacy and the Arab-Israeli Conflict Since 1967* (Brookings and University of California Press, 1993), p. 329.

19 Quoted in Ivo H. Daalder and I. M. Destler, Moderators, "The Bush Administration National Security Council," National Security Council Oral History Roundtable, Center for International and Security Studies at Maryland and The Brookings Institution, April 29, 1999, p. 4. This 60-page transcript includes many other comparable characterizations of the Bush-Scowcroft-Baker process. On the Iraq conflict of 1990–1991, see also Richard N. Haass, *War of Necessity; War of Choice: A Memoir of Two Iraq Wars* (Simon and Schuster, 2009). On the revolution in Europe, see Philip Zelikow and Condoleezza Rice, *Germany Unified and Europe Transformed* (Harvard University Press, 1997).

20 George F. Kennan, *Memoirs 1925–1950* (Boston: Little, Brown and Company), chap. 14.

21 Eli Lake, "Washington Loves General McMaster, But Trump Doesn't," *Bloomberg News*, May 8, 2017, www.bloomberg.com/view/articles/2017-05-08/washington-loves-general-mcmaster-but-trump-doesn-t.

7

HOW WE DECIDE WHAT WE NEED

Planning the future force

David S. C. Chu, with the assistance of Allison F. Taylor

As is well known, the United States' Department of Defense uses a deeply analytic approach to planning its future course, both for the forces it intends to field, and for the personnel so important to the success of those forces. This extensive role of analysis is a modern development, unfolding since the 1960s, and only recently emulated by other militaries.[1]

Like any important intellectual construct, what's subsumed under "defense analysis" has changed over the course of those five-plus decades, as decision makers adjusted its features to deal with its shortcomings and to respond to changing circumstances. But the changes in response to the circumstances of the last quarter century—the end of the Cold War, the rise of terrorism and the advent of what some are calling "hybrid" or "gray zone" conflict—may not have gone far enough.

This chapter attempts briefly to sketch how the U.S. system of defense planning has evolved over the last half-century, especially with regard to balancing needs against resource limits, and in developing "human capital". For each, it offers potential changes that in the authors' view would enhance the Department's ability to respond more effectively to today's challenges, and the likely challenges of tomorrow.

The origins of contemporary analytic practices

The forward planning system used by the U.S. Department of Defense originates from research and reflection at RAND in the 1950s.[2] Charles Hitch brought the ideas he and his colleagues had generated to the Pentagon when he was named DoD Comptroller in 1961, as part of Secretary of Defense Robert McNamara's team. Even today, these ideas are remarkable in the federal bureaucracy, especially the notion that budgets should ultimately be grounded in a view of what's necessary to achieve an agency's long-run objectives, and that the program laying out what's necessary should look several years into the future, to highlight the resource implications of today's decisions. Put differently, budgets should be developed by looking forward (vice looking back at recent experience), and decision makers should understand on a multi-year basis what their choices imply (vice starting programs via the "thin edge of the wedge", as it's cynically phrased, focusing just on the initial requirements).[3] The Planning, Programming and Budgeting System established in the 1960s continues to the present day as a central feature of how the Department of Defense thinks about its future.[4]

The concomitant achievement of the McNamara era was to impose the framework of cost-effectiveness analysis as the basis for defense choices, vice expert judgment. Again, this is not necessarily the norm for public program construction, and it was certainly controversial when introduced in Defense. Indeed, the Systems Analysis staff members (who constituted the core of what might be termed McNamara's "intellectual shock troops") were denounced as "whiz kids", and as late as 1980 the Republican Party platform called for the abolition of the Systems Analysis office (by then relabeled Program Analysis and Evaluation).

But McNamara served as Secretary long enough that the Military Services decided to send some of their most promising officers to the same kinds of graduate programs from which the whiz kids received their training, presumably to be able to defend Service positions the Systems Analysis staff members were challenging, using the same tools. The long-term effect, however, was the reverse of that presumptive intent, with the returning officers adopting a similar outlook as they rose to senior positions—including, at the four-star level, Wayne Downing, Dave Jeremiah and Don Pilling.

Thanks also to Secretary McNamara's leadership, and that of his successors, cost-effectiveness as a test for decisions extended beyond the formulation of how resources might be applied to meet military needs. It became the standard by which investment choices were compared. In fact, the documents reporting on analyses of alternatives (as they now tend to be named) were at one time known as Cost and Operational Effectiveness Analyses.

The use of empirical analysis to guide DoD decisions extends to perhaps its most important resource, its people—at least those in uniform. Since the advent (or really, return) of the All-Volunteer Force in 1973, the central human resource challenge has been ensuring a steady supply of quality personnel for military service. Because an important element in meeting that challenge is establishing a competitive compensation package within the DoD budget constraint, economic analysis has played a central role. Indeed, some credit Walter Oi's estimate that the necessary wage rate would be affordable as critical to the political decision to proceed.[5]

Empirical analysis has sustained the success of the All-Volunteer Force in the succeeding decades. In the 1980s experiments were used to help decide cognitive objectives for the enlisted force (reacting to the weak quality of the 1970s),[6] and experiments were also used to determine optimal enlistment bonus policies.[7]

In later years, the Department turned to the National Academy of Sciences to recommend empirically the balance between desired quality standards and the cost high standards impose.[8]

The Congress mandated Quadrennial Reviews of Military Compensation that typically took on a deeply empirical character, starting even before the decision to return to an All-Volunteer Force. The Ninth QRMC set the cash compensation standard that guided policy for the first decade of the 21st century, correcting the retention shortfalls that had plagued the 1990s, and undergirding the use of an All-Volunteer Force for sustained combat operations.[9]

The analytic emphasis in decision making for the Department of Defense reflects Executive Branch leadership, made possible by the 1958 amendments to the National Security Act (and subsequent legislation) that clarified and strengthened the role of the Secretary of Defense, including his authority over investment decisions. Besides allowing Secretary McNamara to impose cost-effectiveness analyses and the Planning, Programming and Budgeting System, you can see the exercise of that authority in the creation of Defense Agencies and other entities that established central control over key policy decisions (e.g., the creation of the Joint Strategic Targeting and Planning Staff by Secretary McElroy in August 1960).

Nonetheless, in the initial years of strong Secretarial leadership the Congress frequently criticized the analytic approach to Defense decision making. The steadfastness—and adaptations—of Executive Branch practice slowly changed that view, with the result that the 2009 Weapons Systems Acquisition Reform Act celebrated the use of analysis, and mandated its more extensive employment.

How, then, did the DoD analytic environment evolve such that once-controversial practices are now accepted? And how should it focus to confront successfully the issues with which the Department is now wrestling?

Key developments in PPBS

Three changes to PPBS created the essential features of resource analysis and decision making in today's DoD.

First, Secretary Laird adopted the practice of fiscal guidance against which the constituent elements of DoD (including the Military Departments) develop their program proposals (the Program Objective Memoranda, or POMs). *Ex-ante* fiscal limits were not imposed in the early years of PPBS, for fear that innovative proposals might not compete well against established programs.[10] And the initiative lay almost entirely with the staff of the Office of the Secretary of Defense. Besides creating a significant mismatch between desired programs and available resources (with the budget review trimming the program to synchronize with fiscal reality), this approach spawned deep resentment in the Military Departments. Secretary Laird's changes essentially reversed the process. The POMs returned initiative to the Military Departments, but their proposals were constrained by the fiscal guidance, and subject to OSD's review.

Second, consultation on the merits of the POMs and challenges to them took on an organized character with the creation of the Defense Resources Board in the late 1970s.[11] As strengthened in the 1980s by Secretary Weinberger and his Deputy, Frank Carlucci, it brought together all the principals—both from the Military Departments and OSD—for an organized discussion of the issues. While the forum has changed with each Secretary and Deputy Secretary's preferences, the notion that a Board of principals should advise remains a key feature of the system. In essence, the Board gives "voice" to all key elements of the Department.

Third, Secretary Weinberger brought the operating elements of the Department—what we now call the Combatant Commands—into the advisory process. Deeply unpopular with the Military Departments at first, sometimes producing heated disagreements among military leaders in front of the Secretary (to the consternation of the Joint Staff), this ensures that the users of Defense programs have an important say in their formulation, even if the exact mechanism for their advice again varies with the preferences of each Secretary.

Shortcomings of PPBS and the implications for a future agenda

There should be no doubt that PPBS improved the process of deciding what DoD needs. Perhaps the best compliment to the contemporary model of PPBS was paid by the recent Secretary of the Department of Homeland Security. Secretary Johnson adopted that model, with little change, as his instrument for pulling together the disparate elements of his Department into a more coherent and focused whole.

Nonetheless, critics of PPBS cite a number of shortcomings; these criticisms create an agenda for future improvement.

First, it can be slow, making it difficult to respond to a quickly changing security environment. Some of the difficulty in reacting quickly reflects the Constitutional authority of Congress over appropriations, and the restrictions Congress has imposed legislatively on their execution. But some reflects a failure to automate the translation of decisions into program and budget detail. Why, for example, is the Budget Estimate Submission (BES) submitted by the Department's constituent elements as a separate document once program decisions are made? Why could not the BES be generated automatically through estimating equations once those decisions are taken, then adjusted for any important factors omitted from the software? Not only would this cut perhaps several months from the process, it would improve discipline (no longer could one hide an evasion of decisions in the BES). And it would make it straightforward to create alternative budget proposals quickly as circumstances change.

Second, the PPBS time horizon (currently five years) is short relative to the time needed to realize the effects of the investments it authorizes (typically several years). It's long been observed that some of the most important issues lie just beyond the edge of that horizon (e.g., the "bow wave"). In the early years the Department sought to deal with this issue via Extended Planning Annexes, and in 1992–1993 created the first Defense Program Projection, intended to cover for three program periods (then 18 years) the resource needs associated with established policy choices. (At least one observer credits the DPP with changing President Clinton's view of the needed budget trajectory for Defense.[12]) The Department's use of this mechanism has waned—although the Congressional Budget Office publishes its similar analysis, often raising important concerns about the Defense program.[13] It would be straightforward to re-energize this process within DoD, and to use the projection as a key element in deciding what DoD needs.

Such use is critical if DoD is to deal with a third criticism: That the current process largely ignores two-thirds of the resource requirements, the operating costs of the force.[14] It is now widely recognized that unless operating costs are confronted systematically, likely budget limits will sharply constrain DoD's ability to invest in new systems. The concern is expressed typically about personnel costs, which alone comprise over half the Defense budget (and the next section of this paper takes up the personnel issue).

The operating cost challenge involves more than the compensation cost per military person (the current commotion), however. Operations and Maintenance costs have been rising in real terms about 2.5 percent per year per active-duty member for several decades. Each new weapon system costs more to operate per platform than its predecessor (although it's hoped that's mitigated by delivering more capability per platform). The Chairman of the House Armed Services Committee recognized the need to deal with operating costs early in the development of systems in language for the FY2017 National Defense Authorization Act.[15]

A fourth criticism of PPBS is that shares of the constituent elements change little from year to year, especially the share of the Military Departments in "peacetime". You could argue this reflects a competitive equilibrium, with the Military Departments competing successfully against each other for budget share; if they're equally good competitors, you wouldn't necessarily expect shares to change.

But it's possible that deciding fiscal guidance on a mission basis would produce a different result. The Department attempted using mission allocations to set fiscal guidance in the first post-Cold War Defense program. Although the allocations had the *ex-ante* support of the principals, once it became clear how the mission allocation would affect the individual Military Departments, it lost the support of a key player, and the Secretary was compelled to adjust the guidance accordingly.[16]

By itself, challenging shares is not necessarily a reason to refocus PPBS on missions (vice forces, the current organizing principle). But mission budgeting is attractive for two important reasons: It focuses the debate on outcomes, and it helps the Department understand the resources needed to accomplish its missions. That might lead to different decisions about what's needed.

While planning and allocation of resources on a mission basis are not central elements of the American PPBS process, some of our allies approach this issue differently. Both the United Kingdom and Australia conduct capability-based planning and resource allocation on a mission area basis in advance of program development. In both of these countries, the analyses are conducted at the joint level of warfare, with integrated teams of ministry staff (i.e., Joint Staff), and Service experts.[17] Among other ministries with which the United States works closely, Colombia and the Philippines are implementing capability-based planning, and the Republic of Korea is actively considering its adoption.[18]

Focusing on outcomes would also deal with a fifth criticism of PPBS—that the leading "P" is largely silent. Yes, there is a planning process, but the public documents in which its conclusions are reflected typically are denounced as containing too little of real value. And the internal guidance documents, which are the basis for the POMs, are often notable for their lack of quantitative content.

One of the corollary criticisms of the Defense planning process is its slowness in reacting to real-world developments. That's certainly a problem for the formal "war plans"—technically separate from the documents guiding resource allocation. One might ask why such a separation exists, and why in similar fashion decisions about deploying forces are taken without reference to the Military Department Secretaries, whose function is to "organize, train and equip". Recognizing this dysfunction, the Defense Science Board recommended their inclusion in what amounts to a "war council".[19]

A final criticism of PPBS is that it unduly focuses on future budgets, without appropriate consideration of the lessons from implementation of past budgets—lessons that might affect what we think we need. (Some do call it PPBES, with "E" representing execution.) When the Congress mandated a two-year budget in the 1980s, the Department did use the "off" year to begin exploring implementation issues. (A two-year budget might also improve responsiveness to changes, and execution generally, if there were sufficient flexibility for the Department to reallocate funds based on changing circumstances.) But when Congress failed to enact a two-year budget, and later dropped the requirement for its submission, the notion of an "Implementation Review" likewise perished.

Decisions about the most important resource, and creating a "force of the future"

"Human capital"—people, their skills and esprit—lie at the heart of any successful military endeavor. Deciding whom you want to serve in your military establishment, how you wish to develop their "capital", and how you expect them to perform, are essential elements in meeting the nation's security needs. The answers to these questions, in turn, should derive from the future military at which you wish to aim, the capabilities you wish it to possess, and the challenges you believe it must be ready to confront.

Those answers include basic decisions about how many actually wear a uniform (and are therefore governed by the laws of war), how many will be civilian employees of the national military establishment (therefore performing with the authority of the government), and how the private sector might provide key services on which both military and civilian functions depend, perhaps in a partnership arrangement. For each community, you will want to specify the characteristics of the personnel you wish to recruit, the preparation and ongoing education and training they should receive, and the service trajectory you expect them to follow.

Despite the labor-intensive nature of military matters, human capital issues rarely figure in defense planning debates, outside the personnel management domain itself. For the American military particularly, this is an astounding omission: As noted earlier, operating costs account for two-thirds of the Defense budget, and personnel costs (military and civilian) for at least two-thirds of that total. Indeed, in their retrospective review of the 1960s experience, Enthoven and Smith cite operating costs as a key item of "unfinished business", correctly pointing out that "top management of the Department cannot make good decisions when [these] costs … are unknown."[20] Nonetheless, even their discussion does not tie human capital planning back to force structure decisions, or the nature of procurement choices, despite the focus on those two issues by PPBS, both in its early years and continuing down to the present day.

Grounding the human capital debate in the force you desire also implies it is the force characteristics that should drive personnel policies, not the other way around. This is especially true as today's evolving technology and international security environments alter U.S. needs. It is the responsibility of the compensation system, broadly defined, to produce these desired force characteristics. A key element is the competitiveness of compensation, both military and civilian, with non-government opportunities. But from the enterprise perspective, there is an appropriate concern with costs.

The ultimate cost issue, of course, is not military compensation alone, but what is required overall to operate the Department. Operating costs are driven by military equipment decisions (including the reliability of that equipment); by business practices (including, for example, the statutory floor for government depot work, and the impediments to A-76 competitions); and by choices on the mix of active military, Reserve Component military, federal civilian, and contractor personnel.

Choosing the mix

On the last set of issues (the staffing mix), Secretary of Defense Ash Carter called for more "permeability"—to attract a wider variety of experience and backgrounds in both military and federal civilian personnel. He announced a series of initiatives to address this issue. Some of those confront what his Acting Under Secretary of Defense for Personnel and Readiness identified as difficulties created by the federal civilian personnel system, including limits on appointing authority.

The Department faces two obstacles in considering the optimal mix of personnel, one a planning challenge, one institutional. The planning challenge is defining the structure—the nature—of the force of the future. The Department has struggled to meet this challenge since the end of the Cold War, with its initial responses a scaled-down version of its prior choices (Base Force, Bottom-Up Review). Apart from the growth of Intelligence, Surveillance and Reconnaissance force elements (including cyber), that remains, as a generalization, the case today. Much of the structure is aimed at high-end, state-on-state conflict, for which we must be prepared, but with little devoted to the challenges we face immediately. The structure emphasizes the ability to destroy targets, not necessarily the ability to secure the political or political-military outcomes we desire. Securing a broader range of capabilities within likely budget limits may require accepting hedges vice full-up solutions, perhaps involving greater use of Reserve Component authorities (conceivably new authorities), and of civilians.

The second obstacle is institutional. The Department's planning processes, as long constituted, do not adequately consider the "total force" solution space in arriving at the mix. Military personnel are decided and budgeted for in terms of a central account (end strength), and once the strength level is established, military personnel are "free" to the using elements of DoD. (Conversely, they cannot easily trade military personnel for federal civilians or contractors.) In this situation, it is not surprising that in most Military Departments the demand for military personnel, as substantiated in various manning documents, exceeds the planned supply, especially for active duty forces.

At the other extreme sit federal civilians. Their numbers are decided on a largely decentralized basis, but often restrained to produce budgetary savings through ceilings (notwithstanding the statutory provision barring such a practice outside of management headquarters). That leaves contracted services as the safety valve, as organizations strive to meet their needs with the funds available.

Repeated analyses demonstrate that there are significant gains possible from a more systematic approach to deciding on the total force mix.

It would be easy to paint too discouraging a picture about the tradeoff process, and only fair to note some of the exceptions. One interesting development is the Air Force's pursuit of composite units, staffed with a mix of active, National Guard and Reserve personnel, benefitting from the differing levels of service that can reasonably be expected from each community. Another is the long-standing Inherently Governmental/Commercial Activity database maintained by DoD, which allows you to examine military-civil tradeoffs (and whose results argue DoD could make greater use of civilians). Particular Secretaries of Defense have taken an interest in this issue, whether Secretary Rumsfeld in military-civilian trades (to conserve military personnel for the Long War) and in competitive sourcing (an initiative of the George W. Bush administration), or the in-sourcing initiative launched by Secretary Gates. The last two, of course, are now restricted by statutory restraints.

Staffing mix issues extend beyond broad categories of personnel to include structural issues within each community. For example, the Army has solved the conundrum of "up or out" in the context of a pilot force (high training costs, substantial payoff to experience, implying long cockpit tours) by staffing extensively with warrant officers, reserving just a few billets for (classically) commissioned officers who are groomed for leadership positions. Presumably, as the military becomes more highly technical this mechanism—or its analog, the Navy's Limited Duty Officer—could be used more extensively. Mechanisms like these might be used to strengthen the cyber force, and other areas such as intelligence, language and cultural expertise, science and technology, and acquisition.

Indeed, as one opens the aperture on personnel types it's quite possible that some duties that are now thought to require officers could be performed by enlisted personnel, given the high aptitude and performance standards of the All-Volunteer Force. A recent Air Force Chief of Staff speculated about their possible utilization to meet some piloting needs. Indeed, the Army, Navy and Marine Corps already use enlisted personnel to operate Unmanned Aerial Vehicles.

Managing the mix

Some wish to reconsider the Defense Officer Personnel Management Act (DOPMA), and Secretary Carter spoke to this issue, proposing modest but important changes,[21] with Congress giving DoD some new authority.[22]

Notwithstanding the merits of those proposals, we should first focus on the different *results* that are desired. To what degree do the statutory provisions make it difficult to achieve desired results, versus the manner in which the Act is implemented? If alternate regimes appear attractive, the Department might experiment with those regimes (through existing or new waiver authority, or pilot programs), to understand their possible unintended consequences, before making them permanent.

While key elements of enlisted management parallel that for officers, the rules are largely driven by policy, not statute. Enlisted personnel, of course, constitute the vast majority of the force. Perhaps the management paradigm for this element should receive our attention first.

The challenges of the last fifteen years have demonstrated the value of agility—agility at the individual level, and agility on the part of defense institutions. American military personnel, starting with the Battle of Bunker Hill, have been known for their agility. Could we do even better, whether via the standards we set for recruiting, or the manner in which we prepare the force?

In thinking about a more agile mix, the Department should be willing to consider hybrid vehicles—vehicles that embrace the strengths of the different personnel communities. Secretary Carter pointed in this direction with his emphasis on Intergovernmental Personnel Act appointments, but more ambitious models might also be considered. These include the British notion of sponsored reserves (contractor operations in which all personnel hold Reserve Component appointments, and can be shifted to a military status as theater circumstances require), and Government Sponsored Enterprises, where the government retains control but creates an entity that can operate like a private sector actor (the Saint Lawrence Seaway is viewed as one of the more successful examples).

One issue that has not received the attention it deserves is strengthening the skills of existing federal civilians over the course of their careers. The contrast in DoD could not be more striking: Significant investments in further education and training for military personnel, very limited opportunities for civilians. Some of this result derives from the strictures of civil service rules, some from the lack of budgetary allocations to support the necessary costs. Greater investment in federal civilian "human capital" should pay handsome dividends in long-term performance, and in the ability to recruit and retain talent.

The "force of the future" may look different from today's, reflecting both changing needs (think cyber), and the changing nature of our society (think opportunities for women, and changing views of what constitutes a career). As we contemplate change, however, it is worth reiterating that the current system sustained a successful All-Volunteer Force in the concluding stage of the Cold War, in its immediate aftermath (including the First Persian Gulf War), and in the long period of armed conflict that followed the attacks of 9/11. There are clearly elements that have worked well, or that have adapted effectively. Retaining those elements, while making much-needed revisions, is the analytic—and political—task ahead.

Conclusions

While important elements of PPBS should be able to continue to serve DoD well, rethinking the planning phase (long recommended by others), focusing PPBS on missions (vice forces), lengthening its time horizon, paying greater attention to operating costs (based in part on the experience of execution), and increasing its agility should substantially improve its ability to deal with the challenges DoD faces.

One constraint on improved planning involves the well-known difficulty of persuading the Executive Branch's most senior decision makers to identify their preferred choices in a timely way. This issue arose in the very early days of PPBS. It was hoped that the President would make key choices at the start of the process, via presidential memoranda. It was quickly discovered that the President was unwilling to signal his preferences until the last possible moment—that any hope of early presidential decisions was a vain hope indeed. Nonetheless, the process benefited from preparing the materials that would be needed for such (perhaps hypothetical) decisions, and Draft Presidential Memoranda became one of the important elements forcing DoD to think through the available options for resolving the most difficult problems. Something like that process might again be useful. Indeed, the Department has tried a number of vehicles to encourage early analysis of key decisions identified by the Secretary. Expanding such processes to take on issues that ultimately will need presidential sanction, however, would be a constructive further step.

Note that none of these changes require statutory action. They can all be taken with authority the Executive Branch holds today.

Changes in personnel management that would help produce better outcomes, in contrast, probably do require some degree of statutory assistance. Certainly that will be the case for new organizational structures, and it is doubtful that the trade process can work well without revised civil service rules, and returning authority to DoD to decide on organic versus contractor performance without the crimping constraints Congress has imposed. The Department can demonstrate to the Congress the benefit of revised practices in those areas where it does possess greater flexibility (e.g., enlisted personnel management, and to a lesser extent, officer management, using the powers Congress recently awarded and waiver authority granted earlier). But an ability to redefine the mix of personnel needed to staff the military establishment will ultimately depend on the willingness of the political process, as reflected in the statute, to admit the need for such trades.

The framework for trades, and revised management, of course, is the set of capabilities the United States must build to deal with contemporary challenges, and to anticipate the challenges of tomorrow. That is ultimately the responsibility for which the Department should summon its most imaginative thinking, and not use its existing processes for the defense of successful past solutions, as so often happens. Both the present and the future demand possibly different answers.

Those answers may make us uncomfortable. In some sense, discomfort may be the best indicator that the revised processes are working well, requiring us to explore the new spaces from which innovations arise—the "creative destruction" principle so celebrated in the performance of the commercial economy, that applies just as well to the equally serious challenge of ensuring the nation's security.

Notes

1 DoD encourages an analytic approach to defense planning by other militaries through its Defense Institution Building initiative, succeeding its Defense Resource Management Study Program (DRMS). For a discussion of DRMS, see *Defense Resource Management Study Program (DRMS) 2010 Annual Report* (Irregular Warfare Division, Office of the Secretary of Defense, Cost Assessment and Program Evaluation, July 2010); and Wade Hinkle, Jason Decant, and Charles Fletcher, "Building Partner Capacity," *IDA Research Notes* (Spring 2010): 9–12. For commentary on the Defense Department's more recent experiences in improving planning and other institutional capabilities in security partners, see Aaron Taliaferro, Wade Hinkle, and Alexander Gallo, "Foreign Culture and its Effect on US Department of

Defense Efforts to Train and Advise Foreign Security Forces," *Small Wars Journal* (vol. 10, no. 11, November 2014). For examples of IDA work assisting partner countries in improving defense planning, see Mark Tillman, et al., *Defense Resource Management Studies: Introduction to Capability and Acquisition Planning Processes* (Institute for Defense Analyses Document D-4021, August 2010); C. Vance Gordon and Wade Hinkle, *Best Practices in Defense Resource Management* (IDA Document D-4137, January 2011); William Fedorochko, et al., *The Defense System of Management (DSOM) Republic of the Philippines* (IDA Document D-4785, March 2013); Patrick Goodman, et al., *Observations on the Republic of Korea Force Requirements Verification System* (IDA Document D-5044, October 2013); Martin Neill, Wade Hinkle, and Gary Morgan, *Scenarios: International Best Practice: An Analysis of Their Use by the United States, United Kingdom, and Republic of Korea* (IDA Document D-5665, February 2016); and, Aaron Taliaferro, et al., *Defense Governance and Management Methodology & Practice: Program Budgeting* (IDA Paper NS P-5317, forthcoming).

2 Charles Johnston Hitch and Roland N. McKean, *The Economics of Defense in the Nuclear Age* (Santa Monica, CA: RAND Corporation, 1960). For a concise summary of Hitch's ideas, see C. Vance Gordon, *Basic Conception of a Planning, Programming and Budgeting System* (Institute for Defense Analyses Report NS D-4331, May 2011).

3 The classic account of the early years of the Planning, Programming and Budgeting System is provided by Alain C. Enthoven and K. Wayne Smith, *How Much is Enough? Shaping the Defense Program (1961–1969)* (Santa Monica, CA: RAND Corporation, 1971).

4 Indeed, in the George H.W. Bush administration, when the then-Deputy Secretary of Defense expressed skepticism about the value of PPBS, the Military Departments made clear that they would continue using it to shape their futures even if the Secretary of Defense's office abandoned it. Deputy Secretary Don Atwood then relented.

5 See John T. Warner and Paul F. Hogan, *Walter Oi and His Contributions to the All-Volunteer Force: Theory, Evidence, Persuasion* (Prepared for The All-Volunteer Force: A Symposium in Honor of Walter Oi, Sponsored by CNA Corporation, Arlington, VA, September 23, 2014).

6 John D. Winkler, Judith C. Fernandez and J. Michael Polich, *Effect of Aptitude on the Performance of Army Communications Operators* (Santa Monica, CA: RAND Corporation, 1992). www.rand.org/pubs/reports/R4143.html. Also, Orvis, Bruce R., Michael Childress and J. Michael Polich. *Effect of Personnel Quality on the Performance of Patriot Air Defense System Operators* (Santa Monica, CA: RAND Corporation, 1992). www.rand.org/pubs/reports/R3901.html.

7 J. Michael Polich, James N. Dertouzos, and S. James Press, *The Enlistment Bonus Experiment* (Santa Monica, CA: RAND Corporation, Prepared for the Office of the Assistant Secretary of Defense/Force Management and Personnel, April 1986). www.rand.org/content/dam/rand/pubs/reports/2006/R3353.pdf.

8 Bert F. Green and Anne S. Mavor, eds., with the Committee on Military Enlistment Standards, Commission on Behavioral and Social Sciences and Education, and the National Research Council, *Modeling Cost and Performance for Military Enlistment: Report on a Workshop* (Washington, DC: National Academy Press, 1994).

9 Department of Defense, Office of the Under Secretary of Defense for Personnel and Readiness. *Report of the Ninth Quadrennial Review of Military Compensation*, Vol. 1 (Washington, DC: March 2002).

10 Author interview of Alain Enthoven 1981.

11 Donald B. Rice, et al., *Defense Resource Management Study: A Report Requested by the President and Submitted to the Secretary of Defense* (Washington, DC: Government Printing Office, February 1979). Subsequently adopted by Secretary of Defense Harold Brown in April 1979.

12 Robert Soule, Director of Program Analysis and Evaluation (1998–2001), to author.

13 *Long-Term Implications of the 2016 Future Years Defense Program*. Congressional Budget Office, January 2016. www.cbo.gov/sites/default/files/114th-congress-2015-2016/reports/51050-2016_FYDP.pdf.
14 See *National Defense Budget Estimates for FY 2016*, Office of the Under Secretary of Defense (Comptroller), March 2015. http://comptroller.defense.gov/Portals/45/Documents/defbudget/fy2016/FY16_Green_Book.pdf.
15 See www.congress.gov/bill/114th-congress/senate-bill/2943/text.
16 Author's recollection.
17 Goodman, et al., op. cit., chap. 3; UK Ministry of Defence, *Defence Reform Report* (London: The Stationery Office, June 2011); UK Ministry of Defence, *Enabling Acquisition Change* (London: The Stationery Office, June 2006); Australian Department of Defence, *Defence Capability Development Handbook* (Canberra, Australia: Commonwealth of Australia, 2012); Australian Department of Defence, *Procurement and Sustainment Review* (Canberra, Australia: Commonwealth of Australia, May 2008); Australian Department of Defence, *Joint Operations for the Twenty-First Century* (Canberra, Australia: Commonwealth of Australia, May 2007); and, Australian Department of Defence, *Defence Capability Development Manual* (Canberra, Australia: Commonwealth of Australia, May 2006). The authors are grateful to Wade Hinkle for these insights.
18 On Colombia, see Viceministerio para la Estrategia y la Planeación, Ministerio de Defensa Nacional, *Guía Planeamiento Estratégico* (Bogota, Colombia: Ministerio de Defensa Nacional, June 2011). On the Philippines, see Fedorochko, et al., op. cit. On the Republic of Korea, see, Goodman, et al., op. cit, and Neill, Hinkle, and Morgan, op. cit.
19 *Report of the Defense Science Board 2010 Summer Study on Enhancing Adaptability of U.S. Military Forces, Part A: Main Report* (Washington, DC: Office of the Under Secretary of Defense for Acquisition, Technology, and Logistics, January 2011).
20 Enthoven and Smith, op. cit., p. 316.
21 Remarks on "The Next Two Links to the Force of the Future," as delivered by Secretary of Defense Ash Carter, The Pentagon Courtyard, Washington, DC, June 9, 2016. Transcript available at www.defense.gov/News/Speeches/Speech-View/Article/795341/remarks-on-the-next-two-links-to-the-force-of-the-future.
22 See FY2017 National Defense Authorization Act.

8

GLOBAL CHALLENGES AND AMERICAN GRAND STRATEGY FOR THE 21ST CENTURY

Walter Russell Mead

The following chapter was adapted from written testimony delivered to the United States Senate Committee on Armed Services on October 22, 2015.

When the Cold War ended, many Americans thought that foreign policy was about to become much less demanding. Democracy seemed to be spreading around the world. Globalization and free trade were going to unleash universal prosperity, and that prosperity would make peace relatively easy to achieve. There were a few remaining problems out there: the looming danger of climate change, the threat of "rogue states" like North Korea and Iran and their nuclear weapons programs, but on the whole, the world seemed to have moved from an age of turbulence and crisis to one of progress and peace.

One year into President Trump's term, that optimism looks misplaced. Russia, China and Iran seek to revise the post-Cold War world order. The European Union is divided, facing economic, political and security challenges that it does not seem able to overcome. The world's central banks are deep into uncharted waters after years of unconventional monetary policy. The revelry at Davos this year was tempered by a chorus of Cassandras, bleating about the potential fallout of mounting debt. Living standards in the United States and other developed countries are stagnating and in some countries falling, and in both Europe and the United States many citizens seem to be losing patience with the ideas and policies of their respective establishments. Religious war has broken out in much of the Middle East, and the challenge of radical jihadi movements is far from contained.

Young people growing up in the 1990s often felt that they were growing up in a boring world: that history was over, the big questions all settled, and that their task in life would be to execute the plans and run the institutions that their parents and grandparents had built. This is no longer the case. Contemporary students of foreign policy must struggle to make sense of the lapse of America's tidy globalist consensus. Maintained from 1947 to 2016, a longstanding set of compromises among elites sustained their belief in the necessary primacy of the United States abroad. The election of President Trump has opened the prospect of a definitive break with seven decades of this outlook.

Wrenching developments like the drift of Poland and Hungary into new ideological channels, Brexit, and President Trump's professed skepticism about precepts of liberal order are signs of fundamental change in the Atlantic world. Old institutions and ideas are visibly inadequate to the tasks of the 21st century; today's young people will face more challenges, live more consequential lives, and face greater dangers than anyone predicted a generation ago. The liberal world order that the United States and its allies built after World War Two and worked to deepen after the Cold War faces its most severe tests in many decades. The next generation of American and world leaders must understand what this liberal world order is, why it matters, why it is in trouble, and work from there to recast America's national strategy for a new age.

Background

After the World War Two, the United States replaced Great Britain as, in Col. House's phrase, the "gyroscope of world order." The United States assumed the burdens of global leadership not because we desired power—in fact, we had spent twenty years before the war, and two after it, trying to avoid global responsibilities—but because Americans needed the benefits of a stable world order to be safe and prosperous at home. Maintaining an open global economic system is vital to continued American prosperity. Maintaining a stable geopolitical order is vital to continued American security. And promoting values of freedom and self-determination worldwide is a critical element of these two missions.

These realities are still the basis of American foreign policy and national strategy today. While there are many disagreements about how these principles should be translated into policy, and while some Americans seek to turn their backs on the difficult tasks of global engagement, on the whole, the commitment to the principles of liberal world order building that have framed American foreign policy since the Truman administration continues to shape our thinking today. As the world becomes more integrated economically, and as new threats like cyberwar and jihadi terrorism combine with old-fashioned geopolitical challenges to create a more dangerous environment, this postwar American foreign policy tradition is more important than ever, but we must think long and hard about how we address our vital interests in an increasingly turbulent and dynamic world.

The question before us today is whether we can continue to afford and manage the global commitments this policy requires. If, as I believe, the answer is that we can, we must then address questions of strategy. How do we harness the means we possess to secure the ends we seek, what priorities do we need to establish, what capabilities do we need to cultivate, and to what allies can we look for help as we seek to promote a peaceful and prosperous world amid the challenges of the 21st century?

We can begin by examining some of the advantages and disadvantages that the United States and its allies have as we consider how to adapt a 20th-century strategy to the needs of the contemporary world.

Disadvantages and advantages

Surveying the global landscape, we can see several disadvantages that make it difficult to maintain the global system we've built into the 21st century. At the most basic level, one of the chief disadvantages facing the United States is the never-ending nature of our task. America's work is never done. Militarily, whenever the United States innovates to gain an advantage, others quickly mimic our developments. It is not enough for us to be ahead today; we have to continue to innovate so we are ready for tomorrow and the day after.

The United States is challenged by the products of its own successes in ways that extend far beyond weapons systems. The liberal capitalist order that the United States supports and promotes is an engine of revolutionary change in world affairs. The economic and technological progress that has so greatly benefitted America also introduces new and complicating factors into world politics. The rise of China was driven by the American-led information technology revolution that made global supply chains possible and by the Anglo-American development of an open international economic system that enabled China to participate on equal terms. The threat of cyberwar exists because of the extraordinary development of the "Born in the U.S.A." internet, and the revolutionary advances that it represents.

In this way, American foreign policy is like a video game in which the player keeps advancing to new and more challenging levels. "Winning" doesn't mean the end of the game; it means the game is becoming more complex and demanding. This means that simply in order to perform at the same level, the United States needs to keep upping its game, reforming its institutions, improving its strategies, and otherwise preparing itself to address more complex and challenging issues—often at a faster pace than before, and with higher penalties for getting things wrong.

America's competitors are becoming more capable and dynamic as they master technology and refine their own strategies in response to global change. The world of Islamic jihad, for instance, has been transformed by both the adaptation of information technology and adaptation to previous American victories. In both these regards, Al-Qaeda represented a great advance over earlier movements, Al-Qaeda in Mesopotamia yet another advance, and ISIS a further step forward.

In the world of international geopolitics, Russia has also made much of information control and its current leadership possesses a keen eye for the weaknesses of American-fostered successes such as the European Union. And China is also emerging as new kind of challenge, one that on the one hand plays "within" the rules much more than Russia or ISIS, but on the other, is still willing to break the rules—viz. the United States Office of Personnel Management hack or industrial espionage—when Beijing feels it is necessary. Far more than America's other competitors, China has used this combination to develop its own economy and to lay the foundations for long-term power. That China's economy may be slowing should not make Americans complacent. Internal economic challenges can make a country more aggressive and less predictable in the international arena, and recent Chinese actions in the South China Sea suggests that Beijing's current political and economic difficulties are leading to exactly this kind of behavior.

Meanwhile, many of America's traditional allies in Europe are losing ground in the global economic race, and NATO, the most successful military alliance in world history and the keystone of the worldwide American alliance network, is in trouble. Many of Europe's leading economies—which is to say, many of the top-ten economies of the world by GDP—are stagnating, and have been for some time. This has corrosive, follow-on effects on the social fabric of nations like France, Italy, and Spain. Further, the EU's organizational mechanisms have proven inadequate to both the euro monetary crisis and the current refugee crisis, and secession movements (whether from the EU itself, as in "Brexit", or within EU nations, e.g. Scotland or Catalonia) are likely to strain them even more going forward. Finally, prospects for European adaptation to the 21st-century tech economy are dimmer than one would like. Entrenched interests are using the force of government to repress innovation, start-ups are thin on the ground, and major new tech companies—"European Googles"—are nowhere to be seen.

And of course, there is a military side to all of this. Since the Great Recession, the European members of NATO cut the equivalent of the entire German military budget from their combined defense expenditures. Many of our mainland European allies are also at least somewhat ambivalent about the extent of their commitment to defend other NATO members, particularly the new member-states in the Baltic—a fact that has not escaped Russia's notice.

More broadly, the international security system promoted by the United States is based on two principles, alliance and deterrence, that greatly amplify our military capacity—and which we have undermined in recent years. Our alliances allow us to do more with less; they also repress competition among our allies. For instance, mutual alliances with America help to keep Japanese-South Korean tensions in check today just as the American presence helped France and Germany establish closer relations based on mutual trust in the past. Deterrence is key to the alliance system and also to minimizing the loss of U.S. lives as we fulfill our commitments around the world.

Recent events in the Middle East demonstrate what happens when alliances fray and deterrence loses its force. Iranian and Russian adventurism across the region has undermined the confidence of American allies and increased the risks of war. American allies, like Saudi Arabia, who fear American abandonment, have grown increasingly insecure. Saudi freelancing in Syria and Yemen may lead to great trouble down the road; Riyadh is not institutionally equipped to take on the burdens it is attempting to shoulder.

Another significant disadvantage facing U.S. policymakers is that the international order is based on institutions (like the UN) that are both cumbersome to work with and difficult to reform. As we get further and further from the circumstances in which many of these institutions were founded, they grow more unwieldy, but for similar reasons, nations who were more powerful then than now grow more deeply opposed to change. The defects of the world's institutions of governance and cooperation are particularly problematic for an order-building, alliance-minded power like the United States.

Meanwhile, many of our domestic institutions relating to foreign policy are not well structured for the emerging challenges. From the educational institutions that prepare Americans for careers in international affairs (and that provide basic education about world politics to many more) to large organizations like the State Department, the Department of Homeland Security, and the Pentagon, the core institutions on which we need to rely are not well suited to the tasks they face.

In the Cold War era, the challenges were relatively easy to understand, even if developing policies to deal with the threats was often hard. Today, the policy challenges are no less difficult, but the threats themselves are more diverse. A revanchist Russia, competing radical Sunni and Shia jihadist movements, and a rising China all represent important challenges, but they cannot be addressed in the same way or with the same tools. Americans, particularly those in public service but also the engaged citizens whose votes and opinions sway foreign policy, will have to be more nimble and nuanced in their understanding of the problems we're facing than ever before.

In spite of these serious disadvantages and problems, the United States is much better positioned than any other country to maintain, defend, extend and improve the international system in the 21st century. We should be sober about the tremendous challenges facing us, but we should not be pessimistic. We cannot do everything, and we will not do everything right, but we can be more right, more often than our adversaries.

The United States remains an adaptable society that embraces change, likes innovation, and adjusts to new realities with enthusiasm (and often, an eye to enlightened self-interest). Indeed, in many ways, these truisms are more true now than ever. We remain on the cutting edge of technological development. We're better suited than our global competitors to weather demographic shifts and absorb new immigrants. And despite significant resistance to change among some segments of society (in particular, ironically, the "public-service" sector), we are already starting to re-engineer our institutions for the 21st century.

One of the United States' greatest advantages is our exceptional array of natural resources. We possess a tremendous resource base with energy, agriculture, and mineral wealth that can rival any nation on earth. Hydraulic fracturing and horizontal well-drilling have fundamentally transformed the American energy landscape overnight. Oil production is up 75 percent since 2008, and new supplies of shale gas have millions of Americans heating their homes cheaply each winter. New U.S. oil production has been a big part of the global fall in oil prices, and shale producers continue to surprise the world with their ability to keep up output, even in a bearish market. In 2014, the U.S. was the world's largest producer of oil and gas, according to the U.S. Energy Information Administration. Energy policy debates have shifted from issues of scarcity to those of abundance: we're now discussing what to do with our bounty. Do we sell liquefied natural gas (LNG) abroad? End the ban on crude oil exports? These are good problems to have.

The United States also retains the most advantageous geographical position of any of the world's great powers. We have friendly, resource-rich neighbors; Canada is a rising power with enormous potential, and Mexico and many other countries in Latin America have made substantial progress. We face both of the world's great oceans, which allow us to engage in trade while still insulating us from many of the world's ills.

The United States has an unprecedented network of alliances that gives us unmatched global reach and resilience. The vast majority of the world's developed nations are U.S. allies. In fact, of the top 50 nations by GDP according to the World Bank, only four—China, Russia, Venezuela, and Iran—are adversaries. Likewise, only two of the top fifteen military spenders are not friendly to the United States. Largely, we have the kind of friends one hopes to have.

Moreover, the world can see that the United States stands for something more than its own power and wealth. The democratic ideals we honor (even if we do not always succeed in living up to them) resonate far beyond our frontiers. The bedrock belief of American society that every woman and every man possesses an innate and inalienable dignity, and our commitment to ground our institutions and our laws on that truth inspire people around the world. The American creed is one that can be shared by people of all faiths and indeed of no faith; our society's principles stand on common ground with the world's great religious and ethical traditions. This American heritage gives us a unique ability to reach out to people in every land and to work together to build a more peaceful and prosperous world.

The United States also has a favorable climate for investment and business that ensures we will remain (if we don't screw up) a major destination for investment. These factors include: America's traditional devotion to the rule of law; long, stable constitutional history; excellent credit rating; large internal market; 50 competing states offering a range of investment possibilities; rich science and R&D communities; deep financial markets adept at helping new companies grow; stable energy supplies (likely to be below world costs given the advantages of pipeline gas compared to LNG); and an educated workforce. We're not at the top of every one of these measures globally, but no country can or likely will match our broad strength across them.

One of the biggest ways in which America is fortunate is that, as I've written elsewhere, "the ultimate sources of American power – the economic dynamism of its culture, the pro-business tilt of its political system, its secure geographical location, its rich natural resource base and its profound constitutional stability – don't depend on the whims of political leaders. Thankfully, the American system is often smarter and more capable than the people in office at any given time."[1]

One way to look at our position is this: at the peak of its global power and influence in the 1870s, the United Kingdom is estimated to have had about nine percent of the global GDP. America's share today is more than double that—and likely to remain at or close to that level for some time to come.

American power today rests on strong foundations. Those who argue that the United States must accept the inevitability of decline, and that the United States can no longer pursue our global interests do not understand America's strengths. The United States, in association with its growing and dynamic global alliance system, is better placed than any other country or combination of countries to shape the century that lies before us.

Opportunities and challenges

The United States has several opportunities in the coming years to significantly advance its interests around the world. In Asia, a large group of countries want the same kind of future we do: peaceful, full of opportunities for economic growth, and with no one country dominating the rest. Two generations ago, this was a poor, dictatorship-ridden region; today, it's full of advanced, high-income economies and contains more stable democratic states than in the past. The regional response to China's assertive policies in the East and South China Seas demonstrated that many countries are willing and indeed eager to work with the United States and with each other to preserve the way of life they have created from regional hegemonic threats.

Cadets should be cognizant of and make a point of studying how American policy toward China has evolved since 1990. At the end of the cold war, Presidents George H. W. Bush and Bill Clinton solidified a policy to embrace China in a liberal East Asian order based on free trade and the spread of western political norms. Increasingly, Americans of all walks of life have been disappointed by the failure of this approach, and look to balance China's growing influence in East Asia. The change came under the Obama years with the "pivot toward the Pacific," in part because China's regional policy became more aggressive after 2012.

The Trump Administration has moved to a more adversarial stance, pairing greater assertiveness toward China with efforts to strengthen ties with India. Improving U.S. relations with the titan of South Asia has become a major element of the Asian realignment. In a speech in late 2017 immediately before his first trip to New Delhi, Tillerson pointed to areas of common interest and links uniting the United States and India, then spoke of China. "China, while rising alongside India, has done so less responsibly, at times undermining the international rules-based order."[2] Tillerson then elaborated Beijing's violations of international law, rules, and norms. Through these remarks, the president's chief diplomat delivered a critique of Beijing's leadership on the eve of China's momentous Party Congress.

Similarly, the Trump administration's Japan policy seeks to build on shared concerns. Over the last two decades, Japan has taken on an assertive role in East Asian security. China's apparent drive for regional hegemony and North Korea's unpredictable, rogue positions dominate Japanese security calculations. As a result, Tokyo seeks close cooperation with Washington regardless of who occupies the White House, and Prime Minister Abe has made every effort to build a strong personal relationship with President Trump.

In Europe, despite some quarrels and abrasions, our longstanding allies have worked together to build the kind of zone of democratic, peaceful prosperity that the United States hopes the whole world will someday enjoy. But what we're finding, not for the first time in our history, is that Europe works best when America remains engaged with it. While it's tempting to think that a bunch of first-world, prosperous democracies can handle their own corner of the world (and perhaps some of the neighboring bits, please?), America is the secret ingredient that keeps this historically contentious, rivalry-ridden area, full of states of differing size and capacity, with different attitudes toward economics, defense, social organization, and much else, working together. When Europe works well, it's the best advertisement for the American vision to the rest of the world. It offers us the chance to work together with partners who share our belief in rule of law and human rights. From mutual defense to governance issues, it's clear that America needs to invest more time and energy in engagement and cooperation with Europe. The transatlantic community must be strengthened and revived.

Perhaps the biggest opportunity in the 21st century is not geopolitical, however, but economic and social. The tech revolution has the potential to boost standards of human happiness and prosperity as much as the Industrial Revolution did. It will likely give our grandchildren a higher standard of living than most of us today can imagine.

We should not underestimate either the extent of this coming transformation, or the enormous power it has to make our lives better. Take, for instance, the environment: 21st-century technology is moving the economy into a more sustainable mode. The information service-driven economy is rising even as the manufacturing economy becomes less environmentally problematic and shrinks as a portion of the total economy. From telework to autonomous cars, innovations are likely to cut down on emissions in the new economy, even while improving standards of living across the world.

The information economy will be more prosperous, more environmentally friendly, and more globally interconnected than what came before it. The United States can lead this transition—not by hampering economic growth or by instituting expensive subsidies, but by promoting and accelerating the shift toward a greener but richer and more satisfying economy.

Filled with opportunity as it is, the new century also contains threats: conventional threats like classic geopolitical rivals struggling against the world order favored by the United States and its allies, unconventional threats like terror movements spurred by jihadi ideology, regional crises like the implosion of much of the Middle East and a proliferation of failed and failing states, emerging threats like the danger of cyberwar, and systemic problems like the crises in some of the major institutions on which the global order depends—NATO, the EU, and the UN for example. The U.S. government itself is not exempt from this problem; whether one looks at the Pentagon, the Department of Homeland Security or the State Department one sees organizations seeking to carry out 21st-century missions with 20th or even 19th-century bureaucratic structures and practices.

Additionally, the United States faces a challenge of strategy. While the United States has enough resources to advance its vital interests in world affairs, it does not have the money, the military power, the know-how or the willpower to address every problem, intervene in every dispute, or to dissipate its energies in futile pursuits.

The United States faces an array of conventional and unconventional threats, as well as several systemic dangers. Our three principal conventional challengers are China, Russia, and Iran. All aim to revise the current global geopolitical order to some extent. In the years to come, we must expect that revisionist powers will continue to challenge the existing status quo in various ways. Moreover, the continuing development of "second generation" nuclear weapons states like Pakistan ensures that geopolitical competition between regional powers can trigger global crises.

Meanwhile, we are also confronted by an array of unconventional threats. Despite the fondest hopes of many Americans, Sunni jihadism has not proven to be a passing phase or fringe movement. Al-Qaeda was more resourceful and ambitious than the previous generation of radical salafi groups; its Mesopotamian offshoot (AQIM) was still more effective; today, ISIS has leaped ahead to develop capabilities and nourish ambitions that earlier jihadi groups saw only in their dreams. Unfortunately, the radical movements have lost inhibitions as they gained capacities. Wholesale slaughter, enslavement, barbaric and spectacular forms of execution: these testify to a movement that becomes more depraved, more lost in the pornography of violence, even as it acquires more resources and more fighters. This movement could become significantly more dangerous before it begins to burn out.

Yet radical jihadis may well prove to be less of a threat than the emerging dangers of the cybersphere. Cyber conflict is a new arena of action, one in which non-state, quasi-state and state actors are all present. With almost every day bringing stories of utterly lamentable failures of American cyber security, it must be clearly said that the U.S. government has allowed itself to be made into a global laughingstock even as some of our most vital national security (and corporate and personal) information is captured by adversaries with, apparently, impunity.

But problems like these are pinpricks compared to the damage that cyberwar can cause. Not only can industrial sabotage disrupt vital systems, including military command and control systems as well as, for example, the utilities on which millions of Americans depend for their daily necessities, cyberwar can be waged anonymously. Threats of retaliation lose their deterrent power when the attacker is unknown. Worse, the potential for destabilizing first strikes by cyber attacks will complicate the delicate balance of terror, and leaders could find themselves propelled into conflict. Cyberwar could accelerate the diplomatic timetable of the 21st century much as railroad schedules and mobilization timetables forced the hands of diplomats in 1914.

Beyond that, one can dimly grasp the possibility of biologically based weapons as a new frontier in human conflict. It is far too soon to know what these will be like or how they will be used; nevertheless one must postulate the steady arrival of new kinds of weapons, both offensive and defensive, as the acceleration of human scientific understanding gives us greater access to the wonders of the life sciences.

Finally, there are systemic or generic threats, which is to say, dangers that are not created by hostile design, but emerge as byproducts from existing and otherwise benign trends that are likely to pose significant challenges to the United States' interests and security in coming decades. We do not usually think of these as security problems, but they can create or exacerbate security threats and they can degrade our abilities to respond effectively.

For all its promise, the tech revolution entails an accelerating rate of change in human communities that has destabilizing effects. In the United States, and especially in Europe, these take the relatively benign, but still problematic, form of the breakdown of what I have called the "blue social model"—a tightly integrated economic-social model built during the 21st century that linked lifetime employment and fixed pensions into a socio-economic safety net. Now, the structures that were designed to secure prosperity and economic safety in the 20th century are often constraining it in the 21st. There is an increasingly clear danger, in both the U.S. and Europe, of a more abrupt rupture in politics, as apathy and resistance to changing the old systems among elites runs head-first into inchoate, populist dissatisfaction with the decline in living standards among displaced members of the working class. This tension and political dysfunction makes it much harder to build public support for effective foreign policy and fuels populist and radical political movements that threaten to disrupt current systems of Western alliances without replacing them with something more effective.

But elsewhere, the strains of the modern economy may yet be worse, and produce more malign results. In the Middle East and North Africa, government institutions and systems of belief are overwhelmed by the onslaught of modernity. For better or worse, the pressures of modernity will increase on societies all around the world as we move deeper into the 21st century. To date, the

United States has demonstrated very little ability to help failed or failing states find their feet. Failing states provide a fertile environment for ethnic and religious conflict, the rise of terrorist ideologies, and mass migration. The United States will need to be ready to deal with the fallout—fallout that in some cases could be more than metaphorical.

Finally, the United States and its allies must recognize and overcome a crisis of confidence. The West's indecision, weak responses, mirror imaging of strategic competitors who do not share our values, and our tendency to rely upon process-oriented "solutions" in the face of growing, violent threats have encouraged a paradox: our enemies and challengers have become more emboldened, and disruptive to the world order, exploiting the opportunities that the open order supported by the United States and its allies provides.

Western societies have turned inward, susceptible to "there's nothing we can do" and "it's not our problem" political rhetoric. As history shows, the combination can carry a very high cost and take many years to unwind. Grand strategy has to take this into account: American leadership is critical to highlighting and thwarting problems that may fester into major global threats. Even the best strategic planning and the best procurement of equipment to meet serious strategic threats is insufficient should current Western leaders lack the wit to recognize and the will to meet challenges as they arise.

Recommendations

What can the United States government and its armed services do to prepare the country for the strategic challenges of the future? What should the next generation of thinkers, policymakers and military leaders be thinking about as its members prepare to launch their careers? The purpose of this chapter is to start a conversation, one that looks beyond day-to-day problems and takes a longer view. Here are some thoughts:

Examining our history

From its gestation, the presidency of Donald Trump has been characterized by many as an unlikely, unprecedented, and unwelcome deviation from the national story of the United States. No administration in living memory has received such an immediate, caustic response from elites across sectors, industries, and regions. Problematic as certain aspects of President Trump's agenda may be, it is necessary to bring a sober disposition to analysis of where the United States is going and how we got here.

For that reason, I urge you to consider the cultural unities that link earlier periods in our history to the present moment. This has remained a primary goal throughout my career. Many of my thoughts on this subject came together when I wrote *Special Providence*.[3] By crafting my arguments about schools of thought in American foreign policy, I attempted to provide an intelligible description of how the diplomacy of the United States has consistently taken a prominent position in American domestic political debates. I continue to marvel at the resonance contemporary controversies bear to past disputes in our history. Topics like the proper position of the United States in the North American Free Trade Area, the United Nations, and the World Trade Organization resonate with earlier controversies. Developing an awareness of how and why foreign policy has influenced American politics and society, decades before our transition to becoming a world power, is an intellectual investment that will reap dividends for years to come.

Life under the Trump Administration is an ideal time to investigate populist strains in American thought about the role of the United States in the world. In *Special Providence*, I argue that there is school of thought which prioritizes both the economic well-being of the American populace as well as their physical security. I named it after President Andrew Jackson, a figure mythologized with images of martial valor, who still holds great esteem among thinkers skeptical of the wisdom of elites. Jacksonian thought, I believe, has been on the rise for some time. It is no surprise to me that the Tea Party invoked the rattlesnake banner of the Revolution, exhorting us all, as it has in the past, not to "tread on" its standard-bearers. The trends of the last ten years demonstrate the activation of this way of thinking, culminating, some might argue, with the election of our current president. Before dismissing the opinions of others close to this movement, engage with aspects of American history which you think might intersect with their intuitions about how the world works.

Invest in the future

The apparently inexorable acceleration of technological and social change has many implications for the armed services of the United States. It is not just that weapons and weapon platforms must change with the times, and that we must continue to invest in the research and development that will enable the United States to field the most advanced and effective forces in the world. Technological change drives social change, and conflict is above all a social activity. Military forces must develop new ways of organizing themselves, learn to operate in different dimensions, understand rapidly changing cultural and political forces and generally remain innovative and outward focused.

New tech does not just mean new equipment on the battlefield. As tech moves into civil life, the structure of societies changes. Insurgencies mutate as new forms of communication and social organization transform the ways that people interact and communicate.

The need for flexibility is heightened by the diversity of the world in which the armed forces of the United States, given our country's global interests, must operate. American forces must be ready to work with Nigerian allies against Boko Haram, maintain a base presence in Okinawa while minimizing friction with the locals, operate effectively in the institutional and bureaucratic culture of the European alliance system, while killing ruthless enemies in the world's badlands. Our combat troops must work in a high-tech electronic battlefield of the utmost sophistication even as they work to win the hearts and minds of illiterate villagers.

The armed services must continue to reinvent themselves to fit changing times and changing missions, and they must be given the resources and the flexibility necessary to evolve with the world around them. The bureaucratic routines of Pentagon business as usual will be poorly adapted to the kind of world that is growing up around us. A focus on re-imagining and re-engineering bureaucratic institutions is part of investing in the future. Private business has often moved more quickly than government bureaucracy to develop new staffing and management patterns for a more flexible and rapidly changing environment. Government generally, and the Pentagon in particular, will need aggressive prodding from Congress to adopt new methods of management and organization. Investment in better management and organizational reform will be vital.

Address the interstitial spaces and the invisible realms

The United States, like Great Britain, is a power that flourishes in the "spaces between". In the 18th century, think of sea power and the world markets that sea power guaranteed. Britain rose to world power by mastering the "spaces between" the world's major economic zones. In the 19th century Britain added telegraph and cable communications to its portfolio, developing and defending the world's most extensive network of instantaneous communications. Similarly, the British built a global financial system around the gold standard, the pound, and the Bank of England. Again, the focus was less on dominating and ruling large land masses than on facilitating trade, communications and investment among them.

In the 20th century, the nature of this space changed again: air power, radio and television broadcasting, satellites and, in the century's closing years, the internet created new zones of communication. The United States was able to retain a unique place in world affairs in large part because it moved quickly and effectively to gain a commanding position in the development and civil and military use of these forms of communication. Whether it is the movement of goods or of information or of both, Anglo-American power for more than three centuries has been less about controlling large theaters of land than about securing and expediting trade and communication in the "spaces between."

This type of power, most evidently present today in the world of cyberspace, remains key not only to American power but to prosperity and security in the world. Information is becoming the decisive building block of both economic and military power.

American defense policy must remain riveted on the developments in communications and information processing that are creating the contemporary equivalent of the sea lanes of the 18th century and the cable lines of the 19th.

The recent series of high-profile hacker attacks against key American government and corporate targets suggests that we have lost ground in one of the most vital arenas of international competition.

This needs to change; cyber security is national security today, and at the moment, we don't have it.

Notes

1 Walter Russell Mead, "The Seven Great Powers," *The American Interest*, January 4, 2015.
2 Quoted in Carol Morello, "Tillerson Chides China while Calling for Greater Ties with India," *The Washington Post*, October 18, 2017.
3 Walter Russell Mead, *Special Providence: American Foreign Policy and How It Changed the World* (New York: Taylor & Francis, 2002).

9

SECURITY CHALLENGES IN THE POST-UNIPOLAR ERA

Andrew F. Krepinevich, Jr.

It has been 70 years since the 1947 National Security Act (NSA) that established the foundation for how the United States organized for what became a 44-year protracted strategic competition with Soviet Russia. Significant reforms have been made to the NSA from time to time since then. There is, however, a growing recognition that the strategic environment has changed dramatically since 1947, both with the Cold War's end and more recently with the rise of daunting new challenges to America's security.

This is hardly surprising. We are as far from 1947 as 1947 was from 1877, a year that began only a few months after Custer's defeat at the Little Big Horn. Arguably more change has occurred in the past three score and ten years than during the previous epoch. This suggests the need for a fundamental review of the country's national security structures and processes.

Just as U.S. leaders took into account both the lessons of World War II and the rapidly emerging challenge posed by the Soviet Union in crafting the National Security Act, so too should recent geopolitical, economic and military trends inform how the United States adapts its national security apparatus for a new era in global affairs. This paper's purpose is to identify these trends and provide some initial thoughts on their implications for those who are engaged in the reform process.

Geopolitical trends

Today the United States confronts a situation only modestly comparable to the one it encountered in the early days of the Cold War. After a very brief period following the Allies' victory in World War II, U.S. civilian and military leaders were faced with a new great power challenge in the form of the Soviet Union, one that required crafting a long-term national strategy to preserve American security along with the necessary structure and processes to execute that strategy efficiently and effectively. Following the Soviet Union's collapse in 1991, America enjoyed an extended interval of nearly two decades in which its military enjoyed essentially unchallenged dominance. Today, however, as in the late 1940s, the United States finds itself confronting formidable challenges that seem likely to grow even more threatening with time.

Unlike the early Cold War period, however, when Soviet Russia stood out as by far the greatest danger to U.S. security, today's geopolitical challenges are more diverse and complex. Washington now confronts three revisionist powers seeking to overturn the existing order in three different regions long considered by administrations of both political parties as key to U.S. security. American security planners must also account for a minor rogue nuclear power, North Korea, whose arsenal appears to be expanding at an alarming rate.

After nearly two decades of working to recover from its precipitous collapse, Russia has emerged as a revanchist power. Vladimir Putin's Russia poses a less formidable military threat than Soviet Russia during the Cold War. Yet because of its nuclear arsenal, it remains the only power capable of posing a clear existential threat to the United States. Putin's apparent goal is to establish spheres of influence over countries that were once part of the Soviet Union, to include absorbing territory when circumstances permit, and creating serious fault lines in the NATO alliance.[1] Thus far Putin has played a weak hand well. Russia's conventional forces have been upgraded over the past decade and now enjoy a favorable military balance over NATO's front-line East European states. Moscow has also successfully employed proxy forces to seize Crimea and portions of eastern Ukraine. At the same time the Russian military seeks to mask its inferiority to the United States and China in conventional forces through a doctrine of "escalate [to nuclear use] to de-escalate" a conflict, suggesting an increased willingness to employ nuclear weapons.[2]

In the Middle East, Iran looks to exploit the growing internal problems that have emerged in many states of the Arab World, and the power vacuum created by the United States' diminished presence and stature in the region. Tehran is working to expand and deepen its influence, particularly in Gaza, Iraq, Lebanon, Syria and Yemen. Like Russia, Iran seeks to avoid a conventional fight with the United States. Instead it continues employing proxies, often aided and assisted by its special operations forces (the Quds force) to support client states and organizations like Hezbollah who seek to undermine rival regimes.

It is in the Far East, however, that the United States faces its principal security challenge in the form of a rising, revisionist China. Beijing's extraterritorial claims now extend beyond Taiwan to encompass the South China Sea and its islands, and Japan's Senkaku Islands.[3] Chinese military writings speak of establishing a favorable position out to the Second Island Chain, which extends from Japan through the U.S. possession of Guam and down to New Guinea.[4]

China possesses by far the greatest economic and military potential of the three revisionist powers. Indeed, relatively speaking, China's GDP is substantially greater relative to that of the United States than any of its great power rivals of the last century, to include Nazi Germany, Imperial Japan and Soviet Russia.[5] Unlike Iran or Russia today, China is clearly building up its conventional forces to compete with the U.S. military. While Russia struggles to maintain a nuclear arm greatly reduced from its Cold War levels, China has the economic might and technical ability to field nuclear forces on par with Moscow and Washington.[6]

Although China has greater long-term military potential than Russia and Iran, it has thus far chosen to pursue its goals in a manner similar to that of those two states: by engaging in "gray area" or ambiguous low-level acts of aggression that fall below the threshold that would trigger a direct U.S. military response. As is the case with the other two revisionist powers, Beijing seeks to avoid a direct (and very costly) military confrontation with the United States, while it continues efforts to shift the military balance in its favor.[7]

It has been decades since North Korea's conventional forces posed an existential threat to South Korea, especially when U.S. military capability is placed in the balance. Yet thanks to its emergence as a nuclear-armed state in 2006 and its growing arsenal of nuclear weapons over the past decade, Pyongyang's capacity to inflict damage on South Korea and Japan has risen exponentially.

Like the authoritarian rulers of the three principal revisionist powers, North Korean dictator Kim Jong-un's primary objective is regime survival. Yet he also dreams of unifying the peninsula under his control. Kim's nuclear capability, which is believed to number between ten and twenty fission weapons, is far better suited to support regime survival than territorial expansion.[8] Thus he is highly unlikely to risk the former objective to achieve the latter. The principal threat from North Korea may emerge if Kim concludes he must engage in nuclear brinksmanship to gain the military and economic assistance he believes is needed to maintain himself in power.[9]

There is a fifth, albeit significantly less formidable challenge to the existing international order in the form of radical Sunni Islamism reflected most prominently by al Qaeda and, more recently, the Islamic State of Iraq and Syria (ISIS). Although their military capabilities are exceedingly modest compared to those of the three major revisionist states, these radical groups have demonstrated an ability to punch well above their weight and impose highly disproportionate costs on those who oppose them, principally through waging a form of modern irregular warfare, and through acts of terrorism.

Their objectives center on expelling foreign military forces and influences from Muslim lands, which stretch from the Atlantic Ocean at the western Maghreb to the Indonesian archipelago; overthrowing apostate Muslim regimes that have misled the *ummah*; and re-establishing a caliphate that encompasses all lands that have ever been under Islamic control, which include significant parts of Europe.[10] Currently centered in the Middle East, both al Qaeda and ISIS have demonstrated the ability to conduct terrorist strikes beyond the region and to recruit supporters on a global scale, thanks in no small measure to the use of modern social media.

In summary, while there are some similarities relative to the last time a major challenge to U.S. security emerged in the late 1940s, the differences in both scale and form make the current challenge far more substantial.

Projecting power

The United States is an insular power with global interests. Enabled by the advantage it has long enjoyed in the scale of its economy relative to its rivals as well as its portfolio of allies and partners along the Eurasian periphery, the U.S. has sought to project military power to protect those interests and to defend its homeland as far from its shores as possible. Since World War II, the U.S. military has developed a distinctive style of projecting and sustaining large forces overseas. It relies heavily on building up combat power at friendly forward bases, and employing naval and air forces to protect the lines of communication to the United States.

During World War II, however, U.S. military operations to project power onto hostile shores often proved costly, as evidenced by assaults at Omaha Beach, Okinawa and Anzio. During the Cold War large-scale U.S. power-projection operations were conducted exclusively against minor powers at remarkably low cost in casualties and equipment during limited wars in Korea, Vietnam and the Middle East. In the two decades following the Soviet Union's collapse the U.S. military's power-projection capabilities were effectively unchallenged.

This period of relatively uncontested power-projection operations is coming to a close. The maturation of the precision-strike regime, particularly with respect to capabilities being fielded by the three revisionist powers, as well as the proliferation of nuclear weapons to hostile states in the developing world, finds the prospective cost of projecting power along traditional U.S. lines increasing dramatically.

For example, China is currently developing a multi-dimensional anti-access/area-denial (A2/AD)[11] network along its eastern air and maritime approaches. This network includes a variety of capabilities designed to defeat U.S. power-projection forces. They include extended-range, conventional precision-strike weapons and the command, control, communications, computers, intelligence, surveillance, and reconnaissance (C4ISR) systems necessary for accurate, over-the-horizon targeting of both fixed and mobile targets at ever-greater ranges, to include both U.S. forward bases and major surface warships. In addition to increasing its ability to strike the U.S. military's "muscle," China's People's Liberation Army (PLA) is also developing a range of anti-satellite capabilities, cyber and other electronic warfare weapons to attack American battle networks that comprise its military's "nervous system."

As Defense Secretary Robert Gates observed in 2009:

> [W]hen considering the military-modernization programs of countries like China, we should be concerned less with their potential ability to

challenge the U.S. symmetrically—fighter to fighter or ship to ship—and more with their ability to disrupt our freedom of movement and narrow our strategic options. Their investments in cyber and anti-satellite warfare, anti-air and anti-ship weaponry, and ballistic missiles could threaten America's primary way to project power and help allies in the Pacific—in particular our forward air bases and carrier strike groups. This would degrade the effectiveness of short-range fighters and put more of a premium on being able to strike from over the horizon—whatever form that capability might take.[12]

While China is the pacing threat, both Russia and Iran are developing their own A2/AD capabilities to fit their unique circumstances.[13]

Finally, the nuclear monopoly enjoyed by the United States against countries in the developing world no longer exists. North Korea joined the nuclear club a decade ago and Iran is on its way to becoming a threshold nuclear state. Although not hostile to the United States, Pakistan, which became a nuclear power in 1998, is both politically unstable and producing nuclear weapons at a prodigious rate.[14]

Simply put, the return of great power competition combined with the maturation of the precision-strike regime and the slow but persistent proliferation of nuclear weapons is sharply increasing the cost, perhaps to prohibitive levels, the U.S. military would incur in gaining or maintaining access to, and freedom of maneuver in, three regions of vital interest along the Eurasian periphery. In retrospect, it appears the relative ease in which the U.S. military conducted power-projection operations over the last 70 years will be viewed as an anomaly, with the costs associated with conducting such operations increasing substantially, perhaps to levels not experienced since the two world wars.[15]

Irregular warfare

The maturation of the precision-strike regime also seems certain to raise the costs of the U.S. military in waging various forms of irregular warfare. Following World War II, the U.S. military became accustomed to conducting combat operations with secure rear areas. Large U.S. bases such as those in Japan during the Korean War, Cam Ranh Bay in South Vietnam a decade later and, more recently, Camp Victory in Iraq and Bagram Air Base in Afghanistan have been near sanctuaries from attack in the midst of conflict. Just as forward bases are likely to be under severe attack from conventional enemy forces, so too will they be subjected to attack, albeit on a more modest scale, by irregular forces armed with "RAMM" (rocket, artillery, mortar, and missile) weaponry. The 2006 Second Lebanon War waged between Hezbollah and Israel is the proverbial "canary in the mineshaft." It showed how a new, more deadly form of irregular conflict—"irregular warfare under high-technology conditions"—or "hybrid war," may be emerging. The 34-day conflict showed how difficult it is becoming to defend key fixed targets like military bases, critical economic infrastructure, and densely populated areas against well-equipped irregular forces armed with RAMM weaponry. During the 34–day conflict, Hezbollah fired some 4,000 rockets into Israel. Most of these were short-range, and all of them were unguided. Yet more than 100,000 Israeli citizens evacuated their homes.[16] The war's economic impact was considerable. A major disaster was narrowly averted when a Hezbollah Katyusha rocket stuck Israel's Haifa oil refinery. Fortunately it hit an open area in the complex. Had it struck one of the petrochemical storage areas roughly half a million people would have been in danger.[17]

Some of Hezbollah's rockets, although short-range by modern military standards, could be fired over 50 miles. Compare this to the mortars and rockets used by Viet Cong guerrillas against U.S. bases in South Vietnam. To combat that threat, U.S. forces employed patrols to keep the enemy beyond his four-mile mortar range. Applying this approach against an enemy whose rocket range extends out to 50 miles is simply not practical.[18]

The problem seems destined to become even more challenging. Precision-guided RAMMs ("G-RAMMs") are proliferating. As this trend continues, it will vastly enhance the striking power of irregular forces.

The global commons

The U.S. military's ability to project and sustain power far from America's shores also enables its participation in the global economy. Both require access to the global commons—the seas, airspace, space and cyberspace. This access has been generally uncontested over the past quarter-century. In recent years, however, the revisionist powers, as well as hostile minor powers and radical non-state groups, have been fielding capabilities to contest access to the commons.

The A2/AD challenge to forward air and maritime operations has been noted, as has the growing challenge to space-based systems. Cyberspace is another domain where the U.S. military's secure access (as well as that of civil society) is increasingly challenged. The competition is also spreading to the seabed. The development of a global undersea telecommunications network in the 19th century made it a target of military operations in the First World War. Today the backbone of the information economy moves via undersea cables. Moreover, shortly after World War II the United States began exploring for oil and natural gas offshore. Today nearly one-third of the world's oil and gas production comes from offshore facilities.[19]

As with the Internet, seabed infrastructure developers assumed a benign geopolitical environment, or that the government would protect the infrastructure. Yet technological advances are rendering critical undersea infrastructure increasingly vulnerable. Once possessed by only the most advanced navies, autonomous underwater vehicles, or robotic submersibles, are now commercially available and capable of carrying explosives and contraband cargo. Latin American drug runners employ submersible and semi-submersible craft to move their freight, and it appears that other non-state entities will be increasingly able to operate in the undersea domain.[20] This suggests that, in the future, maritime commerce raiding will take on very different characteristics than it has in the past.

Strategic warfare

From the onset of the Cold War until its end over 40 years later, U.S. policy makers, strategists and planners devoted considerable time and mental energy to the nuclear competition with the Soviet Union. The "nuclear balance," as it was referred to in the Pentagon, was generally seen as bipolar in its character, and "stable" in the sense that advantage accrued to, and remained with, the offense. Stability was further enhanced in the minds of many strategists once both super-powers possessed the ability to survive a surprise attack and deliver a devastating counter strike. Robert Oppenheimer described the situation as similar to that confronting two scorpions in a bottle, where one could attack the other only at the risk of its own destruction.

Following the Cold War tensions between the U.S. and Russia declined dra-matically. American policy makers accorded increased emphasis to nuclear non-proliferation and securing nuclear materials. Arms reductions among the nuclear powers remain focused, as they had been during the Cold War, primarily on reducing the U.S. and Russian arsenals. In reality, however, geopolitical and military-technical developments as well as advances in the cognitive sciences are arguably making the goal of avoiding nuclear use significantly more challenging than during the Cold War.

We have moved from a strategic warfare competition dominated almost exclusively by nuclear weapons, to one in which nuclear weapons maintain a dominant position, but in which other capabilities have emerged as significant factors in the balance. Put another way, the "nuclear balance," upon which so much effort was devoted to assessing during the Cold War, has become the "stra-tegic balance." The precision warfare revolution and the rise of advanced battle networks have fulfilled Russian military theorist predictions that conventional weaponry would, in some instances, approach the effectiveness of nuclear weap-ons.[21] This is made clear from Chinese and Russian concerns regarding the U.S. military's efforts to develop conventional prompt global strike capabilities and advanced air and missile defenses. They argue the United States seeks "absolute security" through the use of "strategic conventional weapons."[22] Put another way, the relatively clear "firebreak" between conventional and nuclear war that existed during the Cold War has become progressively blurred.[23] Further com-plicating matters is the uncertain potential of cyber weapons to support strategic strikes against an enemy's nuclear and conventional strategic forces (such as by disabling their command-and-control and early warning systems) and key eco-nomic targets. The bottom line is that traditional ways of assessing the competi-tion among states with respect to nuclear weapons must be expanded to include these new factors that affect states' views on the value of nuclear weapons and the circumstances in which they would be employed.

While the strategic competition is increasingly multidimensional in character, it is also becoming increasingly multipolar. As U.S. and Russian nuclear arsenals continue to shrink, the barrier to fielding a "superpower-size" arsenal continues to fall. It is hardly far-fetched to think that in a decade or two China will have achieved nuclear superpower status, creating an "n–player" or multipolar strategic competition. Such competitions have already emerged at the regional level, as is the case in South Asia between China, India and Pakistan. If Russian military exercises are any indication, Moscow sees itself in a strategic competition not only with the United States and NATO, but also with China. Should Iran deploy nuclear weapons, it may find itself in a competition not only with Israel but with with a nuclear-armed Saudi Arabia and Turkey as well.[24]

The policy and strategy challenges that emerge from these geopolitical and military-technical trends are truly formidable. They extend far beyond making progress toward a world without nuclear weapons and reducing American and Russian nuclear weapon inventories by a few hundred more weapons.

Deterrence

When President Eisenhower ruled out preventive war against the Soviet Union, U.S. national security strategy became increasingly anchored to deterrence. Deterrence relies on a "rational" actor whose calculations of cost, benefit, and risk are sufficiently well understood to enable its rival to establish, with high confidence, a condition in which the object of deterrence views the costs of undertaking a proscribed course of action as exceeding the anticipated benefits. From very early on in the Cold War U.S. strategy relied heavily on deterrence through the threat of inflicting unacceptable punishment. This was particularly the case with respect to a prospective Russian nuclear attack or conventional assault on Western Europe. In the case of threats posed by North Korea against South Korea, it was possible to rely on deterrence through denial: convincing North Korean dictator Kim Il-sung that he could not achieve his objective through aggression, so there was no point in trying. Although deterrence was never a universal remedy during the Cold War, it proved out in the most demanding cases.

The trends described above suggest that deterrence, in both its punishment and denial forms, will not be as sturdy a pillar in U.S. defense strategy going forward as it was during the last period of intense great power competition. In particular, the movement of military competition into relatively new domains— space, cyberspace and the seabed—is characterized by competitions that favor the offense. This means that, given an equal amount of resources, the attacker has the advantage. Hence deterrence through denial places the defender in the position of having to spend disproportionately greater resources to maintain his position. Owing to the rise of major revisionist threats, China in particular, and the erosion of its own financial position, the United States is less able to pursue this sort of "rich-man's" strategy now than it was immediately following the Cold War.

Deterrence in these domains through the threat of punishment is complicated further by the problem of attribution. Increasing numbers of countries and even non-state groups are gaining access to capabilities once reserved for the world's major militaries, such as unmanned underwater vehicles (UUVs) and sophisticated cyber tools. If several oil well heads in the Gulf of Mexico are blown off by bombs delivered by UUVs, or if parts of the U.S. electric grid are disabled by a cyber attack, it may prove difficult to identify the attacker with a high degree of confidence. The same challenge may hold if, for example, a satellite's optics are disabled by an earth-based laser based near the border of China and Russia, or by one positioned at sea. This may encourage risk-tolerant enemies to take their chances and conduct such attacks in the belief that they can avoid being identified, and thus escape retaliation.

Deterrence through the threat of punishment (often referred to as "assured destruction") appeared to hold up well during the Cold War. As the firebreak between conventional and nuclear strategic war continues to blur, however, it may become more difficult to discern when the threshold into strategic warfare has been crossed. This could weaken deterrence to nuclear use. Complicating matters further, in a multipolar nuclear competition, U.S. efforts to deter one rival may have the opposite effect upon another. For example, deploying U.S. missile defenses in Eastern Europe and South Korea to address threats from Iran and North Korea, respectively, are seen by Russia (in the former case) and China (in the latter case) as threats to their nuclear forces.[25]

Strategies relying on deterrence may also become casualties of geography. During the Cold War, the United States and the Soviet Union's land-based ICBMs, population, and industrial centers were separated from one another by thousands of miles. This geographic separation provided each side with between 20 and 30 minutes' warning of a major nuclear attack launched from the other's territory.

Today there are situations in which nuclear attack warning time is reduced to levels that threaten to erode crisis stability, undermining efforts at deterrence. Nuclear powers such as China, India, Pakistan, and Russia lie in close geographic proximity to each other. All have a hundred nuclear weapons or more, possess ballistic missile delivery systems, and are modernizing both their missile forces and their nuclear arsenals.

In the case of India and Pakistan, owing to the speed at which ballistic missiles travel, both sides' attack warning times would be perhaps as little as five or six minutes. This would place enormous strain on their early warning and command-and-control systems—assuming they have the technical, human, and material resources to field, man, and maintain them at high levels of readiness. Depending on how their missile forces are deployed, the same situation could quickly obtain with respect to Chinese and Russian nuclear forces, as well as

Chinese and Indian nuclear forces. A similar problem may arise if Iran acquires nuclear weapons, given its geographic proximity to Israel.

Their ability to deter nuclear use may be compromised by the absence of effective early warning and command-and-control systems. In the case of a multipolar regional nuclear environment, a state could face threats from several nuclear-armed powers.

The means at hand

Given the growing security challenges confronting the United States, it would seem likely that it would increase significantly the resources being devoted to defense. This, however, is not the case. Nor does it seem likely to occur in the foreseeable future, absent some catastrophic event. Even then, the country would face more formidable challenges in generating military power than it would have confronted in the late 1940s.

For the first time since the Great Depression, as the security challenges facing the nation are increasing the United States is cutting its defenses. The defense budget was cut by over 14 percent in real terms between 2010 and 2016, and declined by roughly 30 percent as a share of the nation's Gross Domestic Product (GDP). The independent Congressional Budget Office (CBO) projects a further 19 percent decline over the next decade, from 3.2 to 2.6 percent of GDP.[26]

This is not to say that the United States and its allies should seek to maintain a level of defense spending pegged to a particular percentage of GDP. The level of defense spending should be a function of many factors, among them: the scale and form of the threats to U.S. interests; the level of risk the American people are willing (and able) to accept to those interests; social factors (such as the additional cost incurred for maintaining a volunteer force as opposed to employing conscription); the level of contributions from Washington's allies and partners; how efficiently resources are employed; how effective a strategy is developed; and how well that strategy is executed.

The resources the United States plans to devote to defense relative to those being invested by the revisionist powers finds the United States accumulating ever-greater risk to its security. Robert Gates, defense secretary for President George W. Bush and President Barack Obama, put it bluntly in stating that cutting U.S. funding for defense "certainly sends a signal that we are not interested in protecting our global interests."[27]

America's most capable allies are contributing even less. Only the United Kingdom currently plans to budget more than NATO's declared minimum of 2 percent of GDP. France stands at 1.8 percent, Germany at 1.2 percent and Italy at 1 percent. In the Far East Japan remains tethered to its self-imposed ceiling of 1 percent.[28]

Compounding the problem, the shift in the form of the military competition finds the U.S. military risking several major capital stock assets depreciating in value at accelerating rates. For example, the F-35 advanced fighter aircraft, by far the U.S.

military's most expensive new weapon system, is being built to last for decades. Yet it may have a difficult time getting to the fight in the face of rivals' growing A2/AD capabilities.[29] The Pentagon also remains challenged by how to make use of nearly $50 billion in mine-resistant ambush preventive (MRAP) vehicles that appear to have been "one-trick ponies" in Afghanistan and Iraq.[30]

Funding for readiness and new equipment is being crowded out by rapidly rising personnel costs, which since 9/11 have outstripped even the defense budget ramp-up that followed the terrorist attacks. On a per capita basis, personnel costs have increased by over 50 percent, even after inflation is taken into account.[31]

One might argue that after Soviet Russia detonated its atomic bomb in August 1949 and the Communists seized power in China, the United States persisted in efforts to keep defense expenses and its military force structure at modest levels. What distinguishes the United States during that period from the present was its ability to mobilize vast resources for defense, and to do so with remarkable speed, which it did following the invasion of South Korea in June 1950. The war saw defense expenditures increase from roughly 4 percent of GDP to over 11 percent, with budgets averaging roughly 7 percent of GDP for nearly 40 years until the Cold War's end.[32]

Is the United States capable today of undertaking a sustained defense effort similar to the one it did during the last era of great power competition? Several factors strongly suggest it would prove far more challenging today than in the early days of the Cold War.

Command of resources

The entitlement state

The American people, through their government, have made commitments to themselves and to future generations in the form of entitlements. These commitments, such as Social Security and Medicare, are consuming an increasing portion of the federal budget and are becoming ever more difficult to sustain. The expansion of social welfare programs in the United States, which began with Social Security in 1935 and expanded greatly with the Great Society programs of the mid-1960s, has continued into the 21st century with the Affordable Care Act ("Obamacare") and government-provided prescription drug benefits. Over the past 50 years spending on entitlement programs ("mandatory spending") has increased from 4.5 percent of GDP to 13.3 percent, and is expected to grow to 15 percent over the next decade.[33] Perhaps even more worrisome, both the Social Security and Medicare trust funds are drawing down their reserves.[34]

Debt

Recent CBO baseline projections paint a gloomy picture regarding U.S. debt. They find that growth in the federal government's spending, driven primarily by Social Security, health care, and interest payments on the country's debt—will outstrip revenue growth over the coming decade. Consequently, budget deficits will rise more sharply, from an already high level of $439 billion in FY 2015 to $1.4 trillion in FY 2026, whereupon it will reach 4.9 percent of GDP.[35] The government's interest payments on the country's debt are projected to more than double as a percentage of GDP, from 1.4 percent to 3.0 percent over the next decade. The CBO finds that this level of debt "would have significant negative consequences for the budget and the economy."[36] Even more ominously, some experts believe "We are seeing a vicious cycle in which the unsustainable debts of the future can no longer be rolled over to the next generation."[37] When the projected demands of the Entitlement State are added to debt interest payments, the combined expense—apart from the discretionary portion of the budget—will stand at 18 percent of the United States' GDP.[38]

Should it become necessary, can the United States generate a comparable level of effort for national defense as it did during the Cold War? Despite these sobering figures, it can.[39] That being said, such an effort will be far more difficult to accomplish than it was during the Cold War, requiring significantly greater sacrifices by the American people.

Manpower

America's Baby Boomer generation represented a huge source of manpower during much of the Cold War's early decades. Moreover, conscription—or "selective service"—provided a means of maintaining personnel costs at relatively low levels. A large percentage of American males were both qualified to serve, and did. During the Korean War, roughly 70 percent of draft-age American males were in uniform. Even during the Vietnam War, when a variety of exemptions enabled substantial numbers of young men to avoid the draft, 43 percent served.[40]

Things have changed substantially since then. Conscription ended in 1973, replaced by an all-volunteer military. Today, even if all 21 million men and women in the 17–21 age groups wanted to enlist, less than 30 percent would be qualified for service. About 9.5 million lack basic education skills. Another one-third are overweight, have criminal records, or possess other undesirable qualities. This leaves about 4.5 million qualified to serve.[41] During FY 2015 the U.S. military sought to recruit 177,000 people, mostly from those in the 17–21 age group. They succeeded, but only by the Army advancing those scheduled for induction in FY 2016 to cover the shortfall.[42]

Given social and resource constraints, despite a substantially larger population base than in Cold War era, it is difficult to see how the U.S. can quickly or easily expand the military as it did in World War II, or even during the Korean and Vietnam wars, for that matter.

Allies

Should the United States look to its allies to augment substantially its military capabilities, it is likely to be disappointed. America's major allies, who made significant military contributions to collective defense during the Cold War, are even more challenged in their ability to generate military power. France, Germany, Great Britain and Italy are all further along the path toward welfare-statism than is the United States. Moreover, their demographic profile is far worse than America's, with their populations aging at a significantly greater rate. The trend, which would be difficult to reverse over the next several decades and impossible to do so in the near term, is toward ever-greater numbers of pensioners and ever fewer workers to support them. It also means, as in the United States' case, more of the public purse being diverted into entitlement payments with progressively less available for defense. Declining numbers of young people in these countries also raises the costs of manpower for the military services that have abandoned conscription in favor of all-volunteer forces.

The situation is made worse by these countries' increasing tendency to act as "free riders," relying on the United States to provide for their security.[43] This worked in the immediate post-Cold War period when the greatest threat to peace was Milosevic's Serbia, Saddam Hussein's Iraq or Kim Jong-il's (non-nuclear) North Korea. But the world now is a far more dangerous place.

Popular support

The early days of the Cold War found the American people willing to support the costs of the Marshall Plan, the largest foreign-assistance program in the country's history, as well as defense expenditures that reached high single-digits in terms of GDP percentage. A majority of the U.S. public supported conscription.[44] This willingness to sacrifice other priorities to meet the growing challenge posed by the Soviet Union stands in stark contrast to current U.S. public attitudes. The will to address growing security challenges both in terms of restoring the nation's economic foundation and buttressing its defenses, either through personal or material sacrifice, is generally lacking.[45]

The need for strategy

Given the security challenges outlined above, it seems clear that an overhaul of U.S. national security organizations and processes is needed. Before this can be undertaken, however, the United States must decide upon a strategy to ensure the limited resources at hand are employed as efficiently and effectively as possible. At the time the National Security Act was being drafted, the effort to identify and set U.S. strategic objectives was already underway. George Kennan's famous "Long Telegram" in 1946 set the foundation for the containment strategy that followed.[46] Early in 1947 President Harry Truman's "doctrine" committed the United States to resist Soviet expansion in Europe. Shortly thereafter the Marshall Plan, another key part of the emerging U.S. strategy, was enacted to assist the European democracies' economies to recover from the war's devastation. Before the decade was out the United States became the centerpiece of the North Atlantic alliance (NATO), committing itself to the military defense of Western Europe. These elements of an overall strategy of containment and forward collective defense helped inform the structure and processes needed to execute the strategy.

Simply stated, the experience of the late 1940s suggests that any contemporary effort to restructure U.S. national security organizations and processes must be accomplished in tandem with the crafting of a strategy that addresses the security challenges described above. It is, after all, the strategy that will set forth what the United States is seeking to accomplish, and by what methods and means. Only then can the important work of ensuring the government can execute the strategy successfully be truly completed.

Notes

1 Dmitri Trenin, "The Revival of the Russian Military: How Moscow Reloaded," *Foreign Affairs*, May–June 2016, available at www.foreignaffairs.com/articles/russia-fsu/2016-04-18/revival-russian-military.
2 Nikolai Sokov, "Why Russia Calls a Limited Nuclear Strike 'De-Escalation'," *Bulletin of the Atomic Scientists*, March 2014, available at http://thebulletin.org/why-russia-calls-limited-nuclear-strike-de-escalation.
3 Council on Foreign Relations, "China's Maritime Disputes," available at www.cfr.org/interactives/chinas-maritime-disputes?cid=otr-marketing_use-china_sea_InfoGuide#!/chinas-maritime-disputes?cid=otr-marketing_use-china_sea_InfoGuide.
4 Andrew S. Erickson and Joel Wuthnow, "Barriers, Springboards and Benchmarks: China Conceptualizes the Pacific `Island Chains,'" *The China Quarterly*, January 2016, pp. 11–16.
5 According to World Bank data and research conducted by members of the Maddison Project, Germany had 35.6 percent of the United States' GDP in 1917 when the U.S. entered World War I. In 1944, the year Nazi Germany's GDP peaked during World War II, its GDP was 24.8 percent that of the United States, while Japan's GDP (which peaked in 1943) was but 13.6 percent that of the U.S. In 1980, with the United States suffering from stagflation, the Soviet Union's GDP was still only 40.4 percent that of its U.S. rival. The World Bank, "GDP at Market Prices (Current US\$)," no date. Available at http://data.worldbank.org/indicator/NY.GDP.MKTP.CD; and The Maddison Project, "World Economics: Measuring the World," no date. Available at www.rug.nl/ggdc/historicaldevelopment/maddison/releases/maddison-project-database-2018
6 Estimates for 2014 have Russia's GDP at 18 percent the size of China's. Accessed at The World Bank, "GDP at Market Prices (Current US\$)," no date. Available at http://data.worldbank.org/indicator/NY.GDP.MKTP.CD.
7 Andrew F. Krepinevich, Jr., *Archipelagic Defense* (Tokyo, Japan: Sasakawa Peace Foundation, 2017), pp. 16–42.
8 Some analysts estimate Pyongyang could have as many as fifty to a hundred weapons by 2020. Joel S. Wit and Sun Young Ahn, *North Korea's Nuclear Futures: Technology and Strategy* (Washington, DC: U.S.-Korea Institute at SAIS, Johns Hopkins University, 2015), p. 8. See also David Albright, *North Korean Plutonium and Weapon-Grade Uranium Inventories* (Washington, DC: Institute for Science and International Security, revised October 7, 2015).
9 For a description of how the North Korean nuclear threat might manifest itself in the form of nuclear use, see Andrew F. Krepinevich, Jr., "North Korea," in Andrew F. Krepinevich and Jacob Cohn, *Rethinking Armageddon: Scenario Planning in the Second Nuclear Age* (Washington, DC: Center for Strategic and Budgetary Assessments, 2016), pp. 65–81.

10 Tim Lister, "What Does ISIS Really Want?" *CNN*, December 11, 2015, available at www.cnn.com/2015/12/11/middleeast/isis-syria-iraq-caliphate.

11 "Anti-access" threats are defined at those associated with preventing U.S. forces from deploying to forward bases in a theater of operations, while "area-denial" threats aim to prevent the U.S. military's freedom of action in an area of operations. See Andrew F. Krepinevich, Jr., *Why AirSea Battle?* (Washington, DC: Center for Strategic and Budgetary Assessments, 2010), pp. 8–11.

12 Secretary of Defense Robert M. Gates, Speech to the Air Force Association Convention, National Harbor, MD, Wednesday, September 16, 2009, available at http://archive.defense.gov/speeches/speech.aspx?speechid=1379

13 Andrew F. Krepinevich, Jr., *Preserving the Balance* (Washington, DC: CSBA, 2017), pp. 51–52

14 Tim Craig, "Report: Pakistan's Nuclear Arsenal Could Become the World's Third Largest," *Washington Post*, August 27, 2015, available at www.washingtonpost.com/world/asia_pacific/report-pakistans-nuclear-arsenal-could-become-the-worlds-third-biggest/2015/08/26/6098478a-4c0c-11e5-80c2-106ea7fb80d4_story.html; Paul K. Kerr and Mary Beth Nikitin, "Pakistan's Nuclear Weapons," *Congressional Research Service*, February 12, 2016, available at www.fas.org/sgp/crs/nuke/RL34248.pdf. See also C. Christine Fair, "Pakistan's Army Is Building an Arsenal of 'Tiny' Nuclear Weapons—and it's Going to Backfire," *Quartz*, December 21, 2015, available at http://qz.com/579334/pakistans-army-is-building-an-arsenal-of-tiny-nuclear-weapons-and-its-going-to-backfire/.

15 It should be noted that the costs of projecting power against the Soviet Union were expected to be extremely high. Fortunately such operations never became part of the U.S. military's battle history.

16 Meir Elran, "The Civilian Front in the Second Lebanon War," in Shlomo Brom and Meir Elran, eds., *The Second Lebanon War: Strategic Perspectives* (Tel Aviv, Israel: Institute for National Security Studies, 2007), pp. 104–105.

17 Fadi Eyadat, "Katyusha Rocket Hit Haifa Oil Refineries Complex During Second Lebanon War," *Haaretz*, November 19, 2017, available at www.haaretz.com/news/katyusha-rocket-hit-haifa-oil-refineries-complex-during-second-lebanon-war-1.216336.

18 The "keep out" patrol area against systems with a four-mile range is roughly 50 square miles, while the patrol area for systems with a 50-mile range is over 7,800 square miles.

19 Roughly 30 percent of global oil production and 27 percent of global gas production comes from offshore wells. Planete Energies, "Offshore Oil and Gas Production," available at www.planete-energies.com/en/medias/close/offshore-oil-and-gas-production.

20 Semi-submersibles (which sit very low in the water) and submarines (which are capable of running completely submerged) are used primarily to transport cocaine from mangrove swamps along the Pacific coast of Colombia and Ecuador to transshipment points up the Central American isthmus. Semi-submersibles are typically limited in range to roughly 2,000 miles, but the fully submersible vehicles are assessed to have ranges that would enable them to travel all the way to the United States. Each can carry more $100 million in drugs on a single voyage. By one estimate, semi-submersibles make roughly 120 trips in a year. Less is known about the true submarines, as they have been seized ashore but never successfully intercepted at sea. See Robert Mackey "Advances in 'Narco-Submarine' Technology," *New York Times*, July 6, 2010; Michael S. Schmidt and Thom Shanker "To Smuggle More Drugs, Traffickers Go Under the Sea," *New York Times*, September 9, 2012; "Self-Propelled Semi Submersible (SPSS)," Joint Interagency Task Force South Fact Sheet, 2008; and Lance J. Watkins "Self-Propelled Semi-Submersibles: The Next Great Threat to Regional Security and Stability," unpublished paper, Naval Postgraduate School, June, 2011.

21 N. F. (Fred) Wikner, "'ET' and the Soviet Union," *Armed Forces Journal International*, November 1984, p. 100; Marshal N. V. Ogarkov, "The Defense of Socialism: Experience of History and the Present Day," Красная звезда [*Red Star*], May 9, 1984; trans. Foreign Broadcast Information Service, *Daily Report: Soviet Union*, vol. 3, no. 091, annex no. 054, May 9, 1984, p. R19.

22 Richard Weitz, "The Impossible Quest for Absolute Security," *YaleGlobal Online*, Yale University, July 11, 2017, available at https://yaleglobal.yale.edu/content/impossible-quest-absolute-security.

23 For a detailed discussion of this issue, see Barry D. Watts, *Nuclear-Conventional Firebreaks and the Nuclear Taboo* (Washington, DC: CSBA, 2013).

24 Saudi King Abdullah stated, "If Iran developed nuclear weapons … everyone in the region would do the same." A similar statement was made by Prince Turki al-Faisal, former head of Saudi Arabia's General Intelligence Directorate. In 2012, a senior Saudi source declared, "There is no intention currently to pursue a unilateral military nuclear program but the dynamics will change immediately if the Iranians develop their own nuclear capability. … politically, it would be completely unacceptable to have Iran with a nuclear capability and not the kingdom." There have been unconfirmed reports of a Saudi-Pakistani nuclear connection. Naser al-Tamini, "Clear or Nuclear: Will Saudi Arabia Get the Bomb?" *Al Arabiya*, May 21, 2013, available at: http://english.alarabiya.net/en/News/middle-east/2013/05/21/Will-Riyadh-get-the-bomb-.html; *Chain Reaction: Avoiding a Nuclear Arms Race in the Middle East*, Report to the Committee on Foreign Relations, United States Senate (Washington, DC: Government Printing Office, 2008), pp. ix, 12, 20; and Ibrahim al-Marashi, "Saudi Petro-Nukes? Riyadh's Nuclear Intentions and Regime Survival Strategies," in *Forecasting Nuclear Proliferation in the 21st Century, Vol. II: A Comparative Perspective*, William C. Potter and Gaukhar Mukhatzhanova, eds. (Stanford: Stanford University Press, 2010), pp. 77–78. Turkey has said it will not tolerate Iran acquiring nuclear weapons but has left the issue of whether it would pursue its own nuclear arsenal open. Jeremy Herb, "Ambassador: Turkey 'Cannot Tolerate' Iran Getting Nukes," *The Hill*, December 8, 2011, available at: http://thehill.com/blogs/defcon-hill/policy-and-strategy/198237-ambassador-turkey-cannot-tolerate-iran-getting-nukes.

25 Jane Perlez, Mark Landler and Choe Sang-Hun, "China Blinks on South Korea, Making Nice After a Year of Hostilities," *New York Times*, November 1, 2007, available at https://www.nytimes.com/2017/11/01/world/asia/china-south-korea-thaad.html?_r=0; and Andrew E. Kramer, "Russia Calls New U.S. Missile Defense System a 'Direct Threat'," *New York Times*, May 12, 2016, available at www.nytimes.com/2016/05/13/world/europe/russia-nato-us-romania-missile-defense.html.

26 Unless otherwise stated, budget data presented in this section is derived from CBO, *The Budget and Economic Outlook: 2016 to 2026* (Washington, DC: Congressional Budget Office, January 2016), pp. 20, 151; and Office of the Under Secretary of Defense (Comptroller), *National Defense Budget Estimates for FY 2016* (Washington, DC: Department of Defense, March 2015), pp. 250–51.

27 Fox News Sunday, "Robert Gates on Ukrainian Crisis, 'Reset' with Russia; Sen. Rand Paul Lays Out Vision for America at CPAC," March 9, 2014, available at www.foxnews.com/on-air/fox-news-sunday-chris-wallace/2014/03/09/robert-gates-ukraine-crisis-reset-russia-sen-rand-paul-lays-out-vision-america-cpac#p//v/3319005279001.

28 North Atlantic Treaty Organization, "NATO Publishes Defence Expenditures Data for 2014 and Estimates for 2015," June 22, 2015, available at www.nato.int/nato_static_fl2014/assets/pdf/pdf_2015_06/20150622_PR_CP_2015_093-v2.pdf. See also Kedar Pavgi, "NATO Members' Defense Spending, in Two Charts," Defense One, June 22, 2015, available at www.defenseone.com/politics/2015/06/nato-members-defense-spending-two-charts/116008. During the period 1995–99, the average GDP percentage of key NATO allies devoted to defense finds France at 2.9 percent,

Great Britain at 2.6 percent, and Germany at 1.6 percent. The United States stood at 3.2 percent.

29 For a discussion of the threat posed by A2/AD capabilities to U.S. tactical aircraft positioned forward on major air bases and on aircraft carriers, see Krepinevich, *Archipelagic Defense*, pp. 32–33, 36–40, 56.

30 Max Fisher, "The U.S. Military is Scrapping up to 2,000 of its Mine-Resistant Vehicles, Which Cost $1 Million Each," *Washington Post*, June 30, 2013, available at www.washingtonpost.com/news/worldviews/wp/2013/06/20/the-u-s-military-is-scrapping-up-to-2000-of-its-mine-resistant-vehicles-which-cost-1-million-each/?utm_term=.be10a41a40d3.

31 Andrew F. Krepinevich, Jr., "Overhauling the Army for the Age of Irregular Warfare," *Wall Street Journal*, February 19, 2016, available at www.wsj.com/articles/overhauling-the-army-for-the-age-of-irregular-warfare-1455839486.

32 Robert Higgs, "U.S. Military Spending in the Cold War Era: Opportunity Costs, Foreign Crises, and Domestic Constraints," *Cato Institute,* November 30, 1988, available at https://object.cato.org/pubs/pas/pa114.pdf. See also "Government Spending Chart: Military Defense, U.S. from FY1950 to FY1990," U.S. Government Spending. Com, available at www.usgovernmentspending.com/spending_chart_1950_1990US p_19s2li011mcn_31f.

33 CBO, *Budget and Economic Outlook*, p. 20

34 Current projections find that the Social Security trust fund is projected to be exhausted in 2034. At that point, revenue projections estimate that benefits would be provided at roughly three-quarters of the current scheduled levels through 2089. Social Security and Medicare Boards of Trustees, "Status of the Social Security and Medicare Programs: A Summary of the 2015 Annual Reports," Social Security Administration, available at www.ssa.gov/oact/trsum. The Medicare Hospital Insurance ("Part A") trust fund is projected to be exhausted in 2030, at which point current revenue projections will be sufficient to cover 86 percent of anticipated costs, but will decline further to 80 percent by 2050. The Medicare Supplemental Medical Insurance ("Part B") will be adequately financed since current law enables general revenues to be employed to cover any shortfalls. Nevertheless, Part B costs are expected to rise from 2.0 percent of GDP in 2014 to 3.4 percent in 2035, a 70 percent increase.

35 CBO, *Budget and Economic Outlook,* p. 4.

36 CBO, *Budget and Economic Outlook,* p. 21.

37 Glenn Hubbard and Tim Kane, *Balance: The Economics of Great Powers from Ancient Rome to Modern America* (New York: Simon & Schuster, 2013), p. 211.

38 CBO, *Budget and Economic Outlook,* p. 20.

39 That said, actually being able to wage a protracted *war* against one or more other great powers on the scale of World War II would almost certainly be a far more demanding task than it proved to be in the early 1940s. While the prospect of such a war occurring may be low, should rivals perceive the United States lacks the ability to wage such a war, it could compromise U.S. efforts to deter aggression.

40 "Who Will Fight the Next War?" *The Economist*, October 24, 2015, p. 26, available at www.economist.com/news/united-states/21676778-failures-iraq-and-afghanistan-have-widened-gulf-between-most-americans-and-armed.

41 "Who Will Fight the Next War?", *The Economist*, p. 25

42 "Who Will Fight the Next War?", *The Economist*, p. 26.

43 The most capable U.S. allies have been progressively reducing their defense efforts. In the period prior to 9/11, from 1995–99, the U.S. devoted an average of 3.2 percent of its GDP to defense. The corresponding figure for France during that time was 2.9; for Germany 1.6; and for Britain, 2.6. By 2015 the gap had widened. The United States had increased its share of GDP devoted to defense to 3.6 percent, while the shares of France, Germany, and Britain had all declined substantially. At present only the United Kingdom plans to budget more than NATO's declared minimum of

2 percent of GDP, and it seems increasingly unlikely it will achieve even this modest goal. In the Far East, despite China's massive military buildup, Japan remains tethered to its self-imposed ceiling of 1 percent of GDP for defense. "Information on Defense Expenditures," NATO, updated December 8, 2016, available at http://www.nato.int/cps/en/ natohq/topics_49198.htm.

44 Aaron L. Friedberg, *In the Shadow of the Garrison State* (Princeton, NJ: Princeton University Press, 2000), pp. 178–79

45 When asked to state the issue to which the country should accord top priority, in a poll of American voters before the 2016 elections, economic growth, illegal immigration and health care ranked highest, totaling 43 percent of all responses. "National security" was chosen by 9 percent of those polled. Frank Newport, "Economy Remains Top Priority for Next President," *Gallup News*, June 1, 2016, available at http://news.gallup.com/poll/191960/economy-remains-top-priority-next-president.aspx. In a poll conducted by the Pew Research Center asking Americans to list their top public policy priorities, "terrorism" was listed first. That being said, the potential of terrorists to inflict human, material and financial costs on the United States is, at present, exceedingly small when compared to that posed by revisionist states like China, Russia and even Iran. "Strengthening the military" was eleventh in the overall list of voter priorities. Of note, support for "reducing the budget deficit" as a priority declined between 2013 and 2015, the date of the poll. "Public's Priorities Reflect Changing Conditions at Home and Abroad," *Pew Research Center*, January 15, 2015, available at www.people-press.org/2015/01/15/publics-policy-priorities-reflect-changing-conditions-at-home-and-abroad.

46 Telegram, George Kennan to Secretary of State, 9 p.m., February 22, 1946, available at www.trumanlibrary.org/whistlestop/study_collections/coldwar/documents/pdf/6-6.pdf.

10

GLOBAL CHALLENGES, U.S. NATIONAL SECURITY STRATEGY, AND DEFENSE ORGANIZATION

Thomas G. Mahnken

We live in challenging times. From the increased risk of great power competition and conflict to the persistent threat posed by non-state actors and the recent shocks to the liberal international order, it is hard to imagine a more complicated security landscape. In order to develop an effective strategy that safeguards U.S. interests in this increasingly threatening world, this chapter addresses the challenges that the United States faces, both the external threats of adversaries and competitors, as well as the internal structural impediments posed by our own government. It also examines some of the United States' enduring strengths and the opportunities that they provide us in confronting these challenges. This chapter concludes by offering recommendations to improve our strategic position and frame our national security discussion going forward.

External challenges

In contrast to the Cold War, the United States does not face a single competitor that serves as the bedrock of American national security strategy and planning. Today, the United States faces an array of challenges that often compete with one another for policymakers' attention and resources. These external threats emanate from great powers, regional actors, terrorist groups, as well as unforeseen or unpredictable developments across the globe. Yet there are also very real internal challenges that risk undermining our ability to shape and respond to this increasingly complex security environment.

Great powers

The tide of great power competition is rising, with China and Russia at the forefront. Both possess sizeable and modernizing nuclear arsenals and are investing in new ways of war that have been tailored, at least in part, to challenge the United States. Moreover, the leaders of China and Russia harbor growing ambitions and, increasingly, the means to back them up. China, in particular, a nation with a rich appreciation for the past, presents a variety of challenges. Evoking what it has branded the "Century of Humiliation" at the hands of Western powers in the 19th and 20th centuries, Beijing continues to press territorial claims in the East and South China Seas. In the East China Sea, China and Japan spar over control of the Senkakus (known in Chinese as Diaoyu), an uninhabited string of islands recognized by U.S. officials as under the administration of Japan and therefore protected by American treaty obligations.[1] Over the past few years, China's military has unilaterally declared an Air Defense Identification Zone over the area, violated Japanese airspace, and patrolled dangerously close to Japanese units both in the air and on the sea. In 2010, fears of an accident became a reality when a Chinese fishing boat collided with Japanese patrol ships in the Senkakus, causing a hostile diplomatic incident. The longer China engages in such provocative maneuvers, the greater the likelihood for an inadvertent escalation.

Likewise, in the South China Sea, Beijing and its neighbors are at odds, particularly over control of Scarborough Shoal, the Spratlys, and the Paracels. Despite the ruling of an international tribunal rejecting Chinese claims to waters within its "nine-dash line," Beijing refuses to abide by the decision.[2] China continues to harass Filipino and Vietnamese boats operating in the area, use civilian fishing vessels – under the guise of a grey zone – to monitor foreign ships, and engage in an artificial island-building campaign to develop port facilities, pave large runways, and deploy advanced air defense systems to the islands. Just as in the East China Sea, Beijing's aggressive behavior raises the risk of conflict and puts in danger numerous aircraft and vessels operating in or above the South China Sea.

Unfortunately, these trends are likely to persist. China's provocative approach to these territorial disputes is undergirded by Beijing's ongoing modernization of its military, both to its weapon systems and personnel structure; China, "a big country," is seeking to gain the upper hand against what it perceives as "small countries."[3] Perhaps most worrisome is the increasing investment in Beijing's nuclear arsenal which, when combined with conventional, information warfare, and space capabilities, amount to an "integrated strategic deterrent."[4] In particular, China's military is augmenting both its silo-based and road-mobile intercontinental ballistic missiles, such as the DF-5 and DF-41, respectively, as well as its nuclear-powered submarines, including the Type 094 and its JL-2 ballistic missiles.[5]

On the force structure and personnel front, China's leadership is making noteworthy changes. Announced by President Xi Jinping in 2015, the reforms are shifting the military's command structure from seven "military regions" to five "theaters of operations," have established a headquarters for ground forces, promoted the rocket force from an "independent branch" to a "full service," created a strategic support force to preside over the space and cyber portfolios, and

restructured roles and missions.[6] Overall, the reforms complement Beijing's preference to develop a larger air force and navy, in particular, with new amphibi-
ous ships, submarines, and surface ships, not to mention aircraft carriers. Out of
the reforms Chinese forces will emerge leaner and increasingly expeditionary, a
move that signals Beijing's interest in conducting out-of-area operations, perhaps
from its first overseas base in Djibouti.[7]

Like China, Russia too presents a number of challenges. A country that
seemed to pose little threat following the Cold War has reemerged as a competitive power that seeks to undermine the current global order. In Europe, Moscow
demonstrates an indifference to sovereignty and international law, annexing
Crimea and Eastern Ukraine. Since 2014, Russia has supported a separatist
movement in Ukraine with funding, personnel, and weapons.[8] It also engages
in cyber warfare, has weaponized energy supplies, conducts large-scale snap
exercises along its neighbors' borders (including simulating nuclear conflict),[9]
finances far-right-wing parties across Europe,[10] and stokes resentment among
Russian minorities living abroad. These incitements are designed to poke at the
sovereignty of former Soviet countries and test the political will of the North
Atlantic Treaty Organization and the European Union.

In the Middle East, Russia supports Syrian president and dictator, Bashar
al-Assad, aligning Moscow with the likes of the Iranian Revolutionary Guard
Corps (IRGC) and Lebanese Hezbollah.[11] Under the guise of fighting terrorism,
Russia has deployed S-300 and S-400 anti-aircraft systems, conducted airstrikes
against opposition forces (and civilian targets), and worked with troops on the
ground in Syria. Moscow's involvement contributes to Syria's horrific humanitarian crisis, prevents the international community from finding solutions to end
the years-long conflict, and, perhaps most noteworthy, demonstrates the costs
Russia is willing to accept in order to exhibit its perceived status, in theory, as a
crucial problem-solver.

Anchoring these provocations across Europe and the Middle East is Russia's
willingness – and almost pleasure – to challenge global norms and disregard
landmark international agreements, such as the Treaties on Conventional Armed
Forces in Europe and Intermediate-Range Nuclear Forces.[12] Over the past few
years, Moscow's leaders have casually referred to using nuclear weapons as part
of its "escalate to-deescalate strategy,"[13] and Russian President Vladimir Putin
has even ventured beyond rhetoric, nearly placing the country's nuclear forces
on alert at the start of the crisis in Crimea[14] and later deploying nuclear-capable
missiles to Kaliningrad. Taken together, Russia's current trajectory of unpre-
dictability and reckless stewardship poses enormous challenges for the international community.

Regional powers

Although not global competitors, Iran and North Korea present their own
unique threats as regional powers. Despite Iran's nominal adherence to the

terms of the Joint Comprehensive Plan of Action (JCPOA), Tehran continues to engage in troubling activity in the Middle East writ large. Testifying before the Senate Armed Services Committee, former Chairman of the Joint Chiefs of Staff General Martin Dempsey highlighted five areas of concern: "ballistic missile technology ... weapons trafficking ... the use of surrogates and proxies ... naval mines and undersea activity ... [and] malicious activity in cyberspace."[15] With respect to ballistic missile technology, Iran seeks to overcome gaps in its current long-range weapons in order to hold at risk and strike, if necessary, key targets in the region, such as hangars, fuel storage depots, and runways. To do so, Tehran is acquiring more advanced guidance systems and is in pursuit of operational anti-ship ballistic missiles and longer-range ballistic missiles that would also extend its bubble over the Arabian Sea as well as into Europe and the United States.[16]

Beyond gaining an advantage militarily, Iran engages in weapons trafficking and proxy support in order to extend its sphere of influence. Among other customers, Houthi rebels in Yemen receive supplies of weapons from Tehran via small boats, and Iranian smugglers also deal in drugs and people, complicating the civil war in Yemen further.[17] The use of surrogates too is deeply embedded in Iran's calculus, supplying both weapons and scientific know-how to active proxies in Iraq, Lebanon, and Syria. Iran has provided, for example, approximately 100,000–150,000 rockets and missiles, including advanced-air-to-ground and ground-to-sea missiles, to Lebanese Hezbollah.[18] In return for the weapons, Iran garners ideological and political sway abroad.

On the seas, multiple incidents in the Gulf reflect an irresponsible attitude that puts international commerce in the Middle East at great risk. The year 2015 witnessed the *Maersk Tigris* incident in which the IRCG-Navy seized a cargo ship for political purposes, as well as the near miss of the U.S. destroyer *Harry S. Truman* and a French frigate during a live-fire exercise conducted by the IRGC-N in the Strait of Hormuz.[19] In cyberspace, too, Iranian provocations are well documented. Policymakers point to the 2012 hacking of Saudi Arabia's Aramco as the wake-up call to Iran's growing cyber capabilities, but Tehran is now relying particularly heavily upon this domain following the JCPOA. With dimmer prospects for acquiring a nuclear weapon, the Iranian regime believes developing a robust cyber capability is a central component of its toolkit.[20] Whether probing cyber networks, engaging in reckless maritime behavior, perpetuating conflicts through the use of proxy forces and supply of weapons, or developing technologies that can hit targets in Europe and the United States, Iran continues to pose substantial challenges across the board.

Further east, North Korea has proven to be an unstable and unpredictable country fixated with nuclear power. To fulfill its core goal of regime stability and survival, Pyongyang is developing a sizeable nuclear arsenal and an ability to deliver those weapons. Over the past year, North Korea has conducted a range of both nuclear and ballistic missile tests and, in September 2016 alone, tested three ballistic missiles in a synchronized launch[21] and detonated its fifth and most powerful nuclear warhead.[22] These tests demonstrate Pyongyang's disregard for the crippling sanctions regime targeting the country, as well as contempt for well-established international agreements, such as the Treaty on the Nonproliferation of Nuclear Weapons. Likewise, its preference for saber rattling and elaborate shows of force, whether demonstrated through missile launches or special operations drills, highlights North Korea's aggressive posture. Most importantly, it exhibits Pyongyang's ability to target South Korea and Japan, including U.S. military bases in both those countries, as well as the American homeland. Should the United States enter into conflict with North Korea, Pyongyang could hold these targets at risk and gain important leverage.[23]

Not only is Pyongyang developing these weapons for its own use, but it also expresses a willingness to sell nuclear technology to other states, challenging global norms to counter nuclear proliferation. In the past, North Korea sold missiles and equipment to both Iran and Syria, even helping the latter build a nuclear reactor.[24] More recently, there is speculation that Pyongyang – described by Secretary of Defense Ashton Carter as "a welcome all-comers kind of proliferator"[25] – is developing its relationship with Tehran further, sharing scientific know-how on the development of ballistic missiles. Taken together, North Korea's dogged pursuit of nuclear weapons, bombastic rhetoric, and careless treatment of sensitive technology – not to mention gross human rights violations – present enormous challenges to the United States and its allies and partners in the region.

Terrorism

The challenges we face are not confined to global and regional powers, but rather include non-state actors as well. We remain engaged in a war, whether we choose to call it that or not, with Al Qaeda and its affiliates, as well as other jihadist groups, such as the Islamic State. Al Qaeda's successful execution of the September 11th, 2001 attacks attracted new adherents to its extremist philosophy and spurred its growth worldwide. Although much of its leadership was decimated in the years following the attacks, the group continues to pose a threat, particularly from its branch in the Arabian Peninsula (AQAP). With Yemen in turmoil, partly due to Saudi Arabia's intervention in the country's civil war, AQAP is gaining new fighters, funding, territory, and weapons.[26] There is growing concern that AQAP will indoctrinate its newly established population centers with radical ideology, strengthening the organization and furthering its aims to attack Western targets.

Beyond Al Qaeda, the latest metamorphosis of these extremist beliefs manifests itself in the Islamic State (IS). Controlling a loose network of territory in Iraq and Syria, IS seeks to establish a caliphate and invoke terror as a means of achieving that goal. It employs horrific tactics within the land it controls, using civilians as human shields, committing mass murder, condoning torture, and engaging in the genocide of religious minorities. The vicious crimes committed against the Yazidis are just one example of IS's brutality. To counter these atrocities and prevent its expansion, the American-led coalition of nations from across Europe, the Middle East, Africa, North America, and Asia is targeting IS leaders and fighters with air strikes,[27] and the Iraqi government too is regaining territory. As a result of IS's diminishing caliphate, it now emphasizes two lines of effort externally: for individual citizens either to carry out attacks under the guise of the IS flag or to execute operations that are coordinated by IS leaders.[28]

The former order is particularly concerning. Attacks inspired by IS and undertaken by so-called "lone wolf attackers" are difficult to monitor and ultimately to defend against. Consider the attacks in San Bernardino and Orlando as two examples. With greater access to extremist content on the Internet and an ability to engage with like-minded jihadists as part of online forums, there are few barriers to self-radicalization. Likewise, the plethora of technology platforms provides a useful means for sharing instructions for attacks planned by IS leadership. Over the past year, IS has conducted attacks across Europe, in France, Germany, Belgium, and Turkey. Although its leaders continue to seek a chemical, biological, or nuclear weapon,[29] soft targets, such as restaurants and sports venues, prove easier to attack given lower levels of security. These acts of terror not only leave physical damage and casualties in their wake, but also instill psychological harm in populations. With terrorist ambitions growing larger abroad as IS loses ground in the Middle East, this war is likely to continue for the foreseeable future.

An uncertain future

Finally, beyond the immediate threats that we face as a nation, the United States will encounter challenges that we either do not foresee or cannot recognize today. Perhaps former Secretary of Defense Robert Gates summed up this sentiment best, lamenting "when it comes to predicting the nature and location of our next military engagements, since Vietnam, our record has been perfect. We have never once gotten it right."[30] Today's international security environment serves as the perfect example. Who predicted the rise of the Islamic State? Europe's refugee crisis? Russia's annexation of Crimea? The surge of populist forces across the globe? Or even the result of the American election?

Surely, the United States recognizes that there is no crystal ball to determine defense investments, planning, and strategy, but we must also acknowledge that history can serve as a strong guide of future contours. The past should not serve as a carbon copy of the future, but there is important work to be done to examine current and historical trends and patterns that can inform decisions in the years to come.

Internal challenges

Beyond the challenges we face across the globe, there are also a number of internal, structural barriers to effective strategy formulation within our own government. These include a tension between national and social security spending, an overrun of expenses in weapon systems, and a cost growth in personnel. Without addressing these challenges, the United States will not have the necessary resources to shape and respond to the increasingly complex security environment of today and of the future.

National and social security spending

Preserving our national security is expensive, and it is far from our government's only expenditure. With growing costs for social security and health care, primarily Medicare, the tradeoff between national and social security spending is becoming painfully apparent, and will only increase. The number of recipients of these programs will grow as baby-boomers retire, the population ages, and overall life expectancy increases. In 2026, for example, Americans aged 65 years or older will represent nearly one-fifth of the entire population, more than double that figure fifty years earlier.[31]

With social funding on the rise, national security spending will compete for the government's shrinking dollars. To date, the former is faring better. In the period from 2001 until 2015, for example, government spending on both economic and social programs grew by 61 percent, while that of national security lagged behind at 38 percent.[32] Yet the divisions are not only between these two programs, but also within national security spending itself. As recent events in the Middle East demonstrate, the military is not the only, and may not be the most appropriate, tool to deal with all the challenges of the future. Surely it will play an integral role, but many of the hybrid or grey zone threats in the years to come will require a more balanced approach to national security.

Going forward, lawmakers on Capitol Hill should strive toward equilibrium, both within national security funding and with social security spending. Without a serious effort to strike a balance that enables both programs to coexist, the tension will only grow stronger and leave us more vulnerable in the long term.

Weapon systems

Acquisition reform is perennially at the top of reform agendas, and yet often falls short in effecting real change to the system. Accounting for approximately 20 percent of the Defense Department's discretionary base budget since the fiscal year 2001, procurement costs are growing at an unsustainable pace.[33] According to a recent study by Deloitte related to aerospace and defense program management, "total cost growth of today's MDAP [Major Defense Acquisition Program] portfolio over the original baseline estimates is 48.3 percent and an average delay of 29.5 months."[34] "In dollar terms," the report continues, "the combined cost overrun for all programs in 2015 was $468 billion, up from $295 billion from a similar study eight years ago."[35] Such enormous overrun costs should be unacceptable under any circumstance, but in a time of fiscal austerity they are particularly harmful. These expenses cost the Pentagon and, ultimately, the taxpayer, billions of dollars and manpower that could be applied elsewhere within the department.

Efforts to streamline acquisition costs such as implementing the Better Buying Power initiatives, involving the service chiefs in setting requirements, and standing up a private sector board to spur innovation[36] are important steps in the right direction. However, even with these reforms, the overall trend is clear: our marginal dollar is depreciating. We are faced with a tradeoff, either to purchase fewer platforms, preventing us from supplying the force at our anticipated level, or to acquire the same number of systems, siphoning funds from elsewhere to absorb the higher cost. Whichever option we choose, we are undermining our national security.

Personnel

Like the overrun expenses of many acquisition programs, the growth of personnel costs is not new; yet it is every bit as concerning. We face long-term cost growth in personnel across the services, and military leaders are the first to sound the alarm. In a 2013 testimony to the Senate Armed Services Committee, General Raymond Odierno, then Chief of Staff of the Army, noted that, "the cost of a soldier has doubled since 2001. It's going to almost double again by 2025."[37] Testifying alongside their Army counterpart, the other service chiefs echoed General Odierno's concerns. Admiral John Greenert, then Chief of Naval Operations, stated that nearly half of each defense dollar goes to personnel, while General James Amos, then Commandant of the Marine Corps, suggested that the figure for his service is almost two-thirds.[38] For the Air Force, General Mark Welsh III, then that service's Chief of Staff, estimated that personnel costs are between 30 and 50 percent. Although General Welsh deemed this range acceptable at the time, he expressed concern over the likely increase in the future, warning that compensation will continue to rise at an unsustainable pace and prevent the services from making other necessary investments. The growth in personnel costs, General Welsh lamented, is a "threat to modernization and readiness."[39]

Not only are rising personnel costs a concern, but the distribution of the defense workforce has an important fiscal component as well. With millions of employees across the globe, it is crucial that the Defense Department has the right mix of civilians, contractors, and uniformed military personnel.[40] A recent Congressional Budget Office study found that if the Pentagon were to convert 80,000 full-time "commercial positions that perform support functions" from military billets to civilian posts, it could save the government an estimated $3.1 to $5.7 billion each year.[41] Such savings should be music to defense officials' ears. Yet a mismatch in work allocations and growing costs in personnel continue to divert scarce resources from other crucial elements of the defense budget. It is essential to invest in developing and retaining the men and women who serve in the military, and provide them with the benefits they deserve, but the Defense Department will soon find itself unable to pay for non-personnel related initiatives should it not find a way to reduce these unsustainable costs.

Enduring advantages

All is not beyond hope, however. Despite the tremendous external and internal challenges that the United States faces, our country enjoys a number of enduring advantages. We can find strength in our strategic geography, economic vitality, attractive culture, global society, robust military power, and enduring alliances and partnerships. Taken together, the United States can draw upon these strengths to confront the threats of today and of the future.

Strategic geography

The United States' physical location has provided us with the luxury of being an insular nation for much of our history. Separated from Europe to the east and the Asia-Pacific to the west, the United States enjoys geography that quells the threat of invasion and diminishes the likelihood of attacks from great powers. Likewise, flanked by friendly neighbors to the north and south, we do not have to worry about volatility or expansionist policies from nearby states that threaten our own borders and undermine our own stability. Certainly we have witnessed horrific attacks on our soil – Pearl Harbor and 9/11 are just two examples – but, unlike many countries across the globe, the United States has never faced the threat of a full-scale invasion. The United States' global alliances and partnerships compound our geographic advantage, allowing us to work together with our international counterparts to meet threats far from our shores before they reach the homeland.

Economic strength

The United States is a strong financial power, maintaining the world's largest economy. The American economy benefits from two key ingredients: an abundance of natural resources and a strong labor market. The United States draws upon its resource supply, exporting, in particular, automobiles and, more recently, even natural gas and oil; in fact, the United States is now a leading oil producer. The labor market too is crucial, with a skilled workforce. With these two elements, the United States can sustain growth in a variety of important sectors, such as aerospace, energy industries, manufacturing, and the STEM field – science, technology, engineering, and mathematics. The United States is also the world leader in innovation, attracting talent from across the globe to study at our universities and work in our cutting-edge companies. The booming industry in Silicon Valley, California is just one example of the technological innovation that drives our economy.

Culture

American culture too is a great strength. We cultivate a culture that embodies our ideals and values, and one that much of the world finds attractive. Consider the impact of Hollywood and the broader entertainment business. American movies and television series are popular across the globe, airing in countless languages and inspiring other countries to adapt their own versions, and American music can be heard in cities as diverse as Tokyo and Nairobi. Likewise, American brands such as Apple and Coca-Cola are coveted and easily recognizable, penetrating international society. How different might the world look without the technological revolution of the iPod and iPhone, for example? Fast-food restaurant chains too like McDonald's and Kentucky Fried Chicken are littered across foreign cities, both small and large. The reach of the United States' soft power is vast, and every bit as important as the economic and military might that reverberates across the world.

American society

As a direct result of our integrative culture, or perhaps because of it, the United States also possesses unique demographic strengths. Our population includes immigrants from nearly every corner of the globe, speaking the full breadth of the world's languages. Think of the iconic photos of immigrants arriving at Ellis Island in the late 19th and early 20th centuries, fleeing persecution or poverty in search of the values and freedoms that define the American way of life. Not only do we welcome newcomers to our shores, but we are only one of a handful of states that weave them into the fabric of society. Every immigrant brings with him or her traditions that feed into a broader American culture, enriching it further with each new addition. Most importantly, anyone, regardless of background, ethnicity, gender, race, or religion, can become an American. Ours is a society where a citizen can succeed because of how hard he or she works, not because of who he or she is. Successfully integrating immigrants, without in the process losing their unique identity, is the hallmark of American society.

Military power

To complement the United States' soft power, our country also possesses a robust military. We have the world's largest nuclear force and the most capable Air Force, Army, Navy, and Marine Corps – a historically unique combination of joint strength. Across the Asia-Pacific, Europe, the Middle East, and elsewhere, the United States maintains military bases to deter would-be aggressors, ensure the free flow of global commerce, and build the capacity of our allies and partners. From this international presence, the military can help in times of need. Following a natural disaster, for example, our military can provide humanitarian assistance to the affected area and its population. The United States is also at the leading edge of technological change, exploiting space for intelligence, reconnaissance, and surveillance; communications; and precision, navigation, and timing. Our space capabilities, in particular, multiply the effectiveness of American ground, sea, and air forces, as do our cyber tools. Beyond these advanced technologies and missions, however, the American military would not be the leading organization it is today without its people, primarily the brave men and women who serve our country.

Alliances and partnerships

As noted above, the American military maintains alliances and partnerships across the globe, and among these countries are some of the most prosperous and militarily capable. They include the likes of the United Kingdom, France, Germany, Australia, Japan and South Korea. These states are members of NATO, the European Union, the Association for South East Asian Nations, and many other international bodies. Together, we enact meaningful policies, encourage economic liberalization, support human rights, levy sanctions on revisionist and rogue actors that seek to undermine the liberal world order, work to maintain security across the globe, and for those areas that remain in conflict, strive to conclude them peacefully. American allies and partners have played an enormous role over the last seventy years and will continue to do so in the future.

Despite these enduring strengths, however, all too often we fail to exploit them to the extent that we could or should. When confronting challenges, the United States too often focuses on how our adversaries can leverage their strengths against our weaknesses. Instead, we must focus on how best to use our own strengths to exploit the weaknesses of our competitors. Approaching strategy, planning, and ultimately decision-making with this frame of mind is an important first step to address the many challenges the United States faces across the globe.

Implications for defense policy

Based on the external challenges and enduring advantages outlined above, it is possible to draw three implications for defense policy. First, *we need to think more seriously about risk than we have in recent years*. Developing a strategy is designed to mitigate and manage risk, yet, over the past quarter-century, we have grown reluctant to take risks and bear costs when necessary. In many ways, our nation has become risk averse, which has tremendous repercussions for decisions regarding the use of force and for American national security more broadly. Take the Syria "red line" and Russia's annexation of Crimea and Eastern Ukraine as two examples of the United States' inadequate deterrence posture. The United States and its allies and partners have met these violations of international law largely with sanctions, unwilling to take additional steps that could curtail such aggressive actions in the future. The United States, in particular, should draw upon the full range of tools at its disposal, utilizing its economic might in coordination with both military capabilities and soft power tactics.

Failing to demonstrate a readiness to accept risk will only yield additional hazard in the long term. If the United States does not demonstrate resolve to its stated policy commitments, whether challenging provocative measures by great powers or combatting horrific acts of terrorism, our competitors will view us increasingly as weak and exploitable and our allies and partners as feckless and untrustworthy. When the United States does not remain firm to its pledges in the Middle East, vowing to intervene militarily if Syria's Assad uses chemical weapons, how will the Baltic states, for example, view American promises within NATO to defend the easternmost members from renewed Russian aggression? Likewise, how will these actions embolden Moscow as it seeks to achieve its own goals? These are the questions that American policymakers must ask in order to avoid long-term escalation. The lack of American resolve has grave consequences not only for regional conflict prevention and alliance management, but also for international stability. We need to have a serious discussion about risk – one worthy of our transparent culture – within our government and, most importantly, with the American people.

Second, *we face a series of long-term competitions with great and regional powers alike and with non-state actors.* China, Russia, Iran, and North Korea, in particular, have been competing with us for some time, but we have been reluctant to contend with them. Surely, our intention is not to escalate a situation unduly, but rather to plan for the possibility of conflict as we pursue a range of options to manage tensions, drawing upon both economic and military might. As it stands, however, we find our options constrained and, most worryingly, reactive.

To achieve our aims over the long term and be prepared for any range of contingencies, we must be forward-thinking and meticulous. The United States should clarify its goals, prioritize them – particularly in an era of fiscal uncertainty – and then develop a strategy to achieve them. Such a strategy should seek to expand the menu of options available to the United States, constraining those that are available to our competitors, as well as impose costs upon them, mitigating their ability to inflict harm upon us. Most importantly, our strategy should give us the initiative, forcing our competitors to respond to our actions – and not the other way around. Developing a strategy that incorporates these elements is, of course, easier said than done in Washington. However difficult, it *must* be done if we are to gain maximum leverage from our considerable, albeit limited resources.

Likewise, we need to maintain a better and more comprehensive understanding of our competitors. For example, the Chinese military publishes a vast number of books and articles regarding its approach to modern war, strategy, and operations. These books are freely available for purchase in Chinese bookstores and on Beijing's version of Amazon. Yet they remain beyond the reach of scholars and officers who do not read Mandarin Chinese because translations are not widely available. Similarly, in prior decades, our government invested significantly in building intellectual capital on the Russian military, training a cadre of Americans to speak Russian and understand Russian culture. Today, however, that capital is at dangerously low levels, leaving us surprised or confused by Russian actions that should be neither unforeseen nor mysterious. To compete with these great powers, the United States must invest in developing the military's human capital, investing in a new generation of Chinese and Russian specialists.

Finally, *we need to take seriously the possibility of great power conflict.* Since the Cold War, we have not thought earnestly about a host of national security topics that are now ignored or marginalized. These include the role of nuclear weapons in American military strategy, the mobilization of the nation's resources for war, and the need to wage political warfare and counter its use by our competitors. These are topics that are under scrupulous study by the likes of Russia and China. Moscow is testing – quite successfully – the boundaries of hybrid warfare and propagating its escalate-to-deescalate nuclear strategy, while Beijing is exploring grey zone operations, primarily in the South China Sea, and modernizing its nuclear arsenal.

These realities should prompt the United States – and our allies and partners – to consider new ways to counter such worrisome developments. As a start, we should re-think the educational requirements of our officer corps. Our servicemen and women possess tremendous experience conducting counter-insurgency operations but have fewer opportunities to develop the skills necessary for war with a great power. Similarly, we have a new generation of policymakers who came of age after the Cold War and are less familiar with the elements of great power competition. Both investing in additional educational and training opportunities and attracting regional specialists will be crucial to develop the talent necessary should a conflict with China or Russia become a reality.

Implications for the defense and national security organization

External challenges from great and regional powers, and non-state actors, however, are not the only threats to national security that we need to address; there are very real challenges internal to our government's bureaucratic structure. Tensions between national and social security spending, expense overruns for weapon systems, and cost growth for personnel are just a few examples that demonstrate that today's defense and national security establishment is outdated. Its organizations were conceived during the early years of the Cold War, an era whose security environment was wildly different than the one that policymakers encounter today. Since the National Security Act of 1947, the legislation that ushered in the creation of our defense agencies and organizations, we have made only modest amendments in response to perceived shortcomings. In the mid-to-late 1980s, Capitol Hill ushered in a new wave of national security reform with the introduction of the Goldwater Nichols Act, clarifying the chain of command

and enhancing the "jointness" of the military. It also established U.S. Special Operations Command and a corresponding Assistant Secretary of Defense for Special Operations and Low Intensity Conflict. More recently, following the September 11th, 2001 attacks, Congressional leaders passed the Homeland Security Act, standing up a Department of Homeland Security. Likewise, a number of key congressmen and senators, including Senator John McCain, are exploring a second round of Goldwater Nichols reforms.

Such change is no doubt needed, yet the track record of national security reform is at best mixed. Consider the efforts to transform the defense establishment that began in the 1990s and stretched through Secretary of Defense Donald Rumsfeld's tenure at the Pentagon in the early-to-mid 2000s. The 2001 Quadrennial Defense Review, for example, went beyond earlier rhetoric to enact change, but it was met with mixed reviews overall, including the failure of Capabilities Based Planning.[42] Although Secretary Rumsfeld made important reforms a few years later, notably adding the "execution" piece to the then-Planning, Programming, and Budgeting System, enabling senior leaders to track the implementation of their decisions more efficiently, it is difficult to implement change, even with the support of a department head.

Even with interagency support, reform is not guaranteed. The mixed success of United States Africa Command (AFRICOM) is just one example. Beginning operations in 2008, AFRICOM was designed to assume responsibilities for the African continent, which had been split previously among Central, European, and Pacific commands. Despite its importance, the command suffered from an ambiguous mission early on and was met with skepticism within the region, perhaps best illustrated by the fact that it is headquartered in Germany. AFRICOM's structure provides a unique model for other commands and an example of effective interagency coordination – there is a civilian State Department deputy to the military commander. Yet, despite its potential, AFRICOM is not viewed as a particularly successful undertaking in reform within the national security community.

Likewise, even with presidential support, change is hard to come by. During the late George W. Bush administration, the White House sought to create a cadre of national security professionals to spur whole-of-government strategic planning and implementation. Although the initiative enjoyed both presidential and bipartisan congressional support, it largely failed. The same can be said of efforts to expand and reform the State Department. Secretaries of State in both the Bush and Obama administrations supported these efforts yet they have borne little fruit. Going forward, therefore, it is important that not only the Executive branch endorse any reform attempts, but also that reformers, prior to transforming an organization, take into account three elements: current organizational structure, institutional culture, and barriers to change.

The United States faces mounting challenges, both external to our country and internal to our government. Despite the enormity of the tasks ahead, we have great opportunities, if only we can seize them. In the past, we have relied on acquiring new capabilities and developing novel operational concepts to overcome challenges. This too will be crucial, but our success in the future will lie in cultivating our intellectual capital and capitalizing upon our enduring strengths. To do so will require the sustained support of our President and government leaders, but that of the American people as well. With these investments, the United States can chart a pragmatic course in an increasingly tumultuous world.

Notes

1 The White House, Office of the Press Secretary, "Joint Press Conference with President Obama and Prime Minister Abe of Japan," April 24, 2014, Tokyo, Japan.
2 Mira Rapp-Hooper, "Parting the South China Sea: How to Uphold the Rule of Law," *Foreign Affairs* 95, no. 5 (September/October 2016); Jane Perlez, "Tribunal Rejects Beijing's Claims in South China Sea," *The New York Times*, July 12, 2016.
3 John Pomfret, "U.S. Takes a Tougher Tone with China," *The Washington Post*, July 30, 2010.
4 Michael S. Chase and Arthur Chan, *China's Evolving Approach to "Integrated Strategic Deterrence"* (Santa Monica, California: RAND Corporation, 2016), p. 5.
5 Chase and Chan, p. 21.
6 Office of the Secretary of Defense, *Annual Report to Congress: Military and Security Developments Involving the People's Republic of China 2016* (Washington, D.C.: U.S. Department of Defense, OSD, 2016), pp. 1–3.
7 Jeremy Page, "China Builds First Overseas Military Outpost," *The Wall Street Journal*, August 19, 2016.
8 Maksymilian Czuperski, et al., *Hiding in Plain Sight: Putin's War in Ukraine* (Washington, D.C.: Atlantic Council, 2015), p. 4.
9 Evan Braden Montgomery, *Extended Deterrence in the Second Nuclear Age: Geopolitics, Proliferation and the Future of U.S. Security Commitments* (Washington, D.C.: Center for Strategic and Budgetary Assessments, 2016), p. 20.
10 Alina Polyakova, Marlene Laruelle, Stefan Meister, and Neil Barnett, *The Kremlin's Trojan Horses: Russian Influence in France, Germany, and the United Kingdom* (Washington, D.C.: Atlantic Council, 2016).
11 Michael Carpenter, "Russia's Violations of Borders, Treaties, and Human Rights," *Testimony before the Senate Committee on Foreign Relations*, June 7, 2016, p. 1.
12 Ibid.
13 Dmitry (Dima) Adamsky, "Cross-Domain Coercion: The Current Russian Art of Strategy," *Proliferation Papers*, no. 54 (November 2015), p. 14.
14 Neil MacFarquhar, "Putin Says He Weighed Nuclear Alert Over Crimea," *The New York Times*, March 15, 2015.
15 Martin E. Dempsey et al., "Iran Nuclear Agreement," *Testimony before the Senate Committee on Armed Services*, July 29, 2015.
16 Mark Gunzinger and Bryan Clark, *Winning the Salvo Competition: Rebalancing America's Air and Missile Defenses* (Washington, D.C.: Center for Strategic and Budgetary Assessments, 2016), p. 5.
17 Dan Lamothe, "Iranian Weapons Keep Getting Smuggled at Sea. Stopping Them Isn't Easy for the Navy," *The Washington Post*, April 5, 2016.
18 J. Matthew McInnis, "Iranian Deterrence Strategy and Use of Proxies," *Testimony before the Senate Committee on Foreign Relations*, December 6, 2016.
19 Melissa G. Dalton, *Navigating Gulf Waters After the Iran Nuclear Deal: Iran's Maritime Provocations and Challenges for U.S. Policy* (Washington, D.C.: Center for Strategic and International Studies, 2016), p. 6.

20 Sam Jones, "Cyber Warfare: Iran Opens a New Front," *The Financial Times*, April 26, 2016.
21 Evans J.R. Revere, *Dealing with a Nuclear-Armed North Korea: Rising Danger, Narrowing Options, Hard Choices* (Washington, D.C.: Brookings, 2016).
22 Choe Sang-Hun and Jane Perlez, "North Korea Tests a Mightier Nuclear Bomb, Raising Tension," *The New York Times*, September 8, 2016.
23 Evan Braden Montgomery, *Extended Deterrence in the Second Nuclear Age: Geopolitics, Proliferation, and the Future of U.S. Security Commitments* (Washington, D.C.: Center for Strategic and Budgetary Assessments, 2016), p. 24.
24 Paul K. Kerr, Steven A. Hildreth, and Mary Beth D. Nikitin, *Iran-North Korea-Syria Ballistic Missile and Nuclear Cooperation* (Washington, D.C.: Congressional Research Service, 2016), pp. 3–5.
25 Deena Zaru, "Carter: Bunker Busting Bomb Against Iran Ready to Go," *CNN*, April 30, 2015.
26 Yara Bayoumy, Noah Browning, and Mohammed Ghobari, "How Saudi Arabia's War in Yemen Has Made al Qaeda Stronger – and Richer," *Reuters*, April 8, 2016.
27 Daniel Benjamin and Steven Simon, "The Global Terror Threat in 2016: a Forecast," *CTC Sentinel* 9, no. 1 (January 2016), p. 1.
28 Jessica Lewis McFate and Melissa Pavlik, "ISIS's Global Attack Network: November 13, 2015 – November 9, 2016," *Understandingwar.org*.
29 Hummel, pp. 18–21.
30 Robert Gates, "Secretary of Defense Speech," *Speech Delivered at the United States Military Academy at West Point*, February 25, 2011.
31 Congressional Budget Office, *The 2016 Long-Term Budget Outlook* (Washington, D.C.: CBO, 2016), p. 7.
32 Justin T. Johnson, "Assessing Common Arguments for Cutting National Security Spending: Informing Current and Future Budget Debates," *The Heritage Foundation*.
33 Katherine Blakeley, *Analysis of the FY 2017 Defense Budget and Trends in Defense Spending* (Washington, D.C.: Center for Strategic and Budgetary Assessments, 2016), p. ii.
34 Robin S. Lineberger and Aijaz Hussain, *Program Management in Aerospace and Defense: Still Late and Over Budget* (Arlington, Virginia: Deloitte, 2016), p. 8.
35 Ibid.
36 Robert F. Hale, *Business Reform in the Department of Defense: An Agenda for the Next Administration* (Washington, D.C.: Center for a New American Security, 2016), p. 6.
37 Raymond T. Odierno, Jonathan W. Greenert, James F. Amos, and Mark A. Welsh, "The Impact of Sequestration on the National Defense," *Testimony before the Senate Committee on Armed Services*, November 7, 2013, p. 42.
38 Odierno et al., p. 43.
39 Odierno et al., p. 58.
40 Mackenzie Eaglen, *Framing a Defense Reform Agenda for 2017: Right-Sizing the Pentagon Civilian Workforce, Reforming Acquisition of Services, and Modernizing Military Health Care* (Washington, D.C.: American Enterprise Institute, 2016), p. 3.
41 Congressional Budget Office, *Replacing Military Personnel in Support Positions with Civilian Employees* (Washington, D.C.: CBO, 2015), p. 1.
42 Paul K. Davis, chapter two in Stephen J. Cimbala, *The George W. Bush Defense Program: Policy, Strategy, and War* (Washington, D.C.: Potomac Books, Inc., 2010), pp. 25–26.

11

THE DIFFUSION OF POWER AND THE ORGANIZATION OF THE U.S. NATIONAL SECURITY ESTABLISHMENT

Barry R. Posen

Though the future dimensions of global politics are uncertain, a consensus seems to be emerging that the "post-Cold War" world, in which the United States enjoyed a great power advantage relative to all others, is fading. At the same time, despite the rapid growth of China, now the second-largest economy in the world, a simple return to Cold War bipolarity has not become the organizing principle of those who dare to engage in long-term strategic planning. Instead, the consensus view seems to be reflected in the National Intelligence Council's *Global Trends 2030*: a "diffusion of power" is thought to be in the cards. Among great and middle powers, the world is expected to look "multipolar." At the same time, capabilities to create, to mobilize, and to destroy are all expected to be more widely distributed across the globe, not only to states but to groups and even individuals.[1]

Since the Second World War, the United States has organized itself for sustained participation in power politics, first as the leader of an anti-Soviet and anti-Communist coalition, and after the Cold War ended as an essentially revolutionary state aiming to forge a global, liberal, world order that would integrate the former Soviet bloc, Communist China, and even India and the "non-aligned" movement into an enlarged version of the United States' Cold War coalition. This has been the grand strategy of the United States, and it is not working very well. Reviewing, revising, or replacing this grand strategy should be the most important question on the U.S. national security agenda. Without a change of grand strategy, changing the organization of the U.S. national security effort will not produce markedly different outcomes from those we have experienced.[2]

That said, it still may be the case that the basic structures put in place in 1947, and the subsequent amendments and alterations, have left us less capable of executing either the counter productive grand strategy that we have, *or* any replacement. The task of this paper is to review briefly the major features of U.S. national security organization, summarize the most salient predicted changes limned by the National Intelligence Council, and then ask whether the extant organization seems appropriate for the expected trends. As it is often difficult to tell what role macro-organizational factors play in any major event, this discussion is somewhat impressionistic and speculative. I will argue, however, that the present structure seems inadequate to manage the political complexity of the emerging system, that at the margin the current structure privileges military power over diplomacy, and that the intelligence community privileges "tactical" intelligence over "strategic" (understanding of the domestic and regional, political, social, and economic factors that shape the interests and behaviors of countries of interest to the United States.)[3] It is also equally plausible that the growing complexity of foreign policy problems is simply not easily addressed by structural and organizational changes.

The National Security Act of 1947 and its evolution

The 1947 Act is admirably brief.[4] First, the National Security Council was established to ensure that the United States considered carefully the relationship between its national security means and its strategic ends in the world, and to ensure that the contributions of all relevant branches of the government to those objectives would be "integrated." The NSC is the organ of U.S. administration best suited to the making and enforcement of "grand strategy," which was clearly its purpose. One oddity of the Act is that the Department of State is mentioned exactly once: the Secretary of State is explicitly included as a member of the NSC, but State's role in the overall national security effort is not discussed.

Both World War II experience, and the emerging challenge of Soviet power were the key causes of the Act. U.S. political leaders had experienced global industrialized warfare, and had learned the necessity for management organs to coordinate far-flung national security activities. It is important to note that the industrial mobilization model of warfare still dominated the thinking of the designers. Two organs were created in the Act to manage industrial mobilization. These fell into disuse as U.S. strategists assimilated the nuclear weapon into national security policy. The early 20th-century model of warfare, which required the ability to mobilize an entire economy at relatively short notice, did suggest the need for coordination not merely of political and military instruments of power, but of economic instruments as well.

The creation of the NSC itself proved no panacea. A large staff grew up to serve the Council, and the role of the Director, originally conceived as managerial, evolved into something much more strategic. The balance of managerial and strategic roles changed from Presidency to Presidency, but the President's need for a "strategist in chief" now seems an established fact. There has, however, emerged a tension between the policy role of the NSC Director and that of the Secretary of State. The Department of State should in principle be a source of deep substantive knowledge of allies, neutrals, and adversaries, and the Secretary of State should be in a position to call on that expertise to advise the President, if not to define the purposes of U.S. grand strategy, then at least to advise on practicability. But the role of the State Department in U.S. national security policy was underdeveloped then, and seems underdeveloped now.

Second, the Act created the Central Intelligence Agency, tasked with the purpose of distilling the information gathered by U.S. intelligence-gathering organizations in order to assist the National Security Council in making key decisions, but also to assist the National Security Council in coordinating the activities of these intelligence agencies. The creation of the CIA was motivated in part by the Pearl Harbor surprise, and by the important role that intelligence had played in the Second World War, including the breaking of Japanese and German codes, which was then known only to a few.[5]

Though I am unaware of time series data, the intelligence effort of the U.S. grew quickly during the Cold War. September 11, 2001 precipitated the reorganization of the U.S. intelligence effort, creating a Directorate of National Intelligence to do the job originally given to the CIA.[6] Essentially, the failure to integrate disparate intelligence that might have warned of the attacks of 9/11 convinced legislators and organizational architects that the CIA had been unable to achieve the integration and analytic duties assigned to it in the 1947 Act. Whether the DNI will do any better is difficult to guess. The United States spends some $70 billion a year on "national" and "military" intelligence combined.[7] It is clear that the vast majority of this money goes to intelligence derived either from observation or from eavesdropping, and that most of the money is not only hidden in DoD accounts, it is spent by DoD. The intense desire to avoid a repetition of 9/11 has produced a search for very high-resolution intelligence on quite small and elusive targets. Tens of thousands of people are involved in intelligence, and hence the magnitude of the coordination task makes one a bit humble about placing confidence in any particular organizational solution. It is difficult to untangle the effects on the intelligence community of organizational/ structural factors, vs policy, but it does seem as if the effort to find targets of one sort or another dominates the overall enterprise. Though there have been several sensational leaks of IC efforts to gather political intelligence on foreign leaders, including the leaders of friendly countries, this sort of intelligence appears to be underweighted in the overall effort.

Third, the Act "unified" the armed services, though this proved to be only the beginning of a running battle to reduce the independent power of the services, and produce a genuinely "joint" military effort. Efficiency and effectiveness were the twin goals—the avoidance of redundancy and the mastery of cooperation among all branches and arms. This reflected the experience of the Second World War. For example, early in the war, especially in the North African campaign, U.S. ground and air forces did not cooperate well. They improved significantly as the war unfolded, but the joint effectiveness that was achieved immediately after the Normandy invasion was not to be taken for granted.

The achievement of efficiency and effectiveness through "jointness" proved elusive.[8] The 1947 Act concluded that the central civilian and military management organs of the DoD required strengthening, including the creation of a Chairman of the Joint Chiefs of Staff. By the early 1980s, new doubts emerged from across the national security establishment about the ability of the DoD to function as a cohesive whole in peace and war. The Goldwater Nichols Act strengthened yet again the Secretary of Defense and the Chairman of the Joint Chiefs, as well as the unified and specified commanders, relative to the service chiefs. Though the U.S. military has often been at war since the passage of the Act, it is nevertheless the case that this organization has not had its mettle tested against significant budgetary scarcity in peacetime, a peer competitor in peace or war, or two genuinely simultaneous contingencies. So, it is difficult to judge whether the Act achieved its objectives.

The emerging strategic environment

The diffusion of power suggests that the Cold War organization of the U.S. national security establishment may require reform. In this section I summarize key changes expected in the relations among states, and in the relations between states and peoples, and even individuals. We can expect a world with more politics, and more powerful national and substate actors. From this review, I will infer in the final section of the paper some plausible organizational changes that might ease our way in this changed world.

Diffusion of power I—The structure of global power

Realist international relations theorists have long argued that the distribution of power among the largest nation states impacts the security situation of these states, as well as that of lesser powers. The Cold War was widely understood to have occurred during a bipolar distribution of power; the immediate post-Cold War world saw the "unipolar moment," when U.S. power dwarfed that of any other single actor, and even any plausible coalition. The U.S. National Intelligence Council stated baldly that "there will not be any hegemonic power … Power will shift to networks and coalitions in a multipolar world."[9] Some debate this point, but in case the NIC is right, we should ask what might this mean for the foreign and security policy of the United States?[10]

Multipolar international politics is affected by the simple arithmetic of the strategic environment.[11] For those who predict a future multipolar world, the United States, China, and India are expected to be the main players.[12] The NIC assigns less weight to the European Union, Russia, and Japan, though for different reasons each may remain a consequential player. Theorists would argue that in a multipolar world the presence of three or more proximately equivalent principal competitors should affect the threats that each of these states faces, and the opportunities that each encounters. Perhaps the first rule of multipolar international politics is to avoid isolation. Going it alone, or ignoring a burgeoning coalition, means one may be outweighed, or for that matter outvoted, in international fora, by two or more to one. That arithmetic never looks good. It follows therefore that states act to make themselves attractive allies. This means, among other things, taking into account the interests of potential partners. This also means that one is occasionally asked to take on others' enemies and causes as one's own, which may or may not be a smart move. This is the sort of problem we saw in 1914.

Multipolarity also creates opportunities. For example, one often sees "buck passing" in multipolar worlds: if Great Power A threatens Great Power B, Great Power C may find it in its own interests to sit out the fight until it sees how it might go. A and B might bleed or stalemate each other, leaving C better off. Great Power C might even act overtly or covertly to help assure a stalemate, rather than a victory. Offshore balancers such as the British Empire at its peak, and the United States for much of its history, often defaulted to this strategy. Ocean barriers and great navies provided a margin of security that permitted patience. On the other hand, Power A or Power B may understand C's incentive to buck-pass, and perhaps try to organize itself to achieve a success more quickly than C expects. This is the sort of problem we saw in the late 1930s.

The NIC did not discuss an additional aspect of the emerging multipolar world that makes it different from past multipolar worlds—the existence of nuclear weapons.[13] Nuclear weapons are generally believed to mute the security fears of states, because of the risks that nuclear attackers assume when they target another nuclear power. This will be the first nuclear multipolar world, and it probably has slightly different properties from past multipolar worlds. The fear of isolation noted earlier should be somewhat less intense than in the past, because even a coalition of equals still runs very high risks in a nuclear confrontation with a single great nuclear power. And, though it requires more study, the ability of two great nuclear powers to coordinate a nuclear offensive against a third seems doubtful. If one defects from the agreed plan, the other suffers the full force of the victim's retaliation. The defector probably ends up the global hegemon. The effect of nuclear weapons in the hands of the principal future powers probably makes alliances more rather than less fluid. States will make and unmake coalitions as they compete over limited stakes, but states will not likely fear that a larger coalition can produce the large territorial losses and occasional conquests and occupation that were a feature of past multipolar worlds.

Though nuclear weapons seem to render great powers immune to conquest, they do not on the basis of present evidence end the international struggle for power. Nuclear weapons did not prevent the U.S.–Soviet Cold War, nor even end it when the two sides approached parity in the 1960s. The possession of nuclear weapons has not ended Pakistani or Indian security concerns. The specter of a nuclear-armed Iran was not greeted with equanimity by an already nuclear-armed Israel. It therefore seems likely that a future multipolar world will see some level of global political competition for power and influence, that this competition will be affected by the distribution of power, and that this competition will nevertheless be limited in its intensity.

In a world where true great-power war is incredibly risky, states may nevertheless compete for small stakes, but do so with care. They will likely avoid direct clashes of arms, wage war through proxies, and concern themselves more with weakening their adversaries than making great gains for themselves. The international military competition may be as much about status as it is about combat power. For example, we have seen for years a pattern of military acquisition in the West, and now in Russia and China, that stresses small numbers of very advanced systems, employed by highly trained, often entirely professional, armed forces. If such forces were to meet in a direct clash, it is quite plausible that they would quickly exhaust themselves. They cannot be quickly replenished materially from an industrial mobilization base, nor repopulated with conscripts. These conventional forces seem not really to be built for wars with their equals; they are built for wars with unequals, and to impress each other.

Finally, given the costs and risks of war, and the limited gains to be achieved from it, the making and unmaking of coalitions may prove a kind of proxy war of its own kind. Who sides with whom will provide a pretty good indicator for competitors of whether they are likely to get their way. Though a superior coalition may not threaten conquest in a nuclear world, it does threaten all kinds of minor costs and aggravations. Where the opposing coalition seems stronger, any given gambit—given its limited utility in any case—may fade in importance. Those who specialize in the process of coalition management probably will matter more in the multipolar future than they have in a unipolar or bipolar world. Military power is only one of the currencies of coalition management. Economic power is another. Legitimacy is a third. Because it is uncomfortable to be outnumbered, it is worth investing a good deal of energy in arguing to others that in any particular dispute, you or your coalition have right on your side. Thus, arguments about international law may figure prominently in disputes. Great states will even likely pay close attention to how international law is shaped, knowing that they may someday call upon it as a tool for their foreign policy.

Diffusion of power II—Individuals and groups

Globalization and its twin modernization are causing global improvements in productivity, better health, an increase in education, an intensification of communications, and a growing middle class. These changes are also precipitating another development, the trend toward urbanization, as the share of global population living in cities rises to 60 percent in 2030.[14] Urban areas are powerful centers of economic growth, but they are also places of intense political mobilization.

The diffusion of power thus applies not only to states, but to individuals and groups.[15] The happy part of this story is that millions will enjoy a standard of living higher than they have ever had before. The dark side is that many societies may not be able to cope politically with the pace of change. Individuals and groups may gravitate to various forms of political violence. Better and more diverse weaponry will likely become much more widely available, not only to states but to individuals and groups.[16] By virtue of better education, and intense communication, more people will be able to figure out how to use this weaponry. Better means of communication will allow individuals and groups to concert political action and recruit new followers. Urbanization will bring people together for more intense participation in politics in any case. We would need to be blind to miss the intensification of identity-based politics across the world in recent years in both developing and developed societies. Rapid economic, technological, and social change on a global scale probably has something to do with it. In general "identity politics" is not pretty politics. One aspect of identity politics is quite clear; most self-aware groups resist rule from without. Societies riven by identity politics are the ones that will likely most concern great powers; they are also the ones least susceptible to outside tutelage.

These developments suggest that two major security problems that are already with us will continue and perhaps intensify. First, at least some societies will produce very highly motivated violent actors capable of making trouble not only in their own countries, but abroad in countries that they may come to believe are the authors of their troubles. A second problem is that it will become increasingly difficult and costly for outsiders to employ direct action—occupation and state and nation building—to rectify the social ills that give rise to violent politics. There is a third problem that relates to the emergence of the multipolar system discussed above. Though some states and societies may appear to other states to need rebuilding, the great powers may not all agree. Mustering a consensus to do something will be more difficult. And it will be tempting for some states to view another's intervention in a civil war as an opportunity to impose some costs and weaken another actor.[17] It may not take much by way of financial and military assistance to "rebels" to raise significantly the costs of intervention. This was already true during the Cold War. But the changes noted above assure that these costs will rise.

Though in other work I have recommended against U.S. efforts to address these kinds of security problems at the source, the problems themselves suggest a heightened need for a certain kind of intelligence. Actionable early warning of societies going to pieces seems hard to come by, but knowledge of those countries is far from useless. It will be better to understand what is happening in these places than not, even if one does not wish to intervene directly, and even if one discounts the possibility of preventive action. If and as rapid internal change in any particular country leads first to internal disorder and violence, and then to external violence, the United States and others will need to formulate policies. Each of these states and societies will be different: it will not be productive to impose particular models on them to devise palliatives, much less solutions, to the problems they create. Communication with key actors, finding compromise solutions, or using our own military with discrimination, will all depend on a deep knowledge of these societies. Moreover, because of the spread of education, and the intensity of modern communications means, local political actors have ever more effective tools of political mobilization. Though the West has done a poor job in waging "the war of ideas" in the war on terror, it is nevertheless the case that waging wars of ideas will be an important part of any policy that aims to limit the violence that is often associated with rapid change. One cannot win such a war if one does not understand the other side's ideas, and have a few ideas of one's own that might work with the targeted populations.

The future strategic environment and the organization of the U.S. national security establishment

Both elements of the diffusion of power—the likely emergence of a multipolar world, and the increasing capacity of individuals and groups, coupled with the still unexplained but potent re-emergence of identity politics, may mean that the implementation of U.S. national security policy, whatever that policy is, will require some reforms in the three most important institutions addressed in the National Security Act of 1947, and in the Department of State.

If multipolarity implies a more fluid international political system, then it requires a more agile U.S. diplomacy. In the large, the interests of other powers and peoples will need to be more systematically addressed in the formulation of U.S. grand strategy. It must become more "political." This in turn will require the explicit assimilation of substantive knowledge of other countries and peoples. During the Cold War, the United States could focus this kind of effort mainly on the Soviet Union. That is no longer the case. We have plenty of actual and potential sources of this kind of knowledge within the U.S. government so the task here is reconceptualizing other major powers as strong independent actors with their own interests. This needs to occur across the government. Some organizational changes may facilitate it, but this is an act of imagination, not redrawing organigrams.

The organs most responsible for managing the implementation of policy for high-level diplomacy must nevertheless be reformed—this means the National Security Council and the Department of State. The Obama NSC staff, renamed the National Security Staff, grew larger than that of the Bush Administration, in part due to the absorption of the Homeland Security Council into the NSC. This expansion is said to have produced a less responsive and more cumbersome organization. President Trump reversed this decision. The question, however, is probably not one of size, but of function. Is the NSC staff trying to do the job of the Cabinet departments, or is it coordinating and digesting their contributions?[18] One suspects it was often the former during the Obama Administration.[19] As of this writing, President Trump's National Security Advisor, LTG H.R. McMaster is said to prefer a return to a more coordinating role.[20] Given the increasing magnitude of the task, the management of cooperation is probably the more important problem. This is easier to say than to do. It depends on the President, the NSC staff itself, and the Cabinet Secretaries sharing a model of how the process is meant to work. Given that large organizations such as the Cabinet depart-ments typically value autonomy, and given that the Cabinet Secretaries and their immediate staff of political appointees are few, and are just passing through, this suggestion can only produce limited results.

The State Department is often the object of criticism whenever the U.S. national security apparatus is under discussion.[21] Most of the State Department, including the Foreign Service, is focused on the day-to-day process of U.S. dip-lomatic engagement. A few officials at the highest levels are concerned with developing national security policy, and implementing the larger projects gener-ated by that policy. And a host of senior officials have functional responsibilities. Of necessity, if international diplomacy matters more in the future because of the diffusion of power, then the State Department must become the locus of that effort.[22] The Hart-Rudman Commission's recommendation that the regional bureaus be strengthened at the expense of the functional ones seems even more timely now than it was in 2001.[23] The State Department is the locus of on-the-ground political intelligence about other countries. Only State may have the luxury of systematically training area studies experts in the field in regions where the nation requires expertise.

One recent wave of reform suggestions focused on the "whole of govern-ment" approach to managing U.S. nation-building efforts abroad, which assigns the State Department principal responsibility for managing these efforts. This is understandable. Though these projects may require vast military resources, it is widely acknowledged that they begin and end with politics. State is the only for-eign affairs organization that concentrates such knowledge, though government and administration are *not* its strong suits, even when running its own affairs in the U.S. Given the size of these state- and nation-building projects, the "whole of government" approach risks treating State as a potential colonial administra-tion service, and would divert the organization from its far more important task, the management of relations with the world's emerging power centers.[24]

Reform proposals abound on energizing the public diplomacy efforts of the United States, and they disagree on the wisdom of re-establishing a large semi-independent organization that would resemble the Cold War U.S. Information Agency (USIA), or a range of new nostrums to make the successor organs—the Under Secretary for Public Diplomacy and Public Affairs and the independent Broadcasting Board of Governors—work better.[25] The evidence is not compel-ling on either side.[26] The diffusion of power beyond nation states to individuals and organized groups means that the United States needs to strategize about how to address what others believe about the United States and its policies. If the State Department assumes a somewhat larger role in U.S. national security policy, and that role refocuses on understanding foreign politics, and using that understand-ing for U.S. foreign policy, then State would also be the logical locus for an enhanced public diplomacy effort. In light of Russia's information campaigns to influence not only the U.S. election in 2016, but to influence elections and refer-enda across the Western world, a fresh look at this issue is in order.

The focus of the intelligence community will need to change slightly. Though the very existence of the Global Futures Group in the IC suggests that it does indeed examine long-term, large-scale strategic trends, it is hard not to infer from public accounts of the size, shape, and daily concerns of the IC that it is much more focused on warning and targets than it is on political understanding.[27] Even press reports that U.S. intelligence targets the negotiating positions of other countries have a tactical flavor, though the impulse is right. The question that arises here is whether there is sufficiently strong central management of the intelligence community to produce such a reform. Long-time intelligence scholar Loch Johnson does not believe that the intent either of the original National Security Act that created the CIA, nor the Intelligence Reform and Terrorism Prevention Act (IRTPA) of 2004, which created the DNI, achieved the long-sought objective of integrating "intelligence reporting not only for military matters but on a host of other issues, from global political and economic trends to public health and the environment."[28] It would privilege, slightly, the gathering of a different kind of intelligence—more political than military and more long-term than short-term—and more importantly would promote strategic analysis to provide policy makers with a better understanding of the larger forces they are up against in the rest of the world.[29] Though the reorganization of the Central Intelligence Agency announced by Director John Brennan in 2015 will probably improve the agency's effectiveness against particular problems or particular targets, long-time intelligence practitioner/scholar Mark Lowenthal wonders where is the "intellectual strategic reserve, people not worried about day-to-day stuff but who think about what is going to happen two years out?"[30] The intelligence community has many very capable analysts, and many are possessed of great knowledge of other regions and cultures. That said, the academic community outside of government is doing a poorer job of producing such people than was the case during the Cold War, and the trends are not good.[31] One suspects that regional expertise may be generated increasingly inside the intelligence community. This runs into another problem however; security concerns make it difficult to permit in-house intelligence analysts to spend a lot of time inside the countries about which they are expected to be expert. This probably cannot be helped, but it means that the organ of the U.S. government that can place people in country for long periods, the State Department, will need to play a bigger role in developing, interpreting and exploiting political intelligence.

The principal problem created by an emergent multipolar world for the Department of Defense arises from the U.S. military establishment's size, and presence and purposes abroad. The DoD naturally is governed by a military rationale. Its purpose is to fight effectively. Because of the US's post-Cold War grand strategy the military must be able to fight effectively almost everywhere. The map of the Unified Command Plan (UCP) illustrates this very well. As we consider the problem of fighting effectively in new corners of the world, we generate new combatant commanders.[32] These commanders either do control, or potentially control, vast resources. For the sake of combat effectiveness, they try to develop relationships with most of the militaries in the areas of their purview, except those that oppose our projects directly, or that prefer to maintain their freedom of action.

These efforts to improve our ability to fight effectively alongside partners have several negative consequences. First, rather than mobilizing allies to do more for common purposes, on the whole we demobilize them. The pattern of European and Japanese military efforts since the end of the Cold War testifies to this problem.[33] This did not matter much when we had an overwhelming power advantage; it matters more as that advantage dissipates. We will need others to do more, and the UCP incentivizes them to do less. Second, the UCP hardens our alliance commitments. Most treaties are purposely written with escape clauses: even Article V of the North Atlantic Treaty has escape clauses. These clauses serve a useful purpose; they make the threat of exit plausible, which is a useful diplomatic tool to discipline allies. The UCP makes the threat of exit less plausible. Third, because military engagement involves actual cooperative activities, the military develops close working relations with local militaries. This may contribute to effectiveness in the event of war. We like to believe that it contributes to the knowledge of foreign countries that we may later require. But this knowledge comes with a kind of motivated bias. Working with brother and sister officers from foreign countries creates mutual trust. One's knowledge of the society in question is filtered through these counterparts. But this information is likely biased, and one's foreign interlocutors have their own interests. (It should be noted, however, that the State Department is not immune to similar dynamics.) For example, the U.S. military offered what now seem excessively optimistic appraisals of the effectiveness of the Iraqi security forces as the United States wound down its presence in Iraq. These appraisals were not a little wrong; they were a lot wrong. I do not attribute this to willful deception, but rather the results of thousands of interactions that seemed positive. Hence, I conclude from recent experience, and the analysis above, that the UCP needs to be changed. Put bluntly, we need fewer combatant commanders, not more, and these combatant commanders should live largely in the United States, and whatever forward headquarters they maintain should be as lean as possible.[34] Similarly, engagement opportunities should not be expanded; they should be put on a much tighter rein.[35]

Conclusion

The diffusion of power has already created a very different world from 1947, and for that matter, 1991. By 1947 the Cold War, bipolar competition, was well underway. By the end of 1991 the Soviet Union had collapsed and the "unipolar moment" had arrived. No such dramatic event marks the moment of the "diffusion of power." But we see evidence all around us in economic statistics, diplomatic practice, and the costly endlessness of military interventions in the internal politics of other countries. In other work I have suggested that the post-Cold War grand strategy of the United States is unnecessary, costly, and counter productive.[36]

What the United States actually requires is a change of grand strategy. The diffusion of power makes such a change a more pressing matter, but the commitment to our present course of action seems strong, and change will come slowly.

The diffusion of power, however, creates a changed environment for any national security strategy. In this essay I have tried to connect these big geostrategic trends to the more prosaic matter of the organization of the U.S. national security establishment. Such connections are difficult to draw, because it is not easy to tell how much influence government structure has on outcomes, as opposed to individual leaders and their beliefs. And it is not easy to separate one's grand strategic views from one's view on organization. I venture cautiously the prediction that the demands on the U.S. security establishment for deep understanding of the politics of other countries are destined to grow. Global competition will be diplomatic as much as it is military. Direct use of military force is destined to become more costly and less decisive. Given the number of nuclear powers in the world, direct use of force may also become increasingly risky.

The diffusion of power therefore suggests that some organizational changes may be helpful. The State Department may grow in importance, but internal reforms should focus it more on politics and diplomacy. The intelligence community will need to pay more attention to the gathering and analysis of political, economic, and social information, and less to developing information for tactical purposes, whether those purposes are military or diplomatic.[37] Because there will simply be too much going on in the world to run all national security policy out of the White House, the National Security Council, the National Security Advisor, and the National Security Staff will need to concentrate more on their original purpose in the 1947 Act, which was to coordinate the various bureaucracies that contribute to national security. Finally, the Department of Defense should contract its institutional role: much of what it does is counterproductive to the practice of a diplomacy, in effect binding the United States so tightly to other countries that it loses rather than gains influence.

Notes

1 The National Intelligence Council, *Global Trends 2030: Alternative Worlds*, (NIC2012-001), December 2012, ii, www.dni.gov/nic/globaltrends.
2 Barry R. Posen, *Restraint: A New Foundation for U.S. Grand Strategy*, (Ithaca: Cornell University Press, 2014), 1–20.
3 "A strategy furthers one's advance towards goals by suggesting ways to accommodate and/or orchestrate a variety of variables—sometimes too many for the strategist alone to anticipate and understand. When foreign areas are involved, in-depth expertise is required, which is what strategic intelligence provides. Without the insights of deep expertise—insights based on detailed knowledge of obstacles and opportunities and enemies and friends in a foreign area—a strategy is not much more than an abstract theory, potentially even a flight of fancy." John G. Heidenrich, "The State of Strategic Intelligence: The Intelligence Community's Neglect of Strategic Intelligence," *Unclassified Studies in Intelligence* vol. 51, no. 2 (June 12, 2007), https://www.cia.gov/library/center-for-the-study-of-intelligence/csi-publications/csi-studies/studies/vol51no2.

4 The National Security Act of 1947 – July 26, 1947, Public Law 253, 80th Congress; Chapter 343, 1st Session; S. 758.

5 Mark M. Lowenthal, *Intelligence – From Secrets to Policy,* 2nd edition, (Washington, DC: CQ Press, 2003), 17–19; see also Christopher Andrew, *For the President's Eyes Only,* (New York: Harper Perennial, 1996), 149–170.

6 "Intelligence Reform and Terrorism Prevention Act of 2004", Public Law 108– 458,108th Congress, December 17, 2004 [S. 2845], www.dni.gov/files/documents/ IRTPA%202004.pdf.

7 Director of National Intelligence, Washington, DC, "DNI Releases Budget Figure for FY 2017 Appropriations Requested for the National Intelligence Program," February 9, 2016: "The aggregate amount of appropriations requested for the FY 2017 National Intelligence Program is $53.5 billion, which includes funding requested to support Overseas Contingency Operations." Another 16.8 billion dollars a year is allocated to the Military Intelligence Program: www.dni.gov/index. php/newsroom/press-releases/item/1755-dni-releases-updated-budget-figure-for- fy-2017-appropriations-requested-for-the-national-intelligence-program.

8 Office of the Secretary of Defense, Director, Administration and Management, Organizational Management and Planning, *White Paper: Evolution of Department of Defense Directive 5100.01 "Functions of the Department of Defense and Its Major Components,"* April 2010, revised January 2014, provides a detailed review of the history and rationales for a series of actions, informal and formal.

9 *Global Trends 2030,* ii.

10 Stephen G. Brooks and William C. Wohlforth challenge the "diffusion of power" argument. They critique the use of simple measures of polarity such as GDP, or even composite measures such as GDP+military spending+military personnel+population, in favor of much more refined net assessments of relative military and technological capacity. Global military reach in particular is key to their measure for assessing relative power. Because the U.S. remains comfortably the only state with global military reach, which they assess exhaustively, they conclude that it remains the world's only superpower, and thus that the world remains unipolar. They concede that China is poised, due to its own economic and technological progress, to perhaps someday develop its own global military reach if it continues to grow and if it chooses to do so. This would be the path out of unipolarity, and China's rise matters mainly because we can now see such a path, though they argue that China is the only state plausibly on the path. But unless and until this happens, the world remains unipolar in their view. They seem confident that U.S. power remains sufficiently great relative to all others that it can go on more or less as it has. In the view of those who stress the "diffusion of power," it becomes more and more difficult and costly for the U.S. to be a global power when local powers of resistance cross a certain threshold, especially if this occurs in more than one part of the world. See "The Rise and Fall of the Great Powers in the Twenty-First Century: China's Rise and the Fate of America's Global Position," *International Security* vol. 40, no. 3 (Winter 2015/2016), 7–53.

11 For a brief summary of how modern multipolarity might work, see Barry R. Posen, "From Unipolarity to Multipolarity: Transition in Sight?," chapter 10, in G. John Ikenberry, Michael Mastanduno, and William C. Wohlforth, eds., *International Relations Theory and the Consequences of Unipolarity* (Cambridge: Cambridge University Press, 2011), 317–319, 337–340; see also the seminal discussion in Kenneth Waltz, "Structural Causes and Military Effects," *Theory of International Politics* (London: McGraw-Hill, 1979), 161–193.

12 *Global Trends 2030,* graph: "Aggregate Power of Developing States Set to Surpass US Power by 2030," 16.

13 Posen, "From Unipolarity to Multipolarity," 338–339.

14 *Global Trends 2030,* 2.

15 *Global Trends 2030,* iii–v, 8–12.

16 *Global Trends 2030*, 64, 66–67.

17 Barry R. Posen, "Civil Wars and the Structure of World Power," *Daedalus* vol. 146, no. 4 (Fall 2017), 167–179.

18 For a useful review of the evolution of the Obama NSC, and a relatively favorable assessment of its efficacy by the end of the first term, see Michael Gordon Jackson, "A Dramatically Different NSC? President Obama's Use of the National Security Council," Department of Political Science, Regis College, Annual Meeting of the Western Political Science Association, Portland, Oregon, March 22–24, 2012.

19 Karen De Young, "White House Tries for a Leaner National Security Council," *Washington Post*, June 22, 2015, www.washingtonpost.com/world/national-security/white-house-tries-for-a-leaner-national-security-council/2015/06/22/22ef7e52-1909-11e5-93b7-5eddc056ad8a_story.html.

20 See John P. Burke, "The Contemporary Presidency: The Trump Transition, Early Presidency, and National Security Organization" *Presidential Studies Quarterly* vol. 47, no. 3 (September 2017), 574–596.

21 Though dated, see *Road Map for National Security: Imperative for Change*, The Phase III Report of the US Commission on National Security/21st Century [aka Hart-Rudman], February 15, 2001, 52–63."More fundamentally, the State Department's present structure works at cross purposes with its Foreign Service culture. The Foreign Service thinks in terms of countries, and therein lies its invaluable expertise. But the most senior officials have functional responsibilities." (p. 53). To see that nothing has changed, see "Department Organization Chart," November 2016, www.state.gov/r/pa/ei/rls/dos/99484.htm.

22 Chas Freeman has long argued that the political appointment of ambassadors is a barrier to effective diplomacy. This may have mattered a bit less during the Cold War, as the basic strategic problem of containment and deterrence could be addressed with blunt instruments. He argues, however, that the strategic problems of the post-Cold War world require a bit more diplomatic skill, which can only be achieved through long study and practice. "Judging by results in the complex post-Cold War environment, diplomacy is something the United States does not now understand or know how to do." See "America's Diplomatic Crisis," June 16, 2015, www.theamericanconservative.com/articles/americas-diplomatic-crisis.

23 *Road Map for National Security*, 54–59.

24 For a review of the evolution of this idea, see Otha J. Holmes, "Whole of Government Approach: Maximizing Unity of Effort between the Department of Defense (DoD), Department of State (DoS), and the United States Agency for International Development (USAID)," Master's thesis, USACGSC, December 2013, 19–22.

25 Gordon Adams and Cindy Williams, *Buying National Security: How America Plans and Pays for its Global Role and Safety at Home*, (New York and London: Routledge, 2010), 26–31.

26 Susan B. Epstein and Lisa Mages, *Public Diplomacy: A Review of Past Recommendations*, Congressional Research Service (RL33062), September 2, 2005, 6–7.

27 "Much of today's intelligence is tactical, tangential, or tied to national strategy only by formal references to high-level strategic planning or guidance documents in forewords, prefaces, or other such administrative front-matter." Heidenrich, "The State of Strategic Intelligence."; "The balance between current and strategic analysis has been an issue for as long as I've been an analytic manager, but given the prevailing forces of our customers and our culture, it is likely to worsen without significant management attention." Robert Cardillo, (then) Deputy Director of National Intelligence for Intelligence Integration, "Intelligence Community Reform: A Cultural Evolution," *Studies in Intelligence* vol. 54, no. 3 (September 2010), 5; see also Barton Gellman and Greg Miller, "'Black Budget' Summary Details U.S. Spy Network's Successes, Failures and Objectives," *Washington Post*, August 29, 2013, www.washingtonpost.com/world/national-security/black-budget-summary-details-us-spy-networks-successes-failures-and-objectives/2013/08/29/7e57bb78-10ab-11e3-8cdd-bcdc09410972_story.html.

28 Loch K. Johnson, "Kiss of Death? The Politicization of U.S. Intelligence Under Trump," *World Politics Review*, March 21, 2017, 13–15, www.worldpoliticsreview.com/articles/21597/kiss-of-death-the-politicization-of-u-s-intelligence-under-trump.

29 "A major [community] weakness … is its difficulty in providing strategic intelligence—the comprehensive overviews that put disparate events and the fragmentary snapshots provided by different intelligence sources into a contextual framework that makes it meaningful for the intelligence consumer. This criticism applies to intelligence prepared both for a national policy audience and for more specialized audiences, such as battlefield commanders." *Conference Report: Intelligence for a New Era in American Foreign Policy* (Washington, DC: Central Intelligence Agency, 2004), 3–4, quoted in Heidenrich, op. cit.

30 Quoted in Greg Miller, "CIA Plans Major Reorganization and a Focus on Digital Espionage," *Washington Post*, March 6, 2015, www.washingtonpost.com/world/national-security/cia-plans-major-reorganization-and-a-focus-on-digital-espionage/2015/03/06/87e94a1e-c2aa-11e4-9ec2-b418f57a4a99_story.html; see also the very informative account of the managerial and process lessons drawn from his time as chairman of the National Intelligence Council by Christopher A. Kojm, "Change and Continuity: The National Intelligence Council, 2009–2014," *Studies in Intelligence*, vol. 59, no. 2 (Extracts, June 2015), 9. He notes that while some NIC chairs prioritized the role of thought leader for the administration, looking out into the future for key issues, "I was circumspect about this aspect of my role. Most of the NIC's work is, in fact, in direct response to or in anticipation of policymaker requests."

31 Charles King, "The Decline of International Studies," *Foreign Affairs*, April 9, 2016, www.foreignaffairs.com/articles/united-states/decline-international-studies.

32 Aside from the Northern Command, which covers the continental United States, there are five regional combatant commands, covering Africa, South America, Europe, the greater Middle East and the Pacific. See Unified Command Plan, MAP, "Commanders' Area of Responsibility," www.defense.gov/Sites/Unified-Combatant-Commands.

33 On the propensity of U.S. allies to "cheap ride," see Posen, *Restraint: A New Foundation*, 33–44. For the theoretical explanations for this behavior, see Mancur Olson and Richard Zeckhauser, "An Economic Theory of Alliances," *The Review of Economics and Statistics* vol. 48, no. 3 (1966), 266–79; Timothy W. Crawford and Alan J. Kuperman, *Gambling on Humanitarian Intervention: Moral Hazard, Rebellion and Civil War* (New York: Routledge, 2006); Albert O. Hirschman, *Exit, Voice, and Loyalty: Responses to Decline in Firms, Organizations, and States* (Cambridge, MS: Harvard University Press, 1970).

34 Reform of the UCP is in the policy debate in 2016, but largely as part of a larger argument on reducing the numbers of people committed to headquarters in the American military. See Dov S. Zakheim, "Pentagon Reform: Hope Springs Eternal," *The American Interest*, April 11, 2016, www.the-american-interest.com/2016/04/11/pentagon-reform-hope-springs-eternal. He suggests, however, that the combatant commanders have become too strong. He does not offer specific guidance for how to change the UCP. Benjamin H. Friedman and Harvey M. Sapolsky argue that the regional commands should be abolished because they are wastefully oversized headquarters that serve mainly as regional interest groups, and they note that when wars happen the U.S. usually sets up an actual combat command (a joint task force) to run them. "Shut Down the US Combat Commands," *Defense News,* September 30, 2013, www.cato.org/publications/commentary/shut-down-us-combatant-commands. Offering a sketch of a significant reorganization, which would do away with regional combatant commanders entirely in favor of functional commands, is Major (then) Kelly Houlgate, US Marine Corps, "A Unified Command Plan for a New Era," *US Naval Institute Proceedings*, September 2005.

35 For a longer discussion, see Posen, *Restraint: A New Foundation*, 158–163.

36 Ibid.

4

37 As an aside, this may become necessary in any case. As encryption technologies outpace the IC's ability simply to vacuum up communications intelligence and winnow it with powerful computers and fancy software, the United States government will need to know more of a general nature about other countries and movements to decide against whom to target its technology, and to make sense of the more fragmentary information that it will be able to gather.

CONCLUSION

Looking ahead – The future of national security reform

Erica D. Borghard

This volume set out to explore the extent to which the world has evolved since the early years of the Cold War when the National Security Act of 1947 was enacted, and the implications for debates about national security reform for the future. In the seven decades since the United States solidified its position in the international system as a veritable superpower and built an institutional framework for crafting and implementing a national security policy, the external security context and the domestic political environment have undergone significant changes. For instance, internationally, the distribution of power has shifted from one of bipolarity during the Cold War; to unipolarity in the aftermath of the fall of the Berlin Wall; to, arguably, emerging multipolarity in the second decade of the 21st century. While traditional nation-state adversaries—particularly those equipped with nuclear weapons—remain the primary threats to U.S. national security, technology and the interconnectedness of the international system have enabled transnational and non-state actors to pose national security risks for great powers. The emergence of cyberspace as a domain of warfare in which the U.S. faces near-peer or even peer competitors, coupled with the unique dependence of the U.S. economy and military on IT infrastructure, has created new and potentially catastrophic vulnerabilities that U.S. adversaries could exploit. At the domestic level, on the one hand, national security policymaking is fractured by growing political polarization and division while, on the other hand, the executive branch has grown and centralized control over the national security policymaking process.

These momentous changes naturally engender questions regarding the durability of the National Security Act of 1947 and the extent to which the national security policymaking apparatus to which it gave rise was able to withstand the challenges of the past seventy years, and could continue to do so into the future. Or, put simply, what do these changes mean for the prospects for national security reform, given that the institutions and processes for developing and implementing policy are older than most policymakers? The contributors to this volume offered varying perspectives on this question. While most agreed that there have been significant changes to the national security context, there were a range of assessments regarding the extent to which U.S. institutions and processes could—or even should—change in response. Almost all of the reforms proffered by a diverse set of scholarly experts could be accomplished without legislative intervention.

At the international level, there was consensus regarding the most significant changes to the post-1947 environment. For example, Richard K. Betts and Barry R. Posen agreed that the changing distribution of power and the growing complexity of threats are the key defining characteristics of the current national security environment, although both authors were wary of wholesale change to existing institutions and processes. Posen suggested that some organizational changes, such as focusing more on diplomacy through the State Department than military solutions through the Department of Defense, and prioritizing the production of strategic intelligence within the Intelligence Community, may be necessary to best position the U.S. for the future. Betts asserted, "It's not broke, so let's not fix it."

In contrast, Andrew F. Krepinevich, Jr. called for an "overhaul of U.S. national security organizations and processes," which could not be undertaken in the absence of a clearly articulated strategic vision. Walter Russell Mead similarly acknowledged that the complexities of the strategic environment of the 21st-century demand reform. Thomas G. Mahnken similarly advocated for reform, but was more circumspect about the likelihood of success given the history of prior attempts since 1947. He noted that reform efforts must take into account the existing organizational structure, institutional culture, and barriers to change, and argued for focusing on strengthening intellectual capital and taking advantage of the inherent strengths of the United States.

Deborah Avant drew our attention to the contradictions between U.S. policy goals and the tools that exist to implement them, particularly those between warfighting and governance. These tensions create the conditions for disjointed and ineffective national security policy. Rather than large-scale organizational change, which may be particularly vexing in the current political environment, Avant suggested an approach that focuses on dialogue and process; open conversations about problems that take into account diverse perspectives could drive better outcomes. Risa A. Brooks warned that, seventy years into the National Security Act, there is little agreement regarding the optimal approach for analyzing and choosing strategies within the executive branch, and that there are inherent perceptual and organizational biases that impede good strategic assessment. However, these could be mitigated through improving training of decision-makers in the approaches to weighing and assessing information.

Some contributors focused on specific institutions and processes, particularly the role of the National Security Council, which has grown considerably since its inception, both in terms of the size of the NSC staff as well as the latter's key function in policy development. In her exploration of six different cases of presidential decision-making, Meena Bose found that presidential leadership and clear lines of authority were essential for the effective functioning of the NSC and national security policymaking in general. Good leadership and relationships are difficult to institutionalize through organizational reform; rather, they must be cultivated through precedent-setting and norms. Of course, this begs the question: What happens when a presidential administration chooses to reject precedents and implicit behaviors and norms that have been cultivated over time from one administration to the next? Mac Destler also honed in on the evolving—and growing—role of the NSC staff since 1947. He argued that "policy management staffs work best when they are small" and, therefore, advocated for trimming the size of the NSC staff to 40–45 individuals, while noting that, in the current administration, competence rather than size may be the overriding concern.

David S. C. Chu tackled the issue of long-term planning and capability development within the executive branch through the Planning, Programming, and Budgeting System (PPBS) established in the 1960s. Beyond simply considering the current strategic environment, the U.S. must also forecast future challenges and opportunities and build a force to confront them. This requires, according to Chu, improving the personnel management system, refocusing the planning process to prioritize longer-term thinking, and elevating the mission itself as the primary driver around which planning is organized.

Perhaps reflecting its outsized role, most contributors focused on reforms directed at the executive branch. However, Congress plays a crucial Constitutional role in national security policymaking and, specifically, exercising an oversight function and check on the executive. In exploring the respective roles of the legislative and executive branches, Douglas L. Kriner identified two keys trends that will affect any attempts at national security reform: "the almost unprecedented levels of partisan polarization" and growing secrecy within the executive branch, which has produced an information asymmetry between it and Congress. The key challenge in this domestic environment is how to galvanize Congress to exercise its Constitutional prerogative in national security policymaking. He suggests strengthening the Foreign Relations/Affairs and Armed Services committees, or the Select Intelligence committees. Ultimately, the electorate itself may be the only effective check on the executive branch—a dynamic that may be revealed in the upcoming 2018 or 2020 elections.

This volume was conceived of prior to the 2016 presidential election which, for many in the community of national security experts, raised fundamental questions about the assumptions made about the national security policymaking and implementation process. In many ways, it has been an intriguing intellectual exercise to explore the extent to which diagnoses of the key challenges facing the United States or recommendations for reform that were initially developed by the contributors to this volume in the first few months of 2016 have changed, or remained the same, in the first year of the Trump administration.

One theme across a set of contributors has been that the phenomenon that is the Trump administration has thrown into stark relief the preexisting challenges or impediments to effective national security reform, casting a pall of pessimism over any efforts to change the current system. Revitalizing the diplomatic instrument of power over the military one, building a coherent long-term strategy that can drive organizational overhaul, reforming the NSC staff and process, or simply having open, fact-based conversations about our problems may take the back burner to, in Destler's parlance, focusing on ensuring minimal competence of the national security team.

Alternatively, from the perspective of some contributors, the Trump presidency thus far has only reinforced and reflected long-term trends. According to this logic, the probability of effective national security reform, particularly emanating from Congress, was already slim given the domestic political polarization that had festered for decades prior to the 2016 election. Perhaps an unanticipated wrinkle revealed by the 2016 election is the internal schism within the Republican Party regarding the future direction of U.S. national security policy. President Trump campaigned on a foreign policy platform of neo-isolationism/ nativism that called for a focus inward, ranging from withdrawing from international trade agreements such as the Trans-Pacific Partnership and the North Atlantic Free Trade Agreement, to shedding the burdens of providing for the security of our purportedly free-riding allies, and, of course, building a literal wall to separate the United States from its southern neighbor (although, somewhat contradictorily, simultaneously pressing for even greater militarization of U.S. foreign policy). These policies contrast significantly with the more muscular foreign policy position of many mainstream members of the Republican Party, particularly neoconservatives. The 2017 National Security Strategy reflects these tensions. Yet, convergence around a coherent grand strategy has eluded every presidential administration since the end of the Cold War. This is most likely due to the fact that the U.S. has enjoyed the enviable position of being able to pursue foreign policy objectives free from the constraint of countering threats posed by competing great powers.

Relatedly, the Trump presidency has prompted many in the national security community to contemplate the relative importance of individual leadership versus institutions and the extent to which the latter could or should constrain the former. The original National Security Act of 1947 and the institutions and processes that have evolved since then were constructed to help usher the United States out of the realm of isolationism and into a national security policy of active engagement with the rest of the world as a great power. Currently, then, there is an ostensible mismatch between our Cold War era institutions and processes and the declared national security objectives of the current administration. The President's ability or failure to prevail over decades of formal and informal institutions and processes for making and implementing national security policy will shed light on how important these institutions actually are for constraining and enabling policymaking.

In the current climate, it appears that any real efforts at national security reform will be shelved until the domestic political environment changes—or until external events occur that are of a sufficiently large magnitude to create a moment of reckoning within the national security establishment and, therefore, an opportunity for real reform. Indeed, this is what prompted the enactment of the National Security Act of 1947 and is perhaps what will be required for the National Security Act of the next era. In the meantime, we will continue to depend on those who study and practice national security decision-making to identify problems, propose solutions, and generate the political will to make substantive improvements to our existing architecture. There is plenty that could be accomplished even within the boundaries of existing authorities and the challenges of the contemporary political climate.

AFTERWORD

National security reform for a new era –
An agenda for policymakers

The following report was generated in October 2017 by a group of policymakers, national security practitioners, and scholars, inspired in part by the ideas expressed by the contributors to this volume. The opinions expressed herein do not reflect the position of the United States Military Academy, the United States Army, the Department of Defense, or any other government agency.

Reassessing the National Security Act of 1947: Roadmap to reform

The year 2017 marks the 70th anniversary of the National Security Act of 1947. To commemorate the landmark legislation that powerfully shaped the American national security enterprise, over 60 prominent scholars, practitioners, and national security experts gathered at the United States Military Academy over the course of two years to consider national security reform in the modern era. In April 2016, the group examined how the world has changed since the end of the Second World War and, building upon those discussions in April 2017, endeavored to develop specific, actionable recommendations for reforming our national security institutions and processes.

The recommendations in this report do not represent a consensus among all participants. National security reform is inherently complex and contentious, and the final recommendations reflect only a portion of the vibrant debate among a diverse group of experts. The compiled report provides nine succinct policy recommendations across three broad topics, including the role of the legislative branch in national security, promoting strategic foresight within our national security institutions, and developing a surge capacity in response to unanticipated security crises.

I Congress and national security

Many experts perceive the legislative branch to have acquiesced to a weakening role in national security policy making and oversight. The absence of concentrated power in the U.S. government is by design; the Framers divided the powers of governance among the branches to ensure that no single person or group could dominate national policy, and especially national security. The United States Constitution grants specific powers to the legislative branch in this domain, including war powers, control over revenue and spending, and oversight prerogatives. Originally established as America's "First Branch" by the Framers, Congress has historically wielded these powers in tandem with the executive branch to inform and shape national security policy.

The steady rise of executive branch power relative to the legislature, common during periods of national crisis, along with the severe erosion of bipartisan cooperation in policy that extends beyond the "water's edge," has complicated that constitutional relationship. U.S. national security policy demands are profound, and the legislature appears resigned to a secondary role in addressing those demands.

Focusing specifically on the role of Congress in national security, three factors make it especially difficult for the legislative branch to lead: (1) the structure of the congressional committee and staff system that hobbles efforts to keep pace with the demands of policy in a rapidly changing international security environment; (2) the dual impact of the increased ability of constituents to stay informed of actions taken by their legislators and the rise of party polarization; and, potentially a result of the first two factors, (3) the misalignment of constituents' interests with membership on congressional committees that deal most directly with security policy. Collectively, these realities suggest barriers that impede Congress and also help to explain why members of the legislative branch may have neither the tools necessary to exert greater influence nor the inclination to attempt to do so. Discussions among policy experts, however, reveal the shared belief that the authority and means to address these issues still remain in the hands of the men and women of America's First Branch.

Recommendations for reform

Institute formal education for members and committee staff on national security committees. Only a small subset of the legislative community is focused on oversight of the national security apparatus. At a perennial information disadvantage, congressional committees and their staffs are inundated with detailed reporting from executive agencies that is impossible to review, evaluate, and assess in the time available. A robust and formal national security and defense education program once existed for members of Congress and congressional staff, upon which a future program could be modeled. To encourage a more active and visible role in oversight, an institute for members, selected on the basis of demonstrated interest, would provide comprehensive education and training on national security strategies and global issues. The program would include techniques to achieve parsimony and prioritization among competing national security imperatives, refocus congressional committees on the most important questions about national security policy, and reclaim the legislative branch's Article I responsibilities.

Build an equivalent to the CBO for national security. Create a prestigious congressional research office unconstrained by partisan influence to provide "scores" on various dimensions of national security for disparate policy options. The suggested blueprint for this office is the Congressional Budget Office (CBO). This organization would provide the means for Congress to compare and contrast recommendations for national security developed by the executive branch. The charter of the existing Congressional Research Service may be an appropriate vehicle to provide increased support for evaluating national security policy options.

Create a Select Committee on National Security Affairs as part of a broader reorganization of congressional committee structure. Currently, congressional committees provide inputs to the national security process according to each committee's jurisdictional control, leading to a fractured approach to national security. A Select Committee on National Security Affairs that provides oversight and responsibility of the joint space between Congress and the executive branch would improve focus on a whole-of-government national security policy instead of narrowly defined priorities. Despite the massive reorganization of the executive branch in the wake of 9/11, the legislative branch has yet to undertake a corresponding change to better fulfill its oversight and resourcing role. The existing imbalance could provide an impetus for congressional reform on national security.

II Planning for the future while managing the present

Policy officials in the U.S. government struggle to find the time and space to engage in strategic thinking and forecasting while simultaneously managing current and unanticipated crises. Ideally, our national security professionals consider the future routinely and predict actions required today to prepare for the challenges of tomorrow. Adherence to this ideal is the exception.

Islands of strategic activity do exist within the defense community and other national security agencies, such as the U.S. Marine Corps' Futures Assessment Division and the U.S. Coast Guard's Evergreen program, but efforts to connect and integrate these islands are stymied by the risk of politicization, disproportionate influence by the defense community, and a disconnect between public and private incentives. Strategic foresight and planning is often perceived to be a superfluous luxury within government agencies, given the limits of prediction and the tyranny of the present day among decision makers.

Critical to navigating these risks successfully is a professional ethic among sectors of the national security community and cultivation of professional military and civilian national security intellectuals. Leaders within national security agencies who can articulate priorities and tradeoffs, manage risk, and overcome institutional resistance to thinking about the future are necessary to change the prevalent culture. In particular, greater attention and better processes would be useful to shift attention to profound, strategic issues and away from the merely immediate and urgent.

Recommendations for reform

Identify and strengthen authorities and responsibilities for planning between existing but disbursed communities of strategic forecasters. Uniting islands of strategic forecasters within the national security community is a first step toward promoting a national security culture that values the activity of thinking about the future. Shared expertise, best practices, and an expanded network of forecasting tools, models, and ideas will generate momentum within executive agencies that struggle to prioritize intellectual bandwidth to consider the future and its accompanying threats and opportunities.

Establish a whole-of-government program of interagency exchanges for national security professionals. The capacity for strategic foresight requires a community of agile thinkers sufficiently isolated from the crisis of the day and familiar with the national security community as a whole. In order for strategic planners to take foresight and long-range futures into account when advising senior leaders on potential policy options, they should be provided opportunities to improve their capabilities through education, training, experience, and immersion in multiple agencies, think tanks, or academic institutions. Equipped with broader skills and perspectives, planners are the ideal members of interagency teams focused on strategic foresight tied to current national security decision making.

Integrate strategic planners with national security decision makers. Strategic foresight will never approach parity with crisis management without the attention, organizational discipline, and influence of decision makers. From personnel management decisions that recognize the contributions of strategic forecasters to prioritizing resources to address future challenges, leaders must consciously inculcate a culture that values thoughtful and comprehensive consideration of the future. Leaders must apply ways and means to the concept of the future to create strategy.

III Creating surge capacity for dynamic threats

The contemporary security environment is characterized by dynamism and complexity, forcing the United States to confront an array of diverse and non-traditional threats in addition to conventional, state-based security competition. However, non-traditional threats can be difficult to predict and, when they emerge, require multidimensional responses that challenge existing government structures and authorities. Devising an architecture that enables a surge capacity reduces risk by providing a rapid and effective response to emerging threats that does not currently exist in a systemic way across the national security enterprise.

Examples of scenarios that would require a short-term surge capacity, meaning an ad-hoc team of experts who do not habitually work together in the absence of crisis, include natural disasters, state failure of an ally or a WMD-capable state, asymmetric conflict with a cyber adversary, a mass casualty situation due to a major biological pathogen, or a comprehensive power grid failure. Ultimately, attempts to pre-determine authorities, roles, and responsibilities for all organizations and scenarios would require an unrealistic investment of time and resources.

However, executive responsibilities, authorities, and incentives can be aligned to drive cooperation, reduce response time in the event of a crisis, and develop networks that can be exercised during a surge by the national security community and its partners.

Recommendations for reform

Develop public-private partnerships in advance of crises. Public-private memorandums of understanding, synchronized cooperation between government agencies, and updated protocols for unanticipated crises are already largely implemented among agencies responding to natural disasters, but this model is not widespread within the national security community. Repeated wargaming and planning for contingencies that seem unlikely to materialize is nevertheless a useful and productive exercise, as developing personal relationships and networks will reduce friction in the event of a surge. As a potential model, the much-lauded Interagency Zombie Task Force developed by the Center for Disease Control is one creative initiative resulting in increased surge capacity and pre-existing public-private relationships in the event of a health crisis. The Department of Defense's model of Joint, Interagency, Intergovernmental, and multinational (JIIM) task forces provide a similar template for employing diverse teams in support of organizational planning and execution.

Reform the military personnel system to permit lateral entry from the civilian workforce. Internationally, the Department of Defense holds primary responsibility for surging in response to dynamic threats. The Department of Defense is expeditionary by design, with unparalleled ability to mass and project power globally. What expertise it lacks must be more easily acquired from the civilian sector and incorporated into the military's structure as a matter of routine. Specialized personnel programs that permit lateral entry from the civilian sector will help the Department of Defense recruit and retain a wider array of talents in its active, National Guard, and Reserve components.

Develop incentives for national service. National service can assume many forms. Americans possess skills that could be used across all imaginable sectors in the event of a national security crisis. Incentivizing private citizens' connection to their broader community will not only help Americans feel more invested in their country, but will create a network of capacity that will contribute to the overall strength of the nation.

A call to action

This brief guide to reform is intended to promote further discussion among decision makers within the national security community and those in a position to generate momentum and change. Over the past 70 years, our national security institutions have withstood numerous tests of process and spirit. But perennial debates over the topics included here merit action by the current generation of leaders to keep our institutions ready and capable. We encourage all those in a position to influence or initiate change within the national security enterprise to consider taking steps to implement the agenda for national security reform.

Participants

This guide is based on three days of discussion in April 2017 at West Point, New York about the National Security Act of 1947 and areas of potential reform. The following individuals participated in the conversation that contributed to the proposed agenda. As noted, participation does not necessarily indicate agreement with the report in its entirety.

Colonel Stephanie Ahern National Security Council Staff	Colonel Susan Bryant National Defense University
Mr. Robert Andy Audia Group	Lieutenant General Robert Caslen U.S. Military Academy
Mr. George Beach Superintendent, New York State Police	Dr. Joseph Collins National War College
Lieutenant General (Ret.) Mick Bednarek Former Chief, Office of Security Cooperation-Iraq	Colonel Liam Collins U.S. Military Academy
Hon. John Brennan Former Director of the Central Intelligence Agency	Lieutenant Colonel Heidi Demarest U.S. Military Academy
Dr. Jessica Blankshain U.S. Naval War College	Dr. Jason Dempsey Center for New American Security
Dr. Erica Borghard U.S. Military Academy	Mr. John Doyon National Counterterrorism Center
Dr. Meena Bose Hofstra University	Ms. Malia Du Mont Bard College
Ms. Rosa Brooks Georgetown University	Ms. Jen Easterly Morgan Stanley

Brigadier General (Ret.) Kim Field
Creative Associates International

Mr. Jason Forrester
Jason Forrester Consulting

Dr. Linda Fowler
Dartmouth College

MG Anthony German
Adjutant General, New York National Guard

Hon. Chris Gibson
Former U.S. Representative

Dr. Austen Givens
Utica College

Lieutenant Colonel Scott Handler
U.S. Military Academy

Dr. Kathleen Hicks
Center for Strategic and International Studies

Brigadier General Diana Holland
U.S. Military Academy

Dr. Richard Hooker, Jr.
National Security Council Staff

Colonel Patrick Howell
Duke University

Colonel Suzanne Nielsen
U.S. Military Academy

Dr. Jon Rogowski
Harvard University

Mr. Neilesh Shelat
U.S. Agency for International
Development

Dr. Scott Silverstone
U.S. Military Academy

Dr. Rachel Sondheimer
U.S. Military Academy

Hon. Steven Israel
Former U.S. Representative

General (Ret.) Charles Jacoby
USMA Modern War Institute

Brigadier General Cindy Jebb
U.S. Military Academy

Ms. Katherine Kidder
Center for a New American Security

Dr. Margaret Kosal
Georgia Institute of Technology

Major General Paul LaCamera
VIII Airborne Corps

Dr. Richard Lacquement, Jr.
U.S. Army War College

Dr. Hugh Liebert
U.S. Military Academy

Hon. James Locher III
Joint Special Operations University

Ambassador Douglas Lute
Former U.S. Representative to NATO

Dr. Daniel McCauley
National Defense University

Dr. Douglas Stuart
Dickinson College

Mr. Bill Sutey
Office of the Under Secretary of
Defense for Intelligence

Hon. Frances Townsend
Former Homeland Security Advisor

Colonel Heidi Urben
Joint Staff

Mr. Ian Wallace
New America

Colonel (Ret.) Isaiah Wilson III
The George Washington University

INDEX